Praise for the Second Edition of *First Things Fast*

"Allison Rossett combines thought leadership for the profession with practical guidance. This book, the second edition of a classic in the field, is filled with proven practices and ready-to-use tools that make this a resource you'll use frequently."

—Dana Gaines Robinson, coauthor, *Performance Consulting* and *Strategic Business Partner*

"Any book Allison Rossett publishes is a must-read. *First Things Fast* is a staple in any learning professional's library and this new edition takes all that was covered in the first book to a whole new level."

—Bob Mosher, global learning and strategy evangelist, LearningGuide Solutions USA

"What I appreciate about this book is that it is a straightforward, practical guide to planning, and it embraces new technology and the convergence of learning and work."

—Nancy J. Lewis, vice president and chief learning officer, ITT Corporation

"Allison has done it again! The first edition of *First Things Fast* guided us as we evolved from Training to Learning, and ultimately to Performance. Now she has provided us with a new, easy-to-read, and compelling handbook on how to capitalize on emerging opportunities in the early 21st century."

—Matthew T. Peters, chief, office of learning and career development, U.S. Defense Intelligence Agency

"When someone walks into my office and says 'I need training . . .' the first resource I grab is *First Things Fast (FTF)*! Speed is our priority. *FTF* provides the tools necessary to analyze and evaluate performance gaps quickly and efficiently."

—Brett James Powell, senior manager of training and development, California region, Comcast

"The second edition of *First Things Fast* is sure to address the realities of our workplace, as only Allison can—practical, timely, and relevant."

—Heather A. Morawa, general manager, org effectiveness and talent strategy, Delta Air Lines, Inc.

"This new edition of *First Things Fast* is a must-read for anyone who wants cutting-edge knowledge of the field. Allison makes things understandable, practical, and easy to do!"
—Felipe Jara, director of learning technologies, Center for Innovation in Human Capital, Fundación Chile

"At Procter & Gamble we believe our understanding and use of the 'drivers of performance' described by Allison Rossett in *First Things Fast* enables us to save time and money by creating better, more holistic solutions faster when the phone rings and we are asked to provide only 'training' to solve a business problem. We are looking forward to adding this new edition to our foundation of learning and development work processes."
—Rob Wilson, senior training manager, North America sales capability development, Procter & Gamble

"Rossett offers more than abstract advice. Grounded well in theory, her recommendations reflect years of experience with organizations around the globe. That's why her book translates so well into practice, and that's why the first edition has been on my desk for the past ten years."
—Christian Voelkl, head of consulting, E&E Information Consultants AG Germany

"In *First Things Fast* 1.0, Allison focused on making analysis expedient and palatable to managers and business leaders. In *FTF* 2.0, Allison puts her foot on the accelerator and provides a road map for analysis at the speed of business."
—David C. Hartt, commander, U.S. Coast Guard; and board of directors, International Society for Performance Improvement

"The need for integrating learning into work is increasingly important. *First Things Fast* provides innovative and practical learning approaches that can easily be implemented in any organization, industry, or sector. A must-read for all learning professionals."
—Tamar Elkeles, vice president, learning and development, Qualcomm

"Allison is one of the foremost thinkers of our industry and has succeeded in capturing the most important trends in performance analysis."
—Bjorn Billhardt, CEO, Enspire Learning

About Pfeiffer

Pfeiffer serves the professional development and hands-on resource needs of training and human resource practitioners and gives them products to do their jobs better. We deliver proven ideas and solutions from experts in HR development and HR management, and we offer effective and customizable tools to improve workplace performance. From novice to seasoned professional, Pfeiffer is the source you can trust to make yourself and your organization more successful.

Essential Knowledge   Pfeiffer produces insightful, practical, and comprehensive materials on topics that matter the most to training and HR professionals. Our Essential Knowledge resources translate the expertise of seasoned professionals into practical, how-to guidance on critical workplace issues and problems. These resources are supported by case studies, worksheets, and job aids and are frequently supplemented with CD-ROMs, websites, and other means of making the content easier to read, understand, and use.

Essential Tools   Pfeiffer's Essential Tools resources save time and expense by offering proven, ready-to-use materials—including exercises, activities, games, instruments, and assessments—for use during a training or team-learning event. These resources are frequently offered in looseleaf or CD-ROM format to facilitate copying and customization of the material.

Pfeiffer also recognizes the remarkable power of new technologies in expanding the reach and effectiveness of training. While e-hype has often created whizbang solutions in search of a problem, we are dedicated to bringing convenience and enhancements to proven training solutions. All our e-tools comply with rigorous functionality standards. The most appropriate technology wrapped around essential content yields the perfect solution for today's on-the-go trainers and human resource professionals.

Essential resources for training and HR professionals

FREE Premium Content ▼	Pfeiffer® An Imprint of WILEY

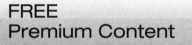

This book includes premium content that can be accessed from our Web site when you register at **www.pfeiffer.com/go/allisonrossett** using the password *professional*.

First Things Fast

A Handbook for Performance Analysis

Second Edition

ALLISON ROSSETT

Foreword by Ruth Clark
Afterword by Marc J. Rosenberg

A Wiley Imprint
www.pfeiffer.com

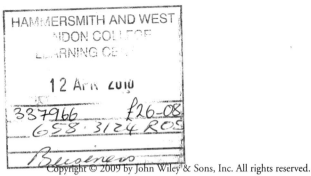
Published by Pfeiffer
A Wiley Imprint
989 Market Street, San Francisco, CA 94103-1741—www.pfeiffer.com

For additional copies/bulk purchases of this book in the U.S. please contact 800-274-4434.

Pfeiffer books and products are available through most bookstores. To contact Pfeiffer directly call our Customer Care Department within the U.S. at 800-274-4434, outside the U.S. at 317-572-3985, fax 317-572-4002, or visit www.pfeiffer.com.

Pfeiffer also publishes its books in a variety of electronic formats. Some content that appears in print may not be available in electronic books.

Library of Congress Cataloging-in-Publication Data

Rossett, Allison.
    First things fast: a handbook for performance analysis / Allison Rossett; foreword by Ruth Clark. —2nd ed.
        p.   cm.
    Includes bibliographical references and index.
    ISBN 978-0-7879-8848-7 (cloth)
        1. Performance standards.   2. Task analysis.   3. Employees—Training of.   4. Training needs.
I. Title.
    HF5549.5.P35R67 2009
    658.4'013—dc21

                                                        2009012605

Acquiring Editor: Matthew Davis
Director of Development: Kathleen Dolan Davies
Marketing Manager: Brian Grimm

Manufacturing Supervisor: Becky Morgan
Editorial Assistants: Lindsay Morton and
Michael Gilbart

Printed in the United States of America
SECOND EDITION
HB Printing   10 9 8 7 6 5 4 3 2 1

CONTENTS

HAVING WRITTEN six books on instructional design and development, I have *never* been tempted to write a book on performance analysis. Why? *First Things Fast* is such a readable and practical resource that to write another book on needs assessment would be redundant. My time is better invested in other projects. But why should "first things," aka performance assessment, be part of your skill portfolio? Read what a recent graduate of my instructional design certification program had to say:

> Needs assessment has never been formally applied or executed with our organization. The approach to training has been focused on fixing a specific issue, but exploring in depth the root cause for training has never been pursued or encouraged. Training has been approached as a stop-gap measure to provide a quick fix for perceived problems. By conducting a needs assessment for my product line, I have been able to uncover significant organizational issues such as lack of capturing solution-based metrics to measure

successful product installations and lack of funding to correct inherent software problems initially identified as a training issue.

Her reflections are not unique. Ask yourself, *What proportion of my recent
training investment has resulted in bottom-line organizational payoff?* You are
unusual if you can answer this question. Unless someone has surveyed the
performance landscape surrounding a training request, any bottom-line last-
ing achievements will occur by chance alone. And today we need not wait for
a training request! Performance technologists (and all of us in the "training"
business are performance technologists) are increasingly taking a proactive
role in business improvement. As part of a profession that collectively invests
close to $60 billion yearly in training in the United States alone, we cannot
afford to waste resources on an expensive solution that won't have a positive
impact on organizational performance. At the same time, most organizational
problems and initiatives are so short fused that there is rarely time to do a
"comprehensive" needs analysis. Here's where *First Things Fast* comes in!

"First Things" means that before you invest time and resources in a training program, you define the operational goals and the various drivers and
barriers associated with those operational goals. After all, if you don't know
where you are going, it's hard to know when you have arrived. "Fast" means
you must be responsive to organizational initiatives. Needs assessments that
take months will find that your business partners have lost interest and the
original need has disappeared or is no longer relevant. Our challenge: to find
efficient and effective ways to define operational goals, identify the processes
and people linked to those goals, and determine whether those goals will
be best realized through working aids, wikis, and other forms of knowledge
management; process changes; upgraded tools; training; or some combina-
tion thereof. And when training is a part of the solution, your assessment
must uncover specific knowledge and skills linked to bottom-line payoff.

If you are new to the training profession, welcome to a much broader
role than you may have realized! You may have thought your job was to produce materials or facilitate—to turn out workbooks, develop e-learning, or
debrief role-plays. Not so. Your real job is to make your organization more
efficient or more effective. You will collaborate with internal stakeholders—
your partners—to define their organizational goals and metrics, identify business processes and teams that support those goals, and ensure that the drivers
needed for success are available. Sound challenging? Yes, but also it's much

more engaging and rewarding than turning out yet another training program that looks good—that's fun, that uses the latest technologies—but in the end costs a great deal to construct and deliver yet gives no bottom-line return on investment. In fact, by giving the *illusion* of solving a business problem, a training program can go beyond being a waste of resources. It can leave the organization in worse condition by preempting the genuine improvement that could accrue from a solution system that addresses root causes.

If you are a seasoned performance specialist or a "graduate" of the first edition of *First Things Fast*, what's new in the second edition? Previously I mentioned that we are evolving from professionals who react to a training request to proactive business partners. As an instructional professional you have probably already made use of resources available in the Web 2.0. While Web 1.0 supported one-way communication, the new social web with blogs, wikis, and twitters offers you opportunities for data mining that were not available when the first edition was written. Consider this: You need not wait for that training request to start your needs assessment. If you are following blogs or discussion boards within your organization or among your customers, you can develop and maintain an ongoing proactive perspective on needs *as they emerge*. If you are "linked in" to your business partners, you can get a pulse on their concerns and initiatives as they evolve. Way before the customer service department contacts you asking for a "refresher on telephone help desk techniques," you may have gathered a portfolio of customer complaints and perspectives on your organization's help desk support. You can provide this data to your business partners *before* customer dissatisfaction turns into reduced sales or wasted resources. And you might be able to derail an unproductive training program before it is requested by suggesting alternative solutions—solutions you harvested from your ongoing Internet or Intranet research.

In summary—ten years after the first edition—first things are still first. And the resources for fast are more available than before. So whether you are an experienced performance improvement professional or just starting your performance journey, an investment of your time in reading and applying *First Things Fast* will yield high returns—for yourself, your business partners, and your organization.

Cortez, Colorado   *Ruth Clark*
February 2009

WELCOME TO the second edition of *First Things Fast*. Much has changed in learning and performance since I wrote the first edition. That is the reason for this second edition. It reflects a world with more technology in just about every aspect of learning and performance. It acknowledges the economic shocks of 2008 and 2009. This new edition addresses the challenges professionals confront today.

Is the new edition really new? Yes it is.

You will find

- New questions and templates that reflect the shift of learning and support into the workplace.

- New approaches that take advantage of wikis, blogs, and online surveys to gather information.

- Recognition of the shift to social networking and the possibilities presented for analysts.

- New cases presented in Chapter Nine, including Search and Rescue for the U.S. Coast Guard; failure investigation for a high-tech device; new hires skill development for The Maids Home Services; and an analysis devoted to finding support and the right blend for a telecommunications company.

- In most chapters, at least one sidebar commentary from a successful leader in our field who explains how he or she uses analysis to advance individual and organizational strategy. Two chapters have two commentaries. Hear from Susan Guest at Ingersoll Rand. Meet veteran consultant Jeanne Strayer. Listen to Mike Taylor; he's had a dozen years of experience in the nuclear industry. And then there's Vanguard University's Catherine Lombardozzi. There are more. Get to know them by digging into the chapters.

- A brand new foreword by Ruth Clark—and an updated afterword by Marc J. Rosenberg.

I've reviewed each paragraph in the book and asked: Is this useful? Does it add value?

Analysis was critical when I published the first edition in 1999. It is even more so today. Why more so? The answer is technology. Today, in harsh economic times, there is pressure to reduce costs while enabling people, sometimes fewer people, to practice with more skills and knowledge. Technology is favored over registrations in hotels and hours in classrooms.

In the good old days, an instructional designer could develop a class, and an instructor would then deliver it to a group in a room, all together, same time and place. When the ideas, examples, or exercises veered off mark, the instructor would fix it, on the fly.

Not so with technology-based delivery. Not yet. There's nobody there to help Marvin or Maria or Minjuan when they avoid, ignore, or dislike their programs. The programs were created before, earlier, in hopes that they would meet the needs of today, now.

Marvin is at home, watching the kids, and taking an e-learning module to introduce him to a new product. Maria now works for a multinational, and is reintroducing herself to her home country, Panama, after three years of work and graduate school in the United States. She uses webinars, podcasts, and online communities to stay up to date and to feel connected. With technology today, the programs are baked in advance. She goes to them, hoping that something of value will appear. Minjuan is a retirement specialist for a large company. She is doing her certification training via a program that blends classes and online experiences. She's been to the face-to-face classes, but now finds herself under some pressure to complete the entire program independently, so she can begin working with a new group of clients.

What do Marvin, Maria, and Minjuan have in common? Choice. They have choices. If a module fails to meet a perceived need, they can do something else—or even nothing at all. If the archived virtual presentation or the podcast doesn't compel, they can skip them. If the examples or practices are not challenging or are too much so, they will have trouble finding time. The programs must fit the work, worker, and workplace.

Analysis is how we find that fit. When we target programs through analysis, we use data to capture and hold attention, and then to contribute to individual performance and organizational accomplishments.

Analysis is obviously important, but it does not always happen. Even though books, articles, and speeches on the topic are plentiful, it is not a stretch to describe analysis as continuing to attract more heat than light. Why is that?

- Leaders often prefer a quick fix. Most executives want what they want when they want it, not after a study of the matter.

- Analysis is even less interesting to leaders in organizations than training. Few executives want to talk about training, and fewer still are intrigued with the planning associated with it. Their eyes glaze over.

- There is little history in the organization of analyses that have made noticeable dents in what matters. Even the telling results of fine analysis studies are often lost in the excitement of rolling out reengineered processes, a new recognition program, and just the right training. Too often, the data gathering and involvement of sources are lost. And that's when such excellent studies even exist. It's not hard to find professionals who can't point to a single result of their planning efforts aside from the frustration of the impatient customer.

- Your customers believe they know what they need. Accustomed to leading, many customers refrain from posing a problem or challenge and instead leap to habitual solutions, often those that are single interventions, such as training or documentation.

- While there is pressure to measure, only a small percentage of measurement efforts (single digits in recent studies) are defined by the eventual impact on strategic goals or even the subsequent delight of the customers they serve. When measurements are taken, most are still fixed on those variables that are easy to discern, such as people in attendance or the number of meetings that are facilitated.

- People don't know what analysis is. There is little agreement about what constitutes effective planning, whether you call it analysis, scoping, diagnostics, auditing, needs analysis, needs assessment, or performance analysis.

- Analysis is not easy to do. It involves many challenges, from figuring out how to plan, to convincing sources to participate, to collecting data, to figuring out what the data mean, to making the findings matter in the organization. Political, interpersonal, and cognitive skills are tapped during analysis.

- Analysis takes time, and time is in short supply. Little explanation is necessary here. We all know the number one reason for avoiding analysis—there's no time for it.

- The number two reason is leadership. Leaders are not yet convinced. Now is the time to convince them, by conducting lean, actionable analyses.

This book attempts to address each of these barriers. It is meant to be a practical guide to handling every one of them through examples, explanations, tools, and templates. If you're new to the field, this handbook will help you anticipate resistance and deal with it. If you're a veteran, I hope you'll appreciate my efforts to bring clarity and concreteness to an often murky topic. Borrow some of these examples. Use them to help make a case for study prior to action.

I try to make a case for performance analysis by telling stories and offering dialogues about our business. Some are true. Some are imaginary. All are familiar and plausible.

I've always enjoyed Greek mythology, thanks to Edith Hamilton (1993). I've taken that appreciation into my current work, continuing to savor themes that put people at the heart of the story, that recognize flashes of the monstrous and miraculous in most circumstances and individuals, and that honor the critical struggle to make the unknown known.

Isn't this what performance analysis is about?

I hope that this book helps you ask and answer better questions for yourself and for your organization or the organizations you serve.

San Diego, California   *Allison Rossett*
March 2009

ACKNOWLEDGMENTS

I'VE LEARNED important lessons from my academic colleagues and students at San Diego State University. I have been blessed with smart colleagues who nudge me and our graduate students to consider emergent approaches, ideas, and technologies. In particular, I want to thank Marcie Bober, Elsa Tapia, Bob Hoffman, Pat Harrison, Rebecca Frazee, and Jim Marshall for their support and their kindness.

One blessing of teaching at the university has been my contact with generations of graduate students in educational technology. Some have read chapters from this book and offered suggestions. Others provided the grist for the tales that pepper the book. Joe Williams was a significant contributor to Chapter Seven. Rebecca Frazee added much to Chapter Eight. Lisa Schafer, with whom I have worked on many projects, was always there with an example or a citation. Marcie Brown, one of the SDSU EDTEC online graduate students, helped enormously by soliciting, editing, and communicating with the sidebar experts. This is a new feature in the book, and I could not have done it without Marcie and those contributors, now sprinkled throughout the book.

I've continued to work with many of our alumni long after their graduation. Their ideas advance my thinking every day: Jordan Baldueza, Ed Beale, Terry Bickham, Randy Bland, Audrey Bloom, Jeff Brechlin, Betsy Bruce, Antonia Chan, Caleb Clark, Colleen Cunningham, Carl Czech, Ann Derryberry, Nancy Dosick, James Frazee, Fernanda Gimenez-Groenendijk, Shirley Gresham, Chris Hall, Liz Herrick, Cathy Kang, Doug Lucas, Paul McManus, Erica Mohr, Matt Moore, Marty Murillo, Milagros Noy, Marci Paino, Dawn Papaila, Rudy Robles, Lou Sanchez, Jeanne Strayer . . .

Not everybody I know is a former student. I also have professional colleagues and pals who deserve acknowledgment. Some posed interesting consulting problems on which we worked together, others helped me through their writings and professional contributions, still others have been wonderful conversationalists: Roger Addison, Cynthia Anderson, Sarah Beers, Sven Blomberg, Bill Brandon, Bryan Chapman, Susan Considine, Kathy Dardes, Joe Durzo, Heidi Fisk, Rob Foshay, Marguerite Foxon, James Frazee, Gloria Gery, Michael Glass, Tony Gleeson, Susan Greenberg, Ruhe Hao, Paul Harmon, Sam Herring, David Holcombe, Joe and Julie Hymes, Roger Kaufman, Ann Leon, Dave Merrill, Becky Monroe, Santhiru Murugiah, Kevin Oakes, Brian Patterson, Deb Pettry, Sandy Quesada, Rena Robey, Patty Schutt, Janice Simmons, Katie Smith, Tim Sosbe, Tom Stewart, Ruth Stiehl, John Stormes, Will Thalheimer, Ellen Wagner, Pat Weger, Deb Wharff, and Diana Wright.

I'd also like to acknowledge the antecedents of this book in what Ruth Clark, Tom Gilbert, Joe Harless, Erica Keeps, Robert Mager, Dave Merrill, Marc Rosenberg, Harold Stolovitch, and Ron Zemke have written and said. Their contributions are woven into the way I approach my work.

I've acknowledged many people. There are others. I fear I've forgotten many. I apologize if you are not included in these long lists. You know who you are. Please know that I am appreciative.

Finally, I want to thank Sue Reynolds for everything, absolutely everything. I'm happy there is no need to update anything about that sentence.

THE AUTHOR

DR. ALLISON ROSSETT, longtime professor of educational technology at San Diego State University, is in the *Training* magazine HRD Hall of Fame, was recently a member of the ASTD International Board of Directors, and was honored by selection as an ISPI Member-for-Life. Recipient of ASTD's singular recognition for lifelong contributions to workplace learning and performance and designated a 2008 LEGEND, Allison coauthored *Job Aids and Performance Support: Moving from Knowledge in the Classroom to Knowledge Everywhere* in 2007.

Rossett edited *The ASTD E-Learning Handbook: Best Practices, Strategies, and Case Studies for an Emerging Field.* She is the author of four awardwinning books, including the first edition of *First Things Fast: A Handbook for Performance Analysis.* Prior award-winning books are *Training Needs Assessment* and *A Handbook of Job Aids.* Some of Allison's recent articles are "Performance Support Tools: Delivering Value When and Where Needed,"

"Moving Your Class Online," "Confessions of a Web Dropout," and "Training and Organizational Development, Siblings Separated at Birth."

Allison has conducted research and published articles on needs analysis, learner engagement, and persistence in online learning. Her client list includes IBM, HP, the Getty Conservation Institute, Fidelity Investments, Deloitte Consulting, BP, the IRS, Amgen, Royal Bank of Scotland, the National Security Agency, Transportation Security Administration, and several e-learning start-ups.

1

Introduction

Nancy Lewis, then IBM vice president for sales and on demand learning and now the executive in charge of learning for ITT, contributed to the LearningTown blog on April 11, 2008:

> Business leaders know that the rate of information change is accelerating, growing faster than our ability to consume it. The result being that we will all have skill gaps, all the time, and that skill gaps will be a constant state of life in the future. We also know that our roles are becoming as complex as the knowledge we work with. There will never be enough time to learn everything we need to learn. There is such a consistent and rapid churn of the skills and knowledge required to maintain job performance that learning can no longer be provided as a set of events. This is the new challenge for learning: enabling people to capitalize on new technologies, discoveries and business insights, to be first to the marketplace with new solutions that exceed our clients' needs and expectations. At the heart, therefore, the essence of any company's ability to adapt and grow is its ability to learn. And that involves new ways of thinking about an approach to learning.

What Lewis is touting is not computers, although technology, of course, plays a starring role in the delivery of learning and support. Lewis's focus is learning in juxtaposition with the work and workplace: "We looked at where learning actually takes place most of the time. It's in the workplace, not in the classroom. We learn naturally on the job. We learn by doing, by solving problems. There will always be a need for formal training, but it will likely be much more in direct support of the capabilities that cannot be learned in the workplace."

Placing learning and references closer to the work is brilliant, except when it is the wrong learning or references. Executives favor such an approach, especially in harsh economic times. Employees reject programs that are extraneous, bloated, or obsolete. That's true in the classroom and online. The big difference is the instructor, present for face-to-face experiences. Instructors typically fix instruction when it is not right. An instructor adds an example to make it more relevant. Another reminds the employee of all that he already knows. Yet another instructor provides an opportunity to tackle a problem that is within the student's abilities, to ensure a success experience. And another links the example to the concept, when the students' faces are blank. Finally, a savvy instructor would recognize when a class, as now written, ignores a critical new product or geopolitical reality. She makes fixes to ensure that the class is timely.

When we diminish instructor centrality in favor of on-demand and workplace-based resources and experiences, more responsibility falls on us. We must be certain about the resonance of our programs. What do our people need? What is top priority? What is already known? For what do they clamor? What will add value? What must they know by heart? What can they seek as they need it? It is performance analysis that answers these questions.

In April 2008, Delta and Northwest Airlines announced their intentions to merge. A Delta learning leader, in a personal email that very morning, shared feelings about the merger. She expressed enthusiasm for it, and closed by remarking that she now needs to get her arms around what Northwest learning is all about and what their people require. She has to figure out how to make this merger work at 550 mph. How does she gain insight into their people, challenges, and programs? What should she do first? What next? And how does she engage colleagues in the process, so that her ideas are not just Delta ideas or habits? It is performance analysis that answers her questions.

A former student provided another example. After a dozen years in training and development in financial services, he reports that he is now, finally, getting more control over the "juicy" projects. "I want to use technology to meet the needs of the far-flung IT community. When their executive asked me to look for ways to improve awareness about system security, I immediately thought about Second Life." Why was Second Life (http://secondlife.com/) such a natural here? I asked. He had reasons that began to bring me around, such as the interest the approach would generate in a skeptical audience and the immersive and vivid nature of the experience. But how would he direct their experiences on his corporate island? How would he rivet their attention, since other even "juicier" opportunities lurked on nearby islands? Given all that could be done, how would he decide what they see, tackle, and do? It is performance analysis that answers his questions.

You could be at IBM or Delta, or even contemplating the design of your corporate island in Second Life. Perhaps your organization is rolling out a new product. Or maybe you are tasked with getting more value from the current learning management system or with squeezing cost out of the current enterprise. Or consider the executive who wants assurance that what his people are studying in class will transfer to the manufacturing floor. Then there is the sales leader who notes that great things are going on across the world and laments that the rest of the salesforce rarely profits from these breakthroughs. Your job is to embrace these requirements as opportunities and to customize programs to ensure performance and results. How do you make that happen? No surprise. The answer is performance analysis.

Where once human resources and training professionals enjoyed a niche defined by familiar activities, such as offering classes or facilitating meetings, now there are urgent expectations about results, speed to competence, benefits and efficiencies from technologies, and eagerness to distribute smarts everywhere, accessible where and when needed.

These expectations define us by customers and causes, not by history, habit, or job title. They lead to tailored services. They lead to data and perceptions gathered from associates, managers, experts, leaders, and benchmarking groups. They lead to solutions enlightened by causes and drivers. They lead to uncovering data in unexpected places, including blogs and wikis. They lead to cobbling together solution systems from across the organization, including assets and experiences that compel attention over time and geography.

The basis for all of this is performance analysis. An effective performance analysis delivers the information and support you need to chart a fresh, tailored approach.

Jeanne Strayer never underestimates the value of a training intervention. With her background as a teacher of English as a Second Language (ESL), she understands the importance of a structured curriculum to address a specific knowledge deficit. But what she found upon entering the business world was that training could just as easily be the *wrong* solution to a problem. Whether working as an independent consultant or an in-house instructional designer, Jeanne expanded her repertoire of skills "to include other interventions to solve performance problems."

In her current position as a partner with the Six Degrees Company, Jeanne finds that even repeat clients often think first of training as the solution to a problem, rather than imagine other possible solutions. To address this illogical leap, Jeanne uses one of several techniques to get a client to slow down, step back, and acknowledge the need for some good, old-fashioned analysis.

1. *Ask the right questions in order to lead clients to discover the value of analysis.* Performance consultants have a need and a knack for asking questions about a problem that "bring to light" the unknowns and uncertainties of a situation. Asking those questions together with the client helps the client see the value of doing analysis. Jeanne had a client who wanted to reach a very large target audience of real estate agents, numbering in the thousands. The client wanted an e-learning product to lead the agents to use a new software product. Jeanne said to the client, "Well, let's see. You say the agents need online training on the new software system, but they never used point-and-click training offered in the past. What makes you think it will be different this time? Why do you think they didn't use it last time? Do they not understand how to do it? Or do they not see the value in the training?" Asking questions can create an "Aha!" moment so that clients see the value of investigating further before investing in a solution.

2. *Demonstrate that budgets are easier to develop after analysis.* Sometimes the scope of a project is so big that it's hard to place an actual dollar figure on a solution without some serious initial analysis. In the situation above, the client *thought* that e-learning was the best way to reach the many real estate agents. After a few questions, Jeanne discovered that the problems were due to motivation, marketing, and implementation—in addition to training. Once the client accepted those drivers, it was clear that further analysis was needed to scope the project and to put some budget numbers together. Jeanne used data to show that a live event was the best way to market the new software. With this information, the client was able to budget for the cost of x number of events in a targeted geographic area, as well as the marketing campaign to promote the live events.

3. *Use the Gilbert model to de-emphasize training.* The Gilbert Behavior Engineering Model, created by Thomas Gilbert, classifies performance problems into one of six categories: information, resources, incentives, knowledge, capacity, and motivation. Jeanne uses this model as a way for project leaders to think about the performance problem. She then asks, "Before committing project dollars to a training program, doesn't it make sense to see if any of these other factors are at work so that we can use those to leverage performance?"

> **Jeanne Strayer** is a partner with the Six Degrees Company, a firm specializing in sales strategy, marketing, and performance improvement. She holds an MA in educational technology from San Diego State University, and a Certified Performance Technologist credential through the International Society for Performance Improvement. You can reach Jeanne at jeanne@strayer.net.

Is This Book for You?

This book is for you if you've found yourself thinking or saying,

I don't know where to start.

I don't know what to do.

I must get it right or I fear they won't use it.

What is performance analysis?

Why should I spend time on performance analysis, when my clients want ACTION?

What would competence look like, really look like?

A certain amount of analysis is critical, I guess. OK, what's the minimum?

They've reorganized, and now I'm in this unit called "client relationships," and we're supposed to be doing performance consulting. What should we do? How might analysis help here?

How do I avoid analysis-paralysis?

How do I get a better fix on what to do first, second, and next?

It's all about technology around here now. How does the shift to technology and independent learning influence the way we plan?

We have online communities, wikis, blogs . . . should I use them in my analysis? How would I do that?

This analysis is just a small part of my job. I don't have time for all of this analysis. What's the least I can do and still derive value?

Whom do I ask? What do I ask?

What's analysis got to do with evaluation?

My customer says she knows what she needs and that it's not analysis. How can I make a case with her for study prior to action?

They want some courses, and one customer wants scenario-based e-learning. But I have my doubts about whether an isolated course, in the classroom or through high technology, is going to solve this problem. How can I make them see this?

The challenges are numerous: a world economic crisis; skepticism from clients; time pressures; the strength of habits; unfamiliar roles in changing organizations; cultural, language, and time zone differences; uneven technology platforms; and expectations regarding cost recovery and collaborations across units. Whereas the traditional roles of human resources and training were functional, tactical, and blissfully familiar, this new world of performance analysis, consultation services, and solution systems is more fluid and strategic. It demands more of you. The changes won't be easy.

That paragraph ends the sympathy. From here on we talk about how to think about and succeed in these new roles and services, and we'll focus on analysis as the strategy to enable you to do just that.

This book is written for human resources and training professionals who are eager to choose solutions based on the situation, not on habits and inclinations; who are interested in analysis prior to action; who seek to consult with line organizations to establish field-based cases for their recommendations; and who are operating under time constraints. Many are called trainers by their organizations. Some are internal or external organizational developers and process reengineers. Many call themselves instructional designers or performance consultants or even performance technologists. Some have another position entirely, but find themselves tasked with or attracted to solving problems. Still others are human resources generalists. What all share is a desire to shift from predetermined activities and events to consultation and customized solutions. They are working to establish partnerships. Their efforts begin with performance analysis.

Performance Analysis and Needs Assessment?

In the past I've written about needs assessment in a way that defines it as a large, overarching concept that is arguably synonymous with good human resources planning. Although I still hold by that definition, I was, I fear, overly optimistic about the welcome that such a demanding process would receive in the field. As practical experience and numerous studies of practice have shown, my own included, needs assessment is honored more in theory than in practice. What to do? Do we abandon this critical planning simply because so many report that they fail to do much of it? I don't think so.

I'm no longer convinced it is helpful to define needs assessment so broadly, because when you do, a commitment to needs assessment will necessitate the expenditure of significant resources up front. Professionals run up against a wall of resistance when they attempt to gather large quantities of information from many sources at the get-go. Instead, I'm proposing that we reduce the daunting size of the effort by carving the planning process into more manageable and iterative bite sizes: *one swift, targeted bite up front and then subsequent mouthfuls of assessment for subsequent associated programs.*

It's hard to argue with the hundreds who've said in one way or another, "Sure, I'm for assessment. I just don't get to do it. What else do you have for me? I want to make better decisions, do some planning, but not jump into so much study." What I have for this typical professional is performance analysis, that smaller, focused bite.

Performance analysis, then, becomes the front end of the front end. It is an elegant and swift look at the situation. It matches changes happening in human resources and training organizations where a group of professionals, who might be called relationship consultants, requirements consultants, or performance consultants, are tasked with facing the customer and helping them get what they need to achieve their goals. They continuously scan and respond, turning projects over to other human resources and training professionals, depending on the challenge or opportunity. Their job is to swiftly figure things out, as the late, great Ron Zemke put it in his classic text, *Figuring Things Out* (Zemke & Kramlinger, 1982). What these professionals are doing is performance analysis, a precursor to the substantial planning involved in the needs assessment associated with the production of a particular solution, like a class or a reengineered policy or a multimedia program.

Only after it is certain that a training, coaching, or information solution is appropriate does the organization make the investment in more lengthy, substantive training needs assessment. Table 1.1 is a comparison of performance analysis and training needs assessment.

In Table 1.1, note the difference in why, when, and how. In performance analysis, we are attempting to make a preliminary sketch of the opportunity, to figure out what is involved in serving a customer, and then to bring the necessary partners together to collaborate on producing and delivering the solution system. Performance analysis is what we do before we invest in needs assessment or what we can finally, accurately dub training needs assessment. Once we have determined that education, training, or information will contribute, the lengthier training needs assessment can commence.

Performance analysis guarantees doing the right things. Training needs assessment is about doing those right things right.

Table 1.1. Performance Analysis and Training Needs Assessment.

Performance Analysis	Training Needs Assessment
Is a process for partnering with clients to figure out what it will take to achieve their goals	Is a process for determining what is in and what is out of an instructional or informational program
Results in a data-driven rationale and the description of a solution system	Results in classes, job aids, coaching, documentation, electronic performance support, and so on
Is an initial response to the opportunity or request from the client or customer	Is a follow-on study that takes performance analysis findings and turns them into the "right" instruction and information
Focuses on defining the limits of the problem or domain in broad strokes and then determining what to do	Focuses on texture and authenticity, on what performers need to know and do in detail
Defines the opportunity or problem and what to do about it	Defines the details necessary to create concrete solutions
Defines cross-functional solution systems	Identifies the details of exemplary performance and perspectives so that they can be taught, included in knowledge-management systems, and communicated

This book focuses on performance analysis. My previous book, *Training Needs Assessment* (1987), covers the more extensive assessment efforts in more detail. Please see Chapter Two for more about these two concepts.

There are precedents for chopping the front end into targeted and related parts, so that what you learn in the first phase enlightens subsequent efforts. General practitioners, for example, do it when a patient presents with a problem such as fatigue. They ask questions to determine likely causes and then turn to more extensive testing to confirm educated hunches. Subsequent contact with specialists, and related intensive diagnostics, are based on that initial once-over.

Another example is the early opportunity analysis conducted by entrepreneurs. In real estate development, an experienced developer quickly reviews the characteristics of a potential site to identify the issues most likely to be fatal to the project. Using as little time and money as possible, the developer confirms the "deal-killer" issue and moves on to another site, or finds that the issue is tolerable and moves on to the next potential deal killer for that site. Only when the largest, easiest-to-investigate killers are retired does the developer invest "real" money and time in the project.

Perhaps you have some questions now. In Table 1.2, I anticipate some of your questions and answer them.

How Does the Book Work?

In this chapter and in Chapters Two and Three, I define performance analysis and explain why, why now, why you, and why do it quickly. I present the performance analysis basics, along with examples, job aids, and templates. What questions should you ask? To whom should you address those questions? Why do it this way? The next two chapters answer those questions.

Chapter Four focuses on handling typical situations, such as a request for support in the introduction of new software or the need to plan to ensure that engineers' skills are contemporary. The chapter highlights four kinds of requirements: (1) a rollout of a new system, approach, or perspective; (2) a problem with performance or results; (3) development for a particular group of people; and (4) strategic planning. We look at strategies for carrying out performance analysis linked to these standard, familiar requests for assistance.

Chapter Five is all about speed. It describes strategies for putting the pedal to the metal and reviews ways of capturing useful data without large numbers of sources or lengthy processes.

Chapter Six acknowledges that performance analysis is a planning process with two primary purposes. The first is to figure out what needs to be done to serve the client and organization. The second is to establish relationships in

Table 1.2. Concerns About Speedy Performance Analysis.

Concerns	Responses
"I like needs assessment. Will I still get to do it?"	Of course. Performance analysis sets the table for needs assessment, finding the right places to direct that focused study. In some organizations, the analyst passes the project on to others who will do the needs assessment. In others, the work is done by the same person.
"It would take me hours to figure out how to do this performance analysis."	This handbook will provide templates matched to the kinds of opportunities you're likely to have. Adapting the template and sample questions will shave time off your study. Use the book in a just-in-time way, if you prefer. Besides, you owe yourself the professional development.
"This doesn't give me enough time."	PA probably doesn't give you enough time to feel certain. What it will do is give you a general picture of what's happening, enabling you to recommend likely, but not certain, directions and approaches. Remember, PA is the beginning, not the end, of your work with your customers.
"I have projects in Palo Alto, Capetown, and Singapore. Will this planning process help me?"	I intend it to. We'll talk about the issues that many countries, cultures, and settings impose on you. Although there are no easy answers, there are some strategies, including the use of technology, that will address issues raised by distance and difference.
"I prefer surveys. Can I do one in performance analysis?"	Yes, you can, especially if you are seeking priority directions, and after you've done sufficient study to be able to present options in the survey. Technology is also useful here. See Chapter Seven for ideas about how to use technology to speed up and extend your reach.
"Performance analysis. Needs assessment. Get serious. My management won't give me that much time."	Take the bull by the horns. Although it is difficult to justify lengthy studies, it is even more difficult to justify hasty actions. Use architects and doctors as analogies. Would your customer respect a physician or architect who plunged into surgery or a building project without diagnostics?

the organization and readiness for subsequent interventions. In this chapter, while reviewing interviews, focus groups, observation, and surveys as methods for performance analysis, we concentrate on the perspectives of executives, managers, employees, experts, and solution partners during analysis. What we'll see is that they are not usually as keen on analysis as we are.

Chapter Seven looks at technology and analysis. This chapter describes the ways that new and familiar technologies can be used for analysis. It makes sense that blogs, wikis, and online communities are influential in how we deliver training and support. But what do they mean for analysis effort? How can we use them to save time? To capture more and better opinions? Chapter Seven presents technology basics and extends to more exotic possibilities.

Chapter Eight describes ways to present the results of your performance analyses and includes examples of both performance analysis reports and briefings. This chapter discusses the challenges related to influencing others and presents touchstones for making analysis efforts more actionable in the organization.

In Chapter Nine, many professionals write about their experiences with analysis. They describe what happened, why they think it happened, and what they'd do differently if they had to do it over again. Their experiences take us to elementary school classrooms, and to the worlds of finance, fish, franchising, technology, and consulting.

Chapter Ten describes trends in our business and how they relate to performance analysis. A source and reference list closes the book.

First Things Fast Is a Handbook

- It's handy. The book is meant to be easy to use. It responds to the needs of two kinds of people: those who want to do performance analyses and those who don't yet want to but might, given good tools and reasons. The book is oriented to your challenges, questions, successes, and concerns.

- It's functional. If you want to know where to start on a performance analysis, the options are here. If you want a sample executive interview for a technology rollout, you can find one to tailor to your situation. If you are confronting resistance from experts, you'll find an example here that's similar to what you're experiencing and suggestions for how to respond. If you are intrigued with blogs, we'll describe how to use the approach for planning.

- It's chock full of practical stuff. There are many examples, charts, anecdotes, and quotes. Job aids are everywhere. There are also exceptions and irreverent commentary.

- It includes the voice of the customer. Sprinkled throughout the book are typical conversations and anecdotes. There are dialogues between trainers, performance analysts, customers, and experts. They provide a quick way to witness and thus prepare for the perspectives of others and for what you have confronted or will confront when you plan. Most chapters include a sidebar story contributed by a practitioner. Chapter Nine is seven extended analysis cases.

- It's stripped down. I've vacuumed out nonessential details. I've eliminated introductions and foundational materials. Unfortunately, this means I've pulled out many references. I apologize to the wise people whose thinking has influenced this book (such as Joe Harless, Robert Mager, Peter Pipe, Tom Gilbert, B. J. Fogg, Jack Phillips, Dana Robinson, Geary Rummler, Marc Rosenberg, Ruth Clark, Ron Zemke, and many others) for not making the frequent allusions to their contributions that I've offered in earlier writings. My purpose here is to make it easier for human resources professionals to get their jobs done—to get to the heart of the matter, as Robert Mager put it (1970). The references that are included are meant to provide more perspectives and examples, not historical underpinnings.

- It's relevant. We'll visit computer companies, banks, oceans, and government agencies. We'll talk about sales, diversity, teams, software, and management development in this country and others. We'll talk about the implications of global settings for analysis. Examples and dialogues come from real projects in real organizations, and, where possible, I will identify the company or agency. Often, I'll take experiences and combine and even exaggerate them to illustrate points.

Given the choice of several examples or quotes, I'll pick the more irreverent.

- It's fun. Well, maybe fun is too strong a word, but it is lighthearted. I'll write as I would talk to you, as if we were sitting in your office together, chatting about a project, looking at work products, planning interactions with an executive, touring the web, considering the reactions of managers or job incumbents, wondering if we can make a case based on talking to seven people instead of seven hundred.

———————————

Performance analysis is your interface with the organization. It is the systematic way that performance professionals understand opportunities and problems and extend themselves into the organization and the field. It is relationships, questions, data, dissection, conversation, synthesis, collaboration, and, yes, marketing too. It is a systematic strategy for figuring out what to do in a swift fashion. I know you will find many uses for it today.

2

What Can We Do First and Fast?

Paula: I want to understand what's going on before I start on this project. Maybe I'll do one of those whatchamacallits, a performance analysis, but I have hardly any time and not much experience doing it either.

Fritz: I know what you mean. People say we should do analysis, but when I mention it to my customers, they often resist. One rolled her eyes last week.

Paula: I know you did one first quarter. What should I do first? How are we supposed to do one?

Speedy Performance Analysis

Paula and Fritz are expressing concerns that probably sound familiar to you. What should they do first? How do they do it fast? How does it fit into the job of someone charged with building training and development programs? Managing a learning management system? Creating scenario-based e-learning programs? Shifting from classroom events to blends that move lessons and messages into the workplace?

Then there is the issue of quality. How is performance analysis done well—as well as quickly? How is it done in a way that demonstrates value to the organization? Just this morning, a former student now working at a telecommunications company admitted, "You know I believe in analysis, but my manager wants product, product, product. If there's a way I can do it really fast, so that maybe management doesn't notice I'm doing it . . ."

Another associate who works at a consulting firm noted, "Sometimes I think that my clients are more interested in getting something—anything—done than in getting it right."

These perceptions are typical. Often, there is scant enthusiasm for analysis from clients. We hear, "We know what we need, and it's not analysis."

Those are words from leaders whose metrics are too often limited to enrollments, completions, and satisfaction, with impact and outcomes trailing behind, if at all.

Fortunately, there are many who believe in analysis, not just as nice to have but as absolutely critical to planning successful programs.

Count training luminaries Donald Kirkpatrick, Robert Brinkerhoff, Jack Phillips, and Jac Fitz-Enz as four who are very much in favor of planning prior to action. On March 6, 2008, they, in a panel chaired by Qualcomm's chief learning officer Tamara Elkeles, spoke about the profession at a conference sponsored by Knowledge Advisors.

Robert Brinkerhoff reminded the audience about how important it is to deliver value and to align services with organizational strategy. Jack Phillips pointed to the turnover in learning leadership positions and lamented passivity, as we "wait for the next request to come along." Donald Kirkpatrick reminded us of the importance of line leaders. Planning must seek insight from the line. Measurement of success must reflect line priorities. And successful programs engage them throughout.

Fitz-Enz emphasized the importance of understanding the business and using that knowledge to add value. When asked why organizations should invest in learning, his answer returned to the business: "It's not all about learning. It's about business problems."

Qualcomm's Elkeles asked her panelists to forecast the future. Jack Phillips spoke urgently about growing pressure to prove results. His example was

UPS. Their executives, Phillips noted, have every right to wonder about the return they are getting on the US$6,000,000 invested annually in learning and development.

Brinkerhoff's response to the question about the future admitted our past stumbles. In a metaphor reminiscent of manufacturing, he remarked that we produce too much scrap in our learning ventures and that so many failures would not be accepted in another industry. He said of our business that it is "not rocket science." Brinkerhoff urged more attention to analysis and to execution on the indicated solutions.

In this book, we applaud study prior to action and an approach that admits to not studying in meticulous detail. Our purpose isn't to know with absolute certainty, but to describe and sketch, to provide fresh views, and to ask questions that push the project in practical and systemic directions. The beauty of this formula for performance analysis is that it allows analysis when you confront scant time and halting organizational support. Thus this book will help you fulfill three purposes: (1) conducting performance analysis, (2) doing it well, and (3) doing it fast.

A trainer for many of the past twelve years, Mike Taylor has worked in the electric utility industry for six of those. He spent the first decade of his career as an IT trainer, but now he serves more than four thousand employees as an instructional designer and developer for the fossil and hydro generation business unit of American Electric Power (AEP). "It's very different from IT," Mike confesses. Not that the principles and processes of human performance technology differ, but the business relationships, regulatory environment, and mission-critical initiatives present different challenges and opportunities. Mike's group consists of thirteen learning professionals, three of whom do everything from analysis to development to delivery.

Safety initiatives often take on an urgency not seen in soft skills or systems-related training. Mike points out that AEP "has a safety goal of zero occurrences," and when an incident does take place, "addressing the performance issue becomes the number one priority." Although the safety professionals are in a different group, Mike and his learning team members work closely with those subject matter experts (SMEs) to design and conduct safety training for the generation business. AEP is fortunate to have an executive team strongly supportive of both the safety and training professionals.

Mike initiates a safety-related analysis when one of three things happens:

1. *A safety SME approaches the learning group to request a performance solution.* For example, safety-related policies are updated regularly. When an update occurs, a safety representative informs the training group. A brief analysis usually reveals whether instruction is needed to communicate the policy update, or information will be sufficient, typically on the basis of the magnitude of the change. At a minimum, Mike works with the SME to develop some question-and-answer sheets about each change.

2. *Someone from the learning group realizes that a performance solution is needed.* A trainer may recognize that company instruction or documentation are open to interpretation, as did happen with the *confined space entry* training materials. Confined spaces, which according to OSHA have limited egress, require very precise procedures about appropriate means of entry and exit. Mike's group pulls together some experts to clarify the policy, and then to ensure that the training materials reflect the clarified intent.

3. *A safety-related incident occurs.* When this does occur, the performance issue quickly "shoots to the top" to be addressed immediately. Eighteen months ago, a hydrogen delivery contractor did not follow AEP policy guidelines, and serious injury occurred. Executive staff demanded the issue receive immediate attention; the safety and training groups decided to change how the policy was enacted.

Contractors present unique challenges for Mike and those in his group, since AEP does not have the ability to enforce every contractual provision or train all of the more than one thousand contractors. Mike's management recently became part of a contract review team, looking at environmental construction contracts for potential training and performance issues. Reviewing contracts from a training perspective may mitigate some performance problems in the future.

The analysis process is made easier for Mike and his colleagues by plentiful and easily accessible internal data. Because so many regulatory agencies require frequent safety-related reports, data is regularly collected and organized in a number of

AEP databases. "Getting information about the actual state is easy," explains Mike, "since all we have to do is manipulate existing data. Getting information about the optimal state is easy, too, since AEP has a 'zero incidents' goal!"

Because Mike comes from an IT background, he sometimes finds himself lacking subject knowledge in the power generation business. "This is sometimes a disadvantage," he confesses, "but mostly it's a good thing. It means that the field operations people don't see me as an 'inspector' or someone trying to tell them how to do things. I tell them that I'm a partner to help them solve performance problems—and then they get on board."

Mike Taylor works as a learning development consultant for the Fossil and Hydro Generation business unit of American Electric Power. With wind, coal-fired, nuclear, and gas generating facilities, AEP is the nation's largest electricity generator and one of the largest utilities in the United States, with more than five million customers. Mike recently completed a master's degree in educational technology, and he applies his new knowledge daily to performance-based problem solving at AEP. You can reach Mike at tmtaylor@aep.com.

Performance Analysis in Context

Performance analysis is critical because it is the process that enables us to provide data-driven advice about performance. That is what matters in every organization. Wasted efforts—scrap, according to Brinkerhoff—must be minimized.

It is time for human resources and training professionals to turn from their habitually favored interventions, like training, to solutions that match the customer and situation, even if it is not what was originally requested. Performance analysis is the study done to define that solution in ways that go beyond the automatic to create fresh, grounded approaches for clients. That is what IBM did when it recreated training for thirty-eight thousand global salespeople. Not surprisingly, IBM has a long and honored history of sales training. To rethink past efforts, IBM used analysis to find a way to transform its young, mobile workforce to become more like the most savvy sales veterans.

On April 7, 2008, in a keynote presentation at ISPI in New York City, IBM's Brenda Sugrue and Nancy Lewis described how they did it. What Sugrue and Lewis attempted was to uncover the foundational capabilities of their stars. The purpose was simple: they intended to clone their top performing salespeople. They did this by asking the top people about their thoughts, smarts, tools, and resources. Through intense interviewing, the IBM team attempted to find out what sales stars knew, did, and relied upon to accelerate sales.

That's IBM. Why not you?

Today we serve colleagues who work far from headquarters, even across the globe. One day the employee is in an airline club. The next day she is with customers, then back at the airline club. And the third day, she is working from home or a hotel room on a proposal that absolutely has to get out.

Their learning and support needs are as large as they have ever been, and palpable to executives and to the individual. How do we meet them? How do we help mobile, diverse employees? How do we provide support for the challenges that matter to them and the next career step that they can't quite imagine? What we must do, sometimes in person and often via technology, is understand the situation today and tomorrow in order to add value to the effort. We do all this through performance analysis.

Defining Performance Analysis

Performance analysis (PA) is partnering with clients and customers to help them define and achieve their goals. PA involves reaching out for several perspectives on a problem or opportunity; determining any and all drivers toward or barriers to successful performance; and proposing a solution system based on what is learned, not on what is typically done.

Let's look at each component of the definition.

Partnering

In the past, a sure sign of success in our business was a magnificent training edifice. In those days, my first visit to a company would leave me stunned by the size and aesthetics of the training center. When I commented on the lush wood, furniture, rugs, and setting at one corporate training center in the eastern United States, a director explained that the beauty was necessary to lure executives and managers from the operating units to headquarters.

The problem was that the posh setting did not lure participants. Busy line leaders did not find fancy rugs or chef-carved roast beef an attraction. Often the problem that consumes human resources and training professionals is how to get people to come and partake of what we know they need. We know it is good for them, that they would be better if they took the class on time management or tuned into the webinar on client services. We know, but alas, they don't.

It is them and it is us, and it shouldn't be. Healthy human resources units are aggressively directing their perspectives and services at the needs of line organizations so that success parallels the priorities of the line organizations, not marketing schemes for training. Our focus is on hearing their priorities and needs, not marketing our perspectives to them.

That doesn't mean that we salute when they speak. What it means is that we are using many methods to see things from their vantage point and to bring new views and data to their attention. In a world with extreme competition and financial dislocation, we must be devoted to understanding them and to helping them understand themselves and their opportunities. Ultimately, we are partners, and our goal is to add value to their endeavors.

In 2006, Cal Wick and colleagues wrote the influential book *The Six Disciplines of Breakthrough Learning*. One key message, out of many relevant to analysis, is the importance of partnerships with people close to the business challenges.

Partnership is established in many ways: through the physical placement of people in the field in permanent or itinerant roles; in the use of HR and training advisory committees composed of line managers; in cross-functional process action teams assembled to solve particular problems; and in assignment of individuals to develop specialized knowledge about the business and concerns of particular line units, even while these individuals still reside in centralized HR or training. Another possibility is to blow up the centralized entity and permanently house performance professionals closer to where the work gets done, perhaps with "dotted-line" relationships to a stripped-down central unit.

Take a moment to assess your progress on partnering in Exhibit 2.1. Where do you stand with a line unit that you and your group are charged with serving? How much of a partner are you today? For each item, give yourself a score from 0 to 10, with 10 representing strong agreement and 0 representing no truth at all in the statement. Total your scores.

A perfect partnering score is 130. How close did you get? Are you satisfied? Would your customers and clients give you similar ratings? Would they express satisfaction with you as their partner? Can they point to ways that you add value to their efforts? Can you use these items to stimulate discussion and improvements?

Exhibit 2.1. Partnering Self-Assessment.

—— I consider myself knowledgeable about their business.

—— I'm as comfortable in the field as I am at headquarters.

—— Many people in the line unit know me and my work.

—— When a new technology or perspective or product is on the horizon, I get involved early and often in the decision making.

—— I know what is of concern to line managers right now. I know what keeps them up at night.

—— I know what is likely to emerge as a concern for line managers in the next year or two.

—— When line managers have a problem, they ask my opinions.

—— I get invited to informal and social events in the field.

—— I know what line leaders are reading, and I'm reading it too.

—— I know what web sites line leaders consider useful, and I visit them regularly.

—— When I talk about the unit, I naturally use the word **we**, because that's how I perceive our relationship. They would feel the same way about me.

—— My colleagues in the field can describe what I do with and for them.

—— If they had to pay for the work I do for them, the business unit would be willing to do so.

Goals

Often, the goals that drive our work do not immediately or overtly match organizational strategy. The best example is measuring viability using the proverbial "butts in seats" or the more contemporary "hits on web sites." What those conventional metrics do is encourage training and HR professionals to become masters of marketing their products and services. Few customers would cheer that goal.

On the other hand, performance analysis directs attention to the customer's priorities. Often this involves working with customers to clarify, define, and make concrete the directions in which they want to go. That might entail reviewing relevant policies, scanning the literature, participating in online communities, and interviewing internal and external subject matter experts. Although there are other rich sources that describe excellent performance in detail, such as benchmarking reports and observations of master performers, they are time-consuming. In this book, we favor those analysis methods that can be carried out quickly.

Customers do come to appreciate the clarity and independence that a performance analyst provides. Century 21 International served as an example (Strayer & Rossett, 1994). Years ago, the real estate corporation sought a major training program for new sales associates. The request was for "twenty-one training modules in a variety of media." Rather than jumping into production mode, we focused instead on what the company really needed, soliciting the perspectives of regional directors, sales experts, brokers, and sales associates. This brought us to more systemic goals than originally conceived by the organization—and to a very different set of solutions. In addition to goals associated with listing, servicing, finance, and the like, we added a new position, the coach, and new perspectives and priorities for the organization.

Several Perspectives

The practice of performance analysis exposes you to diverse views and data. This shift enables you to see things in fresh and complex ways and then to provide that more vivid view to customers. This becomes particularly important when you are constructing programs for dissemination in Indiana,

Frankfurt, Capetown, and Beijing; in offices, hotels, and homes; to groups and to individuals.

A study for a medical manufacturing company provided an example. The executives wanted to know what training to do to help technical supervisors and managers grow in their jobs. By asking hard questions about drivers and barriers, we were able to find out what training was required and to detail significant cultural aspects that had gone awry. Quotes and anecdotes from technical managers told the tale and were used to "sell" management on a solution system instead of just a class on "effective meetings" or "negotiating." These were not our opinions. We were reporting on the views of the very managers they were attempting to influence.

There are many possible sources to be tapped during a performance analysis. They come in animate and inanimate forms. Human sources are executives, managers, supervisors, job incumbents, customers, experts, and colleagues. Inanimate sources are policies, records, tests, exit interviews, work products, reports, printouts, course materials, blogs, knowledge bases, help desk logs, and performance appraisals. It would be unusual to use all these sources in any one performance analysis. The trick is to pick well and to recover from poor selections rapidly.

Here's an example of picking well—eventually. Some colleagues had developed new-product training for a bank. They thought they had created a nifty class for tellers and had that opinion confirmed through course reaction feedback after the sessions. "They loved it," crowed the instructional designers.

Unfortunately, they spoke too soon. A customer and performance focus necessitates waiting for business results before taking bows. On that measure, which in this case was defined as selling more of that particular financial product, things looked dismal a few months later. Soon a director called to urgently request retraining. The professionals wisely demurred, pressing to take a look at why tellers weren't selling the product, rather than automatically scheduling more training.

Because the director was clamoring for action, they decided to schedule one morning of meetings with tellers and branch managers randomly pulled from different branches. The purpose was to find out why tellers weren't selling the product. It was possible that the tellers didn't "get" the new product and thus needed more training, but there were other possibilities as well. After the first focused meeting, a session with tellers, the reason was revealed. A subsequent meeting with other tellers and a group of managers confirmed the cause and provided additional numbers and quotes to use in making the case to the executives. The source of the problem was the incentive system. Branch managers and assistants were measured by wait time during peak times in the branches. Moving people through the line was what garnered supervisory praise and favors, not engaging customers in the more time-consuming relationship selling associated with the new product. Retraining would not make a dent in the problem. Management had to decide what it wanted most, sales or short lines at peak times.

Not all solutions reveal themselves quite this quickly. You will inevitably find yourself with a weak source, a particular threat when you are under severe time constraints. I had this problem during the launch of a management development effort. We were using performance analysis to swiftly scope the situation. We had been directed to a technical manager who was touted as articulate, reflective about management, and able to talk about theory in light of what transpired on the manufacturing floor. But he couldn't, or he wouldn't—not with me. He had recently attended a scientific management conference and was chock full of buzzwords. Specific questions elicited glittering generalities. After about fifteen minutes, we parted. Other sources would be more fertile at this point. In fact, we found that judiciously selected literature on management development served as an excellent and substantive starting point for structuring interactions with managers. Most management sources, technical experts all, were better at reacting to proffered descriptions and examples than they were at generating descriptions themselves.

Problems and Opportunities

This book provides analysis tools for four typical situations, each of which is treated in detail in Chapter Four:

1. *Opportunities,* such as a new technology rollout or an effort to encourage contracts administrators to make more decisions without turning to the legal department to advise them each time.

2. *Problems,* such as missed sales expectations or increases in defective parts or complaints about customer service.

3. *Development of a group of people*—for example, engineers, hospital administrators, or customer service representatives.

4. *Strategic planning,* which occurs when an executive wants assistance in looking at the situation in the midst of a changing competitive environment in order to set a broad, distinguishing direction.

Why these situations? They are in our lives. These kinds of requests are typical grist for the HR and training professional.

Sometimes, however, customers and clients don't ask for anything at all. They do not seek our help. Amanda Scott, then at IBM, described to me the fertile possibilities presented by being proactive and conversant with the client, by not waiting for requests. If you're in a partnering relationship with the line, you're then in a position to anticipate an opportunity, note a problem, and collaborate on solutions. Katie Smith, formerly the practice leader for instructional systems design at Amoco and now a sales training manager at Eli Lilly, described the role that some organizational developers played at Amoco. Assigned to particular business units, they continuously conduct virtual performance analyses, gathering data in formal and informal ways and passing off opportunities to human resources colleagues. Another associate, who chose to remain anonymous, explained that he checks in on several automotive blogs and listservs. As a leader in training for a global car company, he wants to know about problems and opportunities before he hears it in a direct request from line leaders.

Drivers and Barriers

Drivers and barriers are the levers in an organization that encourage, maintain, or impede performance. Although we discuss them in great detail in subsequent chapters, particularly in Chapter Three, a few examples might serve here. Skills are drivers. Access to information is a driver, just as the lack of it could deter performance. Another driver or barrier is the organizational culture, as it either encourages or discourages ways of behaving.

The emphasis on drivers and barriers, current and anticipated, is what distinguishes performance analysis from other planning efforts. Training- and performance-oriented professionals have always worked with colleagues to establish directions through task analysis and strategic planning, for example. What's new and critical in performance analysis is targeting the causes of performance improvement, maintenance, and deterioration, enabling the professional to tailor solutions to these circumstances.

Ideally, the nature of the drivers and barriers defines the services that we propose to provide to customers. We are thus more responsive than if we are doing something because we always have or because we were asked to do so.

Remember the financial product example presented earlier? The initial response to that request for assistance was the opposite of what we're talking about. The bank director said something like this to the instructional designers: "We want a class, something short and snappy. We want them to be able to quickly sell this fairly complicated new account." And that's what the instructional designers delivered. They provided short-term value to the line executive.

But it didn't work. The reason? While they studied up on optimals associated with the new product, the professionals made scant inquiries about barriers and drivers. They assumed that the person who made the request had done the analysis or in some other way divined what was needed. They failed to ask about branch culture, about what mattered in the branches and what might get in the way of the desired sales performance. If they had, both a class and changes in incentives and policies would have taken place. Together, the class, the job aids, and the related incentive changes compose a solution system.

Solution Systems

Solution systems are integrated, cross-functional approaches to solving problems and realizing opportunities. Driven by the nature of the drivers and barriers, interventions are tailored to the situation and coordinated across the organization. A typical solution system involves strategies that develop individual capacity and motivation, such as training and coaching, and organizational readiness and culture, such as recognition programs, workplace technology, processes, and policies.

Consider something you do well and often at work. It might be answering emails, writing reports, coaching a new employee. Why do you do that thing you do well and often? There are probably many reasons: you want to; you believe it is important to do so; you know how to; when you do it, you get recognized for it; you have the necessary tools and materials; the supervisor applauds the effort; you perceive yourself as good at it. . . . How long would you persist if your manager and measurements paid it little mind?

The point is that performance is a complex thing. It happens for many reasons. And when it doesn't happen, that too is usually for several reasons. An example might be dieting. Why don't people enjoy successes in that area? There are many possible reasons: they don't want to; they don't know how to; they love food and the socializing it affords; they don't have low-calorie foods in the house; they are injured and can't exercise; they live with somebody who loves to eat, and they love to eat right along with him or her. If they committed themselves to dieting and hoped for significant long-term improvements in weight control, they would need a solution system. Just taking a class would not get the results. That solution system would probably involve several approaches, including instruction, exercise, food choices, cupboard and fridge purging, negotiating with a partner, and coaching for confidence.

Let's try another example, one that is closer to the work. Imagine that you have been asked to provide some leadership in your organization on the topic of sexual harassment. Although the executive that requested the assistance indicated preference for a "powerful class," performance analysis swiftly revealed that no class on earth, in and of itself, could accomplish such important outcomes. A solution system is essential, likely involving executive stewardship; new policies regarding appraisal, recognition, and promotions; an anonymous hotline; e-coaching; and targeted training, based on where colleagues have erred in the past. Performance analysis reveals the nature of the solution system and provides data to sell such a "full-court press" to the person who wanted that magical class.

A solution system is the opposite of a silver bullet. Terry Bickham, then of the U.S. Coast Guard and now with Deloitte, and I discovered this when we looked at diversity programs for law enforcement agencies. Often, their preference was for a class or a speaker or a counselor. Leadership wanted to do one thing, preferably one self-contained, countable, and laudable event. But most complex changes involve coordinated and significant solution systems executed consistently over time.

Even though solution systems make all the sense in the world, that doesn't mean they happen readily. A 1996 study that Carl Czech, then of SAIC and now with the U.S. Navy, and I completed and published in *Performance Improvement Quarterly* (Rossett & Czech, 1996) made this point: professionals trained in analysis and solution systems are often thwarted in their efforts because their colleagues prefer a silver bullet. The Coast Guard's Cathy Tobias Kang and I followed up and confirmed that study. One striking finding: only 18 percent of ISPI and ASTD respondents described their organizations as boundaryless. The boundaries between IT and HR, for example, and between Marketing and Manufacturing, reduce the inclination toward solution systems.

If your organization does not currently support these systemic approaches, be comforted by the fact that they could be in your future. Look at Accenture, Deloitte, and Intrepid Learning Systems. These consulting houses are organized to facilitate the establishment of targeted solution systems for clients. They are client facing. Boundaries are reduced, and white space is continuously questioned.

Exhibit 2.2 is a self-check that will provide an indication of your likelihood to turn the results of performance analysis into solution systems.

So Many Analyses, So Little Time

Performance analysis. Front-end analysis. Task analysis. Content analysis. Learner analysis. Root cause analysis. We could devote a book to the distinctions so laboriously drawn between these concepts. But this isn't that book. Why?

Making those distinctions isn't necessary for effective practice—and this book is about practice. We'll focus on the kinds of information and sources that you require up front, when you are launching an effort, in order to consult effectively with clients and customers no matter what you dub the

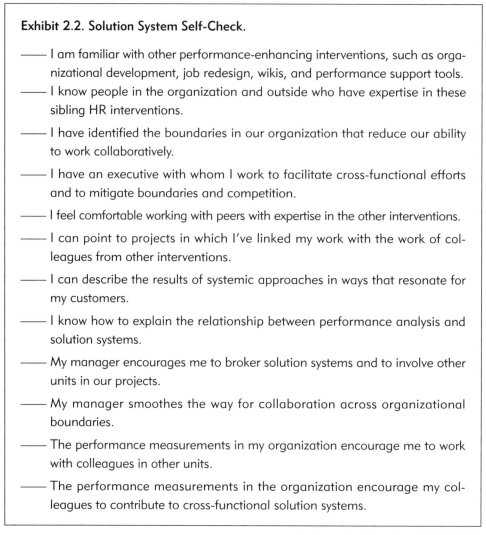

Exhibit 2.2. Solution System Self-Check.

—— I am familiar with other performance-enhancing interventions, such as organizational development, job redesign, wikis, and performance support tools.

—— I know people in the organization and outside who have expertise in these sibling HR interventions.

—— I have identified the boundaries in our organization that reduce our ability to work collaboratively.

—— I have an executive with whom I work to facilitate cross-functional efforts and to mitigate boundaries and competition.

—— I feel comfortable working with peers with expertise in the other interventions.

—— I can point to projects in which I've linked my work with the work of colleagues from other interventions.

—— I can describe the results of systemic approaches in ways that resonate for my customers.

—— I know how to explain the relationship between performance analysis and solution systems.

—— My manager encourages me to broker solution systems and to involve other units in our projects.

—— My manager smoothes the way for collaboration across organizational boundaries.

—— The performance measurements in my organization encourage me to work with colleagues in other units.

—— The performance measurements in the organization encourage my colleagues to contribute to cross-functional solution systems.

analysis. The best place for defining these terms is in a lengthier text or a glossary.

Now that I've convinced you that the fine distinctions aren't important, I'm going to reverse myself a bit and revisit the distinction between performance analysis and training needs assessment. That is one that is important, because both combine to provide planning services in the organization.

Too often, study up front is appreciated more in theory than in practice. Too often, I hear, "They just won't give me time to do any planning. They want what they want when they want it."

In reaction to that, and after observing some nifty practices in organizations such as IBM, Fidelity Investments, British Petroleum, and Wells Fargo, I've cut the front end into manageable bite sizes. One bite is performance analysis. The other and usually lengthier munch is what some call needs assessment and others call training needs assessment.

Performance analysis provides preliminary study of the situation in order to determine if and when training is required, and whether a more detailed training needs assessment is warranted.

Training needs assessment is study to design and develop instructional and informational programs and materials, after the performance analysis has determined that training or informational materials are indeed appropriate. Needs assessments involve subject matter study, audience analysis, determination of prerequisite skills and attitudes, error and work product examination, resolution of disagreements among experts, and definition of the lion's share of the details that will congeal in the learning and reference effort. The effort described by Brenda Sugrue and Nancy Lewis of IBM to dig into the details of how their top salespeople proceed about their work would most typically have belonged in training needs assessment.

We invest in needs assessments only after we are certain that education, training, or information can be critical factors in solving the problem or realizing the opportunity. Thus input for a needs assessment comes from performance analysis.

Performance analysis is what happens up front and immediately, prior to needs assessment. It is the expeditious study that enables you to determine the general nature of the drivers and barriers and thus the related solution system. Performance assessment asks, What should be happening? Why aren't they doing it? What might get in the way if we make these changes? Will training be involved? Will documentation? What about job redesign? Process reengineering? New policies and incentives? Programs for managers and executives? What's it going to take?

There are similarities between performance analysis and training needs assessment. They both represent methods for figuring out what to do. They are efforts to understand and serve customers. And they rely on sources for data. Performance analysis and training needs assessment seek the same kinds

Figure 2.1. PA to TNA.

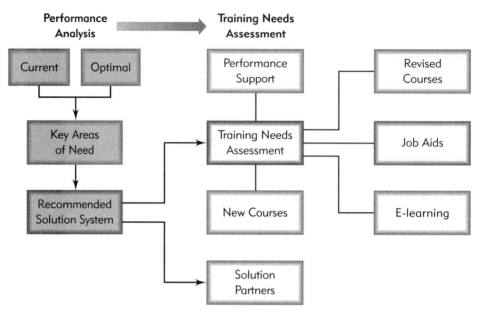

of information but at different levels of detail. The distinction lies in where they are in the food chain, so to speak, as represented in Figure 2.1.

Performance analysis is what you do first and fast. Training needs assessment is what you do to create the tangible solution(s) to the problem or opportunity. Whereas performance analysis is that first response, needs assessment is the more measured and production-oriented effort, something I've described in detail in my older book *Training Needs Assessment.* Performance analysis helps determine what to recommend. If training, coaching, information, or references are indicated, then training needs assessment provides the content for that tailored program.

Performance analysis identifies the people in an organization who must come to the table to develop and coordinate the solution system. It is the initial service provided to customers and clients. The people doing needs assessment receive a hand-off from performance analysts, perhaps a report or a briefing detailing those aspects of the effort amenable to training and information solutions. It is this PA document that will sell and justify the time and expense of meetings with subject matter experts and practitioners, and the lengthier examination of the literature and work products, so often a part of the needs assessment (detailed in *Training Needs Assessment*).

The seductive nature of the new media is another good reason to add performance analysis right up front. Performance analysis keeps the focus on the customers and their purposes. The goal is to find the "right" bundle of interventions, not to take a spin with podcasts or Second Life.

In this chapter we've described the challenges confronting training and human resources professionals:

> Intensified performance orientation—habitual solutions aren't sufficient
>
> Expectations regarding consultation services delivered to customers and clients
>
> Increased emphasis on understanding customer needs
>
> Increased accountability for demonstrating value to clients and customers
>
> Limited time and support for analysis
>
> More study prior to choosing a solution

We've also focused on definitions, particularly looking at performance analysis and then comparing it with training needs assessment. What is performance analysis?

Performance analysis

> Enables you to reach out and understand the organization
>
> Establishes partnerships with customers and clients and sibling colleagues, such as process reengineers and organizational effectiveness experts
>
> Relies on many sources of information, including experts, managers, associates, records, and work products
>
> Produces a picture of what's encouraging or blocking performance in the organization and what must be done about it

Sets the table for needs assessment

Generates solution systems

Does all this swiftly, because performance analysis is a springboard to organizational partners who will then contribute to the effort

Performance analysis helps you determine what to recommend. If training or information or references are indicated, then training needs assessment enables that recommendation to come to fruition.

3

Performance Analysis Basics

Andy: I've been doing analysis for years. That's why I was stunned when a customer accused me of analysis-paralysis.

Marcus: I believe in study before action, of course, but I'm concerned that my efforts are not as focused as they could be, which means I take longer than maybe I ought. And I too have had trouble explaining it to my customers. Each time I bring it up, I have to resell the effort.

Beth: We need to demonstrate more value derived from the process. We tend to stumble around, do a little of this and a little of that. Some days we post a survey on SurveyMonkey. Other times we run focus groups. But we don't have a consistent approach, standard questions, or, most important, a way to communicate back to our customers about what we're doing and why it was worth the time and effort.

In this chapter, we go to the heart of the matter: we talk about the basic principles of performance analysis and about the kinds of information we seek and the sources to which we turn for that information.

Principles of Performance Analysis

Five ideas drive performance analysis:

1. Study prior to action improves the quality of what we do.

2. Incorporation of several sources yields a better program than an approach that relies on fewer sources, such as an executive or an expert.

3. Data, broadly defined, are critical to figuring out what to do.

4. A systematic approach to analysis is good for individuals and the organization.

5. A systemic approach to solutions is good for individuals and the organization.

Let's look at each of these assumptions.

1. Study prior to action improves the quality of what we do.

A doctor would not doubt it. Neither would a reading specialist or a geologist. Is there any question that a reflective examination of the possibilities and the current situation yields a superior effort?

The quality movement has firmly ingrained the value of study and measurement in American organizations. However, a frequent obstacle to analysis is customers' unwillingness to invest time and energy in study that precedes events and programming. Most line managers want what they want when they want it. They want it now, not later, and certainly not if it involves waiting around for the results of a study.

Here is an example. The topic is email etiquette. A line leader sent this email message to a manager in the training department: "That program you brought in on empowerment was good. I've heard some positive things about it. What I want is something like that to deal with the problems surrounding email. You know how it is. We have a problem here and our last cycle of training didn't get it done. When can you get the new training organized? This might be a good one for e-learning."

E-learning might be the answer. And it might not be. What exactly is wrong with the emails? Wrong words? Wrong tone? Wrong signature? Sloppy grammar or word choices? Are responses timely? Are many committing the identified mistakes or just a few? Why are they making these errors? Do they know what is expected of them? Is any feedback provided?

Dana and Jim Robinson (2008), in the second edition of their book *Performance Consulting,* introduce the *gap zapper.* When we function as gap zappers, we are actively and dependably narrowing the chasm between the desired and current situation, between optimal and actual. The gap zapper is devoted to clarifying what is needed and tailoring solutions.

The beauty of performance analysis is attention to answering important questions in ways that make sense to customers. As conceptualized here, performance analysis assumes scant time and organizational support yet bases decisions on the more solid footings that come from taking a data-driven and speedy look at the work, worker, and workplace. That happens through questions, contacts with key sources, and examination of relevant workplace outcomes.

After eleven years in the Coast Guard, Reed Stephenson was selected to attend an educational technology graduate program at San Diego State University. Since graduating in 2001, he has applied his knowledge of human performance technology (HPT) to numerous Coast Guard projects. Reed now manages training at the Coast Guard's major training center in Petaluma, California. Leading more than three hundred personnel, he oversees analysis, course design and development, evaluation, instructor development, learner resources, and instructional support.

The Coast Guard prescribes very specific analysis methodologies that are based on the performance issue, timeline, and scope of the learning or performance scenario. These methodologies include front-end analysis, job task analysis, performance system analysis, and others. Reed points out that regardless of the name, "we always attempt to follow the tenets of good HPT. Our analyses are outcome focused, data driven, objective, measurable, and cost effective."

Many of the apprentice and journeyman programs offered at Petaluma are technically oriented, so skills needed to perform on the job are dynamic. A lengthy Occupational Analysis (OA) is performed on each of seven apprentice programs every three to four years to align curriculum with the current and ideal job requirements.

Much can change between each OA, so Reed uses Level 3 evaluations in the interim to ensure that training is targeted to correct skill sets.

While it is rare that the Coast Guard creates an entirely new apprentice program, existing ones are often split, merged, or enhanced to meet current job requirements. Reed has helped shift the Coast Guard toward online, simulation, and distance-based training opportunities in lieu of or in addition to face-to-face resident training. Here are some of the more interesting distance-based projects Reed managed:

1. *Designing and outfitting a culinary studio to provide live, web-based culinary lessons to Coast Guard cooks across the nation.* The studio is also used for a complete video library of skills and recipes needed by the more than thirteen hundred cooks.

2. *Creating online performance support for a weapons of mass destruction policy and equipment module.* This affects more than twenty-five thousand Coast Guard members who do not now have to attend resident training.

3. *Developing a team training simulator and corresponding curriculum for large ship operations.* This training is intended for teams of six or more working in the communications, command, and control center on the Coast Guard's new line of high-tech ships.

Reed reiterates that all decisions about new training initiatives—traditional or distance-based—undergo cost-benefit analysis that looks at task complexity, task criticality, time, resources, and audience size.

As he looks back on his years of performance consulting and analyzes his successes and failures, Reed points to several lessons learned that continue to hold significance for his work.

- *Get to the decision maker.* If you work with a subordinate of the person who can actually make change happen, you increase your risk of failure. Push to build relationships at the highest level possible.

- *Define the optimal as an outcome.* Too often performance consultants end up with either vague or process-oriented descriptions of optimal states that ultimately cripple a performance project. Decision makers often hesitate to describe measurable and outcome-oriented performance standards, because it requires answering some tough questions, and it asks them to be accountable to those standards.

- *Don't compare apples and oranges.* After defining the optimal as an objective and measurable end state, always keep that state as your reference point and don't be tempted to describe actual performance in other ways. It is not uncommon to see a root cause described as the current state.

- *Communicate.* Communicate early and often with each decision maker. Reed stresses the need to "communicate in their language, *not* the language of HPT. If you keep your client abreast of your status and progress, they can provide small course corrections if needed. They should know what's coming; avoid the Perry Mason moment. Some of my most successful projects have been anticlimactic!"

Reed Stephenson has been a U.S. Coast Guard member since 1990. After working in operations, Reed became an internal performance consultant based in Washington, D.C., focusing on human performance aspects of homeland security missions. He now serves as the chief performance and training officer at Petaluma, where he oversees seven apprentice and thirty-two journeyman programs graduating more than three thousand Coast Guard members each year. Contact Reed at Reed.A.Stephenson@uscg.mil.

2. Incorporation of several sources yields a better program than an approach that relies on fewer sources, such as an executive or an expert.

The quest for information from several sources is an effort to "triangulate." Triangulation increases our confidence about a finding by helping us determine if other sources echo it. Matthew Miles and Michael Huberman (1984), authorities on qualitative research, note that we should draw comfort from the work of detectives who use a modus operandi approach, amassing alibis, fingerprints, hair samples, accounts, opinions, and the like in order to draw conclusions about a case.

In performance analysis we are attempting to do the same thing as we seek the perspectives of several sources on a topic in order to come to more sturdy conclusions. Take the topic of customer service. It is hard to justify installation of a program based on the feelings of a single executive and the impressions of an expert. Don't we also want to talk to the representatives charged with delivering service in the call centers? To their supervisors? To customers too? I would want my program focused by customer complaints and kudos also.

We also profit from inclusion, as we go beyond the executive and expert to solicit involvement from other regions and countries, from the people closest to the work, and from customers. Experience and the literature suggest that people will be more likely to support a solution that they or peers helped to define.

A final benefit is that participation in the up-front study is a form of education for participants. Often I've heard, "You know, that's a good question. I wasn't aware of the nature of the complaints about service, just knew there were some rumblings. I have to look into that before I answer. I'll get right back to you."

A leader in an insurance company issued this request: "We must transform our organization so that our people are doing things in teams. I understand there is a really fine multimedia program that does just that. Buy it, schedule it, whatever. Let's get the transition happening." It is almost laughable to imagine that any single set of materials in any medium could achieve this deep and complex goal—yet the executive was licking his lips over just that idea. And he is not alone. Bringing teaming, or any critical change to an organization, involves eschewing silver bullets, listening to many sources of information, and then birthing a solution system. No question, it takes a village to improve performance. Performance analysis helps define how life and work will transpire in that village.

3. Data, broadly defined, are critical to figuring out what to do.

Data are what we gather from sources. They include facts, attitudes, opinions, results, and actions that turn into information once we organize and infuse them with meaning. Data are the basis for the assumptions that we cobble together to make inferences and derive conclusions.

An example? When you build an email etiquette program, it makes sense to target those emails that have generated complaints. The complaints and emails are data that inspire the program. We look at data to derive a clear picture about where our colleagues are having problems with email and where they are doing fine. We interview employees—yes, more data—to determine their opinions on what is causing their problems and what to do about them.

We collect formal and informal data to make certain that history or whim or habit or politics or metrics isn't pressing us toward recommendations or actions not indicated by the realities of the work, the worker, and the workplace.

During performance analysis, we want to define data broadly, including, for example, letters of complaint and praise from customers, wait time and response rates, conversations enjoyed in the lunch line, employee opinions solicited via climate surveys, mission statements, elevator chats, interviews with randomly pulled supervisors, certification test results, compliments and complaints found on blogs, and focus groups composed of model performers. I examined formal data gathered during performance modeling sessions with financial analysts for a computer company. What resulted from their group meetings was a first-cut picture of their shared goals, skills, and knowledge associated with a top-performing financial analyst. Soon, individual interviews with supervisors and employees will capture data about priorities and perceptions regarding obstacles and barriers. Another data source is the priorities of the two executives most concerned about the productivity and morale of the financial people. Each sliver of data can be thought of as a piece of a jigsaw puzzle, in this case a puzzle focused on the work life of a new financial analyst for a global technology company. The small data elements eventually fit together into a textured picture of the situation.

4. A systematic approach to analysis is good for individuals and the organization.

Performance analysis is systematic. When something is systematic, it has defined purpose, components, data, input, transactions, and output (Table 3.1). It is standardized, consistent, and repeatable.

Table 3.1. Performance Analysis Is a Systematic Effort.

Purpose	The purpose of performance analysis is to help the organization accomplish its goals by incorporating data from varied sources and making effective decisions or recommendations about what should happen next.
Components	The components of performance analysis are sources, kinds of information, data, data-gathering strategies, and solution systems.
Data	The recommendations that result from performance analysis are driven by the data that is gathered from sources, not by whim, politics, or historical precedent.
Defined input, transactions, and output	*Input* is sources' perspectives on the work, worker, and workplace. Examples of input are interviews, records, and work products. Performance analysis *transactions* are the methods used to gather information, such as interviews, review of records and the literature, and focus groups. The *output* of performance analysis is twofold: first, the recommendations regarding what to do and identification of the partners that need to collaborate to do it; second, the involvement and goodwill generated by asking sources to participate in the process—and honoring their opinions.
Output from one phase serves as input for the next	Each contact with a source influences subsequent contacts. For example, what we learn from one expert will influence the way we structure interviews with job incumbents. The information provided by work products helps target the questions we ask about what might be driving the problem.

When systematic, the output from one phase of performance analysis serves as input for subsequent efforts, enlightening decisions about what to do. In the financial analysis example above, the early conversations and focus groups serve as grist for the more formal press for prioritization.

Performance analysis is what enables everything else to happen, serving as the basis for the messages that are conveyed to those who will serve as partners in the effort.

It is not new to think about the work of the human resources professional as a systematic endeavor. Since World War II, on the basis of lessons from Robert Morgan, Robert Gagne, and others, professionals have attempted to use data to identify objectives and then to craft strategies and evaluation items based on the nature of the objectives.

But it is not just the instructional systems development (ISD) movement that offers up lessons about systematic approaches. A workforce improvement model of interest to us is the People Capability Maturity Model (People CMM). Born of the efforts of Carnegie Mellon University's Software Engineering Institute, and adapted to focus on performance alignment in organizations such as Tata, Boeing, and Lockheed Martin, the model presents five levels of maturity and four theme areas. There is more to it than that, but for our purposes, we'll focus on maturity and themes, especially as they concern themselves with systematic performance improvement programs.

Wademan, Spuches, and Doughty (2007) described the five maturity levels associated with the People CMM.

- Level 5 is the optimizing level. Excellence is achieved through continuous improvement of an organization and individuals striving for ever-higher levels of performance.

- Level 4 is the predictable level. In Level 4 effort and improvements are informed by data that are gathered in light of a competency framework and results.

- Level 3 is the defined level. Here workforce improvement is professionalized, with frameworks for competences to achieve business outcomes.

- Level 2 is the managed level, at which stable process and tools are applied, and managers take responsibility for workforce development.

- Level 1 is the initial level, characterized by ad hoc efforts to develop people and the organization. Efforts and outcomes are inconsistent.

Now let's look at the four theme areas as they apply to these maturity levels. Table 3.2 brings the two concepts together and shows how the model might serve as the basis for inquiry during analysis. What I've done here is to insert questions to illustrate the way the People CMM directs our attention.

5. A systemic approach to solutions is good for individuals and the organization.

Performance analysis recognizes that performance occurs within a system. No matter the power of a course or the rightness of the selection of a person for a job, continued excellent performance depends on integrated components that wrap around people. That's the performance system, comprising standards, feedback, knowledge, skills, incentives, recognition, access to information, management, sponsorship, incentives, recognition, technology, tools, processes, and more.

Performance analysis looks into that performance system, as you can see in the questions raised in Table 3.2. The analysis provides details about what is and isn't working within the current system and about what needs to be included in any system to come. Better than customer habit or conventional human resources metrics is a program tailored to enable salespeople to sell and auditors to audit. Table 3.3 describes the elements of a systemic approach.

Jeanne Strayer and I (1994) described an exemplary program for Century 21 International in *Performance Improvement Quarterly.* New sales associates were the focus. Fresh from licensing classes and certification tests, many new associates soon became discouraged as they attempted to make residential real estate sales and failed repeatedly. Not surprising, many quit, creating problems for themselves and the company. After a systematic analysis, the company broke their training habit in favor of a systemic approach to solving the problem. This approach involved selection of the "right" coaches, training for coaches, shared training materials for coaches and new salespeople, and monetary incentives for coaches. The simple and typical thing—training modules for the sales associates—would not have made a dent in the numbers. The performance analysis provided the data needed to sell to management the unfamiliar

Table 3.2. The People CMM Encourages Systematic Performance Analysis.

Culture	Developing Individual Capability	Building Workgroups and Culture	Motivating and Managing Performance	Shaping the Workforce
5. Optimizing	Are individuals learning and referencing in the workflow, as needs emerge?	Are Web 2.0 strategies used to collect the "wisdom of the masses"?	Do managers play daily roles in developing their people? Is the workforce admired by customers?	Do many people want to work there?
4. Predictable	As the world changes, are expectations for skills and knowledge updated?	Is there a system for individuals and teams to share best ideas?	Does performance management match strategic directions?	How long do people stay? Are the people who stay the ones who leaders want to stay?
3. Defined	Do employees have a way to self-assess and plan their development?	Do managers and peers have a way to provide feedback to individuals and the organization?	How do supervisors encourage these competences?	Does the performance management system match competency expectations?
2. Managed	Are skills and knowledge defined for each job?	Are roles specified?	Are roles distinct? Are they recognized?	Are expectations clear? Are career opportunities transparent, known?
1. Initial	No standard approaches			

Table 3.3. Performance Analysis Yields Systemic Recommendations.

Focuses on components and relationships of an entity	Rather than looking at components in isolation, performance analysis looks at the relationships between the entities in an organization. For example, a systemic approach to improved customer services would acknowledge the many organizational and individual levers that must work together to accomplish the business result.
Elements influence each other	Consider the customer service example. Altering the job descriptions and training for supervisors will influence the performance of service representatives and their immediate needs for information and development.
Seeks and addresses root causes	Performance analysis attempts to find and solve underlying problems, not just their symptoms. In the customer service example, the PA might trace the problem of customer complaints to poor service as a result of high employee turnover, which is due in turn to a combination of poorly structured incentive system and outdated tools plus a rapidly changing product database that leaves employees feeling insecure about their ability to help customers.
Acknowledges distinctions between means and ends	Customers say, "We need a coach out there, somebody patient in working with people who are afraid of technology." This is a *means* statement. Although this *might* be the best way to deal with the challenge, we want to focus first on the factors that influence the desired outcomes, rather than do the automatic or habitual thing.
Emphasizes solution systems predicated on causes, barriers, drivers	Performance analysis works on the principle that complex problems typically require multiple, rather than single, solutions. For example, redesigning both the incentives and the tools, often in conjunction with some training, would be likely to produce better results than training without related organization interventions.

and more complicated cross-functional system. When the company looked at the impact of the sales solution system, they found significant differences in offices where the system was in place.

Kinds of Information

During performance analysis, we seek two broad kinds of information, directions and drivers. When we seek directions, we are looking for the performance and perspectives that the organization and its leaders are eager to put in place. Two kinds of information influence our quest for directions: information about "optimals" (where we hope to go) and information about "actuals" (the status quo). We derive directions from perspectives on exemplary or optimal performance and from current or actual performance. Some examples of optimals are what expert salespeople know that enables them to qualify customers, or what a fine chef does to make a plate look especially tempting, or what a master mechanic thinks about when looking at a computer printout associated with an airplane. Some examples of actuals are error rates, help desk inquiries, help desk logs, and retail returns. They indicate what is now occurring in the organization to enable us to focus our attention.

As manager of the Best Practices team for Vanguard University, Catherine Lombardozzi supports the learning professionals at the University and throughout Vanguard. "We keep our finger on the pulse of the industry, and we research new trends and approaches to determine how they might help Vanguard reach its goals." Catherine's team also assists the university in standardizing its own practices.

Vanguard has a strong governance structure that helps the university prioritize and ensure that initiatives are aligned with the most important business needs. The process of prioritizing learning and development projects has several components:

1. *Deans and senior design professionals, who are charged with developing strong partnerships with specific client groups, consult with those groups*

before any decisions are made. These relationships make Vanguard University aware of ongoing goals and objectives as well as specific potential training needs.

2. *Vanguard University requires principal-level sponsorship of all training requests.* Once a project is identified, the dean or senior designer will scope the project at a high level to ensure appropriate sponsorship and to determine how large the project might be and how it will fit into the overall business environment.

3. *Once the project size and scope are fleshed out, the project must be reviewed by the appropriate advisory council, composed of senior business leaders.* Decisions can then be made and priorities set in conversation with the dean or design manager leading the initiative.

Catherine's own analysis work is primarily internal to the University, and she knows the clients quite well. She tends to use prototypes, since "giving the team something to react to is often quicker and more nuanced than gathering data up front." She states that Vanguard employees "are not shy about critiquing a suggested approach!"

Catherine points out that knowing a client group well means that you can tap into key individuals who are very in touch with the team as a whole. Having one or two people serve as conduits is a very useful practice. For example, her Best Practices team recently created an internal course on instructional design. Catherine first attended a line manager meeting and asked critical questions about what the managers wanted their crew members to be able to do. She also inquired about the areas of "greatest need" among new hires. With the information generated from that meeting, Catherine applied her own knowledge of instructional design—and how it's applied at Vanguard—to draw up a set of objectives and a high-level outline for the course. One single manager was then named the business lead for the project, and this manager had final approval of all design details and course materials. Catherine admitted that "occasionally she and I felt the need to consult more broadly," but the relationship served the course and business goals well. "The approach helped us to avoid the paralysis of having too many opinions in the mix."

Catherine believes that a learning professional's value to an organization is directly related to the ability to understand business needs, conceptualize appropriate solutions, and influence business leaders to buy in to those solutions. "The most important influencing strategy we have," she emphasizes, "is asking the right questions and really listening to the answers. We must understand our clients' intended outcomes, and then help them understand that the best solutions might be slightly different than they imagined. Our skill at communicating, with the clients' goals at heart, will help us be better business partners and also better able to position our recommendations."

Catherine Lombardozzi has been a workplace learning professional "for my entire career." In the late 1980s, when the concepts of human performance technology came to the forefront of the learning and development industry, she learned and utilized those skills to help the design teams she managed determine whether training was an appropriate solution to specific business problems. In addition to her work at Vanguard University, Catherine also teaches as an adjunct in instructional design graduate programs at Penn State Great Valley and Chestnut Hill College. You can reach Catherine at catherine_lombardozzi@vanguard.com.

We also seek information about performance drivers. Performance drivers are the factors that block or aid performance or those that might do so in the future. Causes, barriers, and obstacles are synonyms for drivers.

Typical drivers are skills, motivation, articulated expectations, incentives, tools, and work processes. If you think about it, you can see that all are involved in ensuring performance. Let's apply the concept of drivers to the topic of this book. Even if you possess skills and knowledge about performance analysis, you are more likely to do it if you see it as important, are encouraged by your manager or client, are prodded by a criterion within your performance appraisal, and are provided with some technology support in a pinch. The "knowing about it" part is necessary, certainly, but not sufficient.

I am not the only one who is keen on a broad array of performance drivers. Dana and Jim Robinson's 2008 book, a new edition of their classic text *Performance Consulting*, acknowledges that more is involved in performance than training and development. The Robinsons point to five influential factors:

1. Do people know what is *expected* of them? Are *roles clear and vivid?*
2. Are *coaching and reinforcement* available to individuals as they go about their work?
3. Do people get *rewarded* for the desired performance?
4. Are the *work systems and processes* contributing to performance or hindering it?
5. Will people have *access to the information* they need?

Let's look at an example. Consider the Transportation Security Administration. Its members are the people who screen us and our carry-on baggage at airports. What are their likely drivers? What are the components of a system that would strengthen and maintain their critical performance? Certainly, they need to know what to look for, how to screen, how to decipher the computer screens, how to approach passengers, and how to do it all swiftly. They also need to know why their efforts are important and to care enough to maintain energy and performance in a job that is repetitive to the extreme. Yet another factor is technology; it seems obvious that better scanners are critical for doing this job. Finally, these people need to believe that there are incentives for attentiveness. They must know that their performance will be tested, and that feedback, supervision, and ramifications will be swift and certain.

In 2008, directions changed. TSA leadership has begun to encourage more focus on watching travelers in order to discern those who are anxious and perhaps guilty. That will create new instructional objectives, of course. What drivers might get in the way of this new direction? For sure, I wonder if most TSA people know how to discern a person nervous about flying from a person with evil intentions? What of their motivation? While I feel confident that TSA staffers want to do this aspect of their job, I think that their confidence could be questionable. I am also concerned about incentives. What happens to them if they identify somebody with a beard as worthy of further screening and that person pushes back with a charge of "profiling?" Are there incentives to act or to remain silent?

If you are familiar with my work, you are noticing that I've boiled the effort down from a longer list of kinds of information to two. From a quest for information about optimals, actuals, barriers, feelings, and solutions detailed in *Training Needs Assessment* (Rossett, 1987), I'm advising an early emphasis on directions and drivers. The discussion that follows shows how I've streamlined the effort.

We'll examine directions and drivers in the following sections, focusing on methods and sources most likely to contribute to capturing them and furthering the goals of quality and speed.

Directions

Directions set the course for the effort. The task during performance analysis is to determine, from the perspective of judiciously selected sources, what people ought to be thinking about and doing in an ideal situation. "Optimals" are what we want the people to know and do and what the conditions are in which they will be doing them. "Actuals" detail the current situation. What exactly should the TSA people know about anxiety, nervousness, guilt, and impatience? What are the attributes of those concepts, and how do they manifest themselves? What do they already know?

Turn to the sponsor or initiator of the event for definition. One approach focuses on where they hope to go. Here are some sample questions:

What are you attempting to accomplish? Why?

Will effort in other regions or countries be different? How so?

Do you have any documents or policies that explain what it is that job incumbents ought to be doing and why it is important?

Who in the organization must be involved as we move forward on this?

Are there any examples of model work products to which you can direct us?

What experts, inside and outside, should be involved in defining what needs to happen?

What do you think that your more effective people know and do that others perhaps don't? Are there any key resources on which they rely?

Are you or colleagues reading anything that has been particularly influential?

What are the challenges that they will be confronting?

How is the work environment going to shift in ways that matter to [this topic or group of people]?

Another tack on optimals is to approach them from the current situation— the actuals. Seek out descriptions of the current efforts. What does the sponsor seek to maintain or alter? Where are the problems and opportunities? That status quo then becomes the jumping-off point for the effort. The opposite of the problems provides insight into where efforts ought to be focused and where questions about drivers will eventually be focused. Imagine that you are working on a program to improve parents' behavior at their children's sporting events. This latter approach would be fruitful.

Here are sample questions that use current successes and failures to frame the effort and point toward desired directions:

Is anybody here doing it, already talking about it and thinking about it as you wish others would? What about their approaches attracts you, strikes you as model?

Is there anything they are doing that you'd like to increase or change?

As you consider the efforts going on around the globe, what strikes you as particularly useful? How can we learn from these efforts?

Can you describe some of the changes and improvements you'd like to see?

Have there been any examples of flawed performance that concern you? What were the problems, as you see them?

Are there any examples of flawed work products to which you can direct us? What's the problem with them?

What questions do people raise? What concerns? Complaints? Your customers—what improvements do they identify?

How do employees currently handle the work in ways that would be desirable to maintain?

Is there anything about what's going on now that has served as a stimulus for this initiative?

What new products or services are imminent, and how do they affect how you will do business?

What problems do the employees now solve that will continue to be important in the future? Are there any emerging problems to consider?

Here we are attempting to ascertain the focus of the effort, its general outline, and the sweet spots and opportunities to make a difference, and then to identify if there are obvious, critical gaps.

Consider the case of a performance professional who has been asked to do something to improve the writing of engineers. At the get-go, the sponsor suggested that a course might be a good approach, but she is leaving it up to her performance professional. How should one approach this request? The more time-consuming option is to commence with questions about optimals, the essence of good writing for engineers. This sounds like the beginning of a lengthy study.

Wouldn't it be better to begin by finding out where the engineers have been messing up, from the perspective of the sponsor and the clients who raised the issue? That's using the status quo to provide direction and ensure an authentic focus. Here are some questions that could be used with the sponsor and others that she designates: Why are you particularly concerned about their writing now? What's bad about their writing? I asked you to gather some writing samples that were particularly problematic; can you show me where the problems are? Can you randomly pull some examples of their writing and show me instances of the most vexing problems? Do they submit the writing products on time? About what are customers complaining? Is there anything you like about the writing they've done, that you hope to maintain?

The search for a picture of optimals brings us to such sources as the initiator, selected plaudits and complaints gathered from customers, policies and job descriptions, model and flawed work products, and a favored expert who, best of all, has committed his or her ideas to print or electronic

formats. More labor-intensive sources of optimals, such as review of extensive documentation, attendance at vendor courses, lengthy interviews with
subject matter experts, observation and interviews with model job performers, and substantive review of the published literature, are appropriate later,
during training needs assessment, when resources have been committed to
capturing and representing a detailed picture of optimals.

Tap as few live sources as possible. They are expensive and time-consuming. For example, if the problem is the writing skills of engineers, now is
not the time to interview model engineer writers or even to engage with the
literature on technical writing. Save that for training needs assessment, for
after you know that the issue is caused by problems with skills and knowledge or unclear expectations. Far better during performance analysis to talk
to the people who are complaining, see what is making them unhappy, look
at examples of rotten reports, and examine current policies and standards for
what is expected. Then use their problems and concerns to constrain and
focus the quest for optimals. Remember, during PA you're not revealing the
details of the solutions. Rather, you're figuring out what that solution ought
to be, in broad strokes, and who needs to come to the table to enact and
execute on it. That takes us to the issue of drivers.

Drivers

The major purpose of performance analysis is to figure out what to do. During performance analysis, we emphasize the quest for drivers rather than the
detailed definition of the domain or content area, because it is the drivers
that define solutions.

Now we decide what it's going to take to realize the opportunity or solve
the problem. We do this by asking sources for their perspectives on what
has been getting in the way, what it will take to make it happen, or what
will encourage or impede performance. In fact, it is a good idea to ask those
very questions, and then to ask questions specifically associated with the four
kinds of drivers I will be describing shortly.

Think about drivers as everything that it takes to enable performance
to "grow." Just as flowers require consistent exposure to soil, nutrients, sun,
moisture, and the occasional weeding, performance grows and blossoms in

a similarly supportive system. Let's look at four kinds of drivers and then at interventions matched to each driver.

1. Skills, Knowledge, and Information

A successful performer has information about what is expected and knows how and when to do it. Let's start by focusing on knowing what is expected on the job. Recently, Sheila Truesdell, a learning executive with SAIC in San Diego, commented on a lesson learned early in her career. She had responsibility for a teller certification program in a financial institution. She came to believe that the power of the certification program was in its published definition of teller standards and career path, even more than in its training or promotion opportunities.

The most familiar aspect of this first driver is skills and knowledge. A synonym is capacity, the individual's ability to do what is needed, to know what he or she needs to know, to know where to search and find what's necessary, and to handle opportunities and challenges.

In the era of knowledge and mobile work, we've become more conscious of the importance of employees' understanding of their work, not just being able to do it robotically. The employees' comprehension of why they are doing their work and of its fit with other aspects of work contributes to their ability to handle the unforeseen and to do it in settings that aren't closely supervised. Robert Reich, former President Clinton's secretary of labor, emphasized this very issue. He believes that technical training that is purely algorithmic and narrowly defined as how to do something necessitates the need for continuous retraining, an expense most organizations wish to avoid.

Another emergent aspect of this driver is information. Information is useful data available to employees but not necessarily committed to memory through the rigors of training. The data could be provided as performance support, documentation, or job aids. Examples are the GPS available in an automobile or on a personal digital assistant, the Yellow Pages, or an automated online program at Schwab or Fidelity that prompts decisions regarding retirement investments. Another example is the rich databases that the large consulting firms, such as IBM and Accenture Consulting, provide to their employees. These databases make data, information, knowledge, expertise, and wisdom widely available. In his excellent book *Intellectual Capital,* Thomas Stewart (1997, p. 63) described the wealth of intellect within the organization in this way: "The inevitable metaphor is the iceberg. Above the surface, the financial and physical resources . . . Beneath, unseen, something vastly larger . . . but whose contours no one knows."

There are many ways to drive or encourage performance in an organization. After an analysis with the people doing or attempting the work, you then get to choose whether to invest in enhancing memory through training or to provide some form of information support that will be available, as needed. Rossett and Schafer (2007) wrote *A Handbook of Job Aids and Performance Support: Moving from Knowledge in the Classroom to Knowledge Everywhere* on this matter. They provide a free online tool that answers the question, Would performance support be appropriate here? This can be found at http://www.colletandschafer.com/perfsupp/tool.html.

2. Motivation

Motivation is a word that gets bandied about. Every leader wants motivated people. We're all familiar with employees we praise for being gung ho or castigate for being tuned out. But what is motivation, and how can we use it to improve performance?

Motivation can be viewed as persistence of effort by people. A motivated teacher keeps offering up examples, calling parents, and providing feedback. A motivated customer service representative seeks the answer for the caller, even when he doesn't know it off the top of his head and his documentation in that area is out of date. He hunts for it, just because a customer requires it.

Why do some persist and others not? Two factors are typically given credit for motivation. The first is the individual's ability to name, list, and describe the reasons for doing this or that. This is the employee's awareness of the value of the topic or content. She knows why service is important, why answering questions matters, and how her efforts fit into the greater mission. Most important, she buys into all this, not because the boss or the instructor told her so or is hovering but because she shares commitment to the direction.

The second factor is the individual's confidence. This is can-do feeling. Imagine a customer service rep who feels competent regarding computers.

He hears that the organization is moving documentation to automated databases that can be accessed during phone calls. No problem with motivating this representative on this aspect of the job.

The two motivation factors are related. One without the other is a bust. They can enhance each other or cancel each other out. For example, consider the California regulation that all public school teachers must know about computers in education to retain and gain their credentials. Teachers who see the value in technology for teaching and learning and feel confident with it are motivated. They attend classes, read about software and hardware for schools, and use what they glean. Some other teachers, however, aren't at all motivated. When they are queried, we find that most of their reluctance comes because they lack confidence. They doubt their abilities with technology. Even though they are aware of potential benefits for their classrooms, they don't perceive themselves as competent to employ technology. The absence of confidence undermines their motivation. Reiterating the benefits of computers won't bring these teachers to the computer table. They see the value. Threatening them with the loss of a license is not the best way either, although it will bring them haltingly through the door. The solution must address their driver, in this case, lack of confidence. When they walk slowly through the door, the experience must boost their feelings of efficacy.

A pal of mine taught mandated leadership classes for automotive supervisors. The class was written into the union contract. They had to attend. When my friend walked into class, he confronted significant motivation problems caused not by an absence of confidence in this case but by more self-confidence than was appropriate. He's gone so far as to label them "hostile." Because these supervisors thought that their skills were sufficient, even strong, they saw little reason to be doing anything more to buff up. Table 3.4 illustrates this and other situations.

Because motivation has these two related components, questions during performance analysis must get at both. First, there are some overarching questions that you must ask of sponsors and eventually direct to the job incumbents themselves: Do employees share your enthusiasm in this domain? Are they motivated? Do they appear eager to do this? To move in this direction?

Table 3.4. Employee Motivations in Brief.

	Aware of Benefits	*Unconvinced of Benefits*
Confident	"Gung ho"	"Hostile"
Not confident	"Timid"	"Out to lunch"

Here are some questions about the perceived benefits: Why is this important? What is in it for the organization, the unit, the individuals? Do they know the reasons? Have they been informed? Can they tell you why the organization is going in this direction? Are they committed or just compliant?

And some questions regarding confidence: Are your people ready to move in this direction? Would you describe them as confident? What are their related skills and knowledge? Are they able at related things? Has anybody asked what they need in order to handle this? Do they believe that they are capable in this area?

During performance analysis, you parse motivation so that strategies can be targeted. The perception of value and benefit is built by showing employees related, authentic problems that these skills will address. It is also useful to tell them directly why these skills are important. Finally, share data from the performance analysis or the literature documenting the need. Confidence is best built by setting up early, small successes; reminding employees of prior and related learning; sharing the testimonials of others who went from timidity to success; and describing the subsequent support system that will wrap around employees' efforts.

3. Environment, Tools, and Processes

Here we focus attention on organizational issues. Are the policies timely and supportive of the effort? Are the tools in place? Is there sufficient bandwidth so that employees can use and enjoy technology that they are being trained to employ and encouraged to adore? Are the databases up to date? Are jobs and processes set up to facilitate effort? Can employees find what they need to get the work done? Are they encouraged to access and contribute to online communities, such as relevant blogs and wikis?

While working on this new edition of *First Things Fast,* I received an email note from Rob Wilson at Procter & Gamble. Here's what he said about his efforts to help his organization look more broadly at causes or drivers: "This is an acronym that Procter & Gamble Sales created to help us remember your 4 drivers of performance. It was created in a training session run by me and by a participant, Diane Kelly (Diane and I are in Sales Capability Development for P&G). We like your 'First Things Fast' approach, and as we considered your 'drivers,' we asked the group to develop an acronym to remember it by. Diane suggested MIKE:

M: Motivation

I: Incentives

K: Knowledge/skills

E: Environment

Rob continued, "I think M for Motivation is one of the most powerful drivers, since (in my opinion) if someone highly values and has high confidence, they will 'walk through fire' to achieve the performance. I also like that KSA (and therefore a need for training) is further down. Finally, I like how Environment is at the bottom, somewhat 'supporting' the rest of the drivers."

Historically, human resources professionals haven't paid sufficient attention to these larger, critical organizational questions. Yet an infertile environment can block the success of even the most skilled and motivated individuals. A favorite example comes from a situation in which salespeople were trained and exhorted to sell new high-end products when they had no budget to purchase them for demonstration. These salespeople were ready and eager, but they lacked the demonstration systems to show to potential customers.

Another example comes from a telecommunications company that sent its instructional design and delivery people off to classes about how to build e-learning programs. After a class on the authoring system, the designers returned to new, fast, and fabulous hardware and software. They devoted themselves to generating online lessons for delivery to PCs on the desktops of employees across their large organization. Unfortunately, rank-and-file desktop machines were several versions behind the equipment on which the courseware was generated. Their access to the Internet was spotty. Oooops. The lessons looked bad, slow, or unavailable to the people who counted, the users in the field. Good performance was decimated by a badly planned environment. When asked, the people in the field thought that the technology-based training was bad. Was it? We don't know, because the installed platform gave the training no chance to succeed.

I wanted to reschedule a mammography at my HMO. I visited a booth just outside the door of my primary health care provider (a woman formerly known as my doctor). The scheduling booth looked friendly, with pictures of cute animals and smiley faces. And the woman in the booth, she too was friendly, obviously trained and exhorted to treat customers well. I saw an innocuous job aid to that effect tacked near the smiley faces.

Unfortunately, the woman who is the scheduler isn't authorized to schedule, not really, not without specific authorization. I'd possessed this treasured authorization document originally, when they scheduled and botched my first appointment a few months prior, but now I had no clue as to where I'd lost it. What we soon found out was that the friendly scheduler did not have it either, not anywhere in her system. She was also unable to immediately put her hands on the hard copies of my files. Instead, she promised to get back to me later via telephone.

I walked away from the booth certain that she wouldn't get back to me. Do you think that she did? She did not.

When I called a week later, after much button pushing and revisiting this boring story, somebody informed me that I did indeed have a scheduled mammography appointment. With just a little bit of annoyance, she wondered how I was going to diligently appear at my appointment if I didn't know about it. Good question. Do you see a few problems with job description, automated tools, policies, and processes?

4. Incentives

Together with the environment and policies described previously, incentives make up what many label as "culture." I heard Peter Senge of MIT, author of *The Fifth Discipline* (1990), define culture as those aspects of the organization that are so ingrained that we no longer notice them. That definition is useful for us. The performance analyst investigates drivers so as to make such factors manifest and actionable.

This is an important way that we add value. When you have labored within an organization, flaws and strengths become the wallpaper. You do not notice them. It is the questioning process that will reveal to us, and to our clients, what is going on.

How does the organization tell employees what is expected? What is most valued? How does the organization update those expectations for new customers, technology, or opportunities? Does the performance management system applaud efforts? How? Do people throughout the organization think that the leadership cares? Why? What tells employees that this is a top priority? How does the organization express priorities to the employee? Is there anything that the organization does to give a mixed message to employees? Consider team leaders, supervisors, managers, and executives. Are they all pulling in the same direction?

One common problem is that organizations often ignore desired performance. When you ask a group of training professionals about incentives for excellent performance, they will guffaw—or maybe it is a grimace. Too frequently, they perceive none. In fact, some contend that there is punishment associated with excellence, with the best people getting the thorniest clients or challenges.

Sometimes the organization punishes the very behavior that it works hard to put in place. Performance management as a topic itself provides a good example. All the management development in the world about how to fill out performance appraisals cannot compensate for a policy manual that devotes ten pages to how to submit a grievance and one-and-a-half pages to the importance, value, and heroics associated with the appraisal process. Supervisors and managers swiftly figure out that sincere reviews could well cost them time and aggravation. Where does the system encourage the bravery and priorities on which an effective appraisal system is predicated?

Another typical problem with incentives is when they conflict, or when the organization is rewarding behavior that crowds out the desired performance. This happens to customer service people who are often measured and applauded for the quantity of their contacts but exhorted to deliver high-quality, relationship- and loyalty-building interactions. The organization is speaking with two voices. The individual is likely to hear the one that is linked to performance-management metrics.

There are many perfectly reasonable ways to think about the topic of drivers or root causes or barriers. Thomas Gilbert (1978), Robert Mager and Peter Pipe (1984), and Dick Swanson (1994), for example, have done early and excellent work in this area. Dana and Jim Robinson's new book, briefly described earlier, also offers up options. Table 3.5 presents one way of talking about the four kinds of drivers.

Table 3.5. Drivers and Examples.

Type of Driver	Examples
Skills, knowledge, information	Teachers leave their computers in the closet because they don't know how to use them.
	Contracts administrators resist making decisions because they don't know they are expected to.
	Service reps guess more than they ought to because the documentation is out of date.
Motivation	Clerks don't see the value of the new software. The old works just fine, in their view.
	Many teachers fear computers, noting that they're people-people, not techies.
Environment	The documentation and directories are housed way across the office and frequently misplaced.
	Personnel reenter a nine-digit code three different times during an order-fulfillment process.
	Managers don't approve of the approach that the organization is touting during training, and they make it known.
Incentives	Supervisors who rate employees as other than stellar are expected to fill out forms and attend meetings to justify these ratings.
	High-performing human resources professionals are assigned the most difficult clients.

Using Drivers to Define Solutions

There is a superb reason for the quest for drivers: drivers define solutions. They tell us what we have to do now and next. If you know what's causing bad performance or driving successful efforts, you know what you need to do to change or maintain. Table 3.6 links drivers with interventions.

Let's look at an example. Imagine that the problem, in the view of key university administrators, is the failure of professors to use online technology in their university classes. After purchasing the online learning management system BlackBoard, the university scheduled training for professors. Administration offered classes, and some professors attended. In fact, the attendees gave the workshops good ratings. Still, the use rate for BlackBoard showed only the slightest uptick. The administrator is thinking about planning more workshops. You convince her to let you take a quick look at the situation before scheduling training. Here's what your study turns up, presented in Table 3.7. This example presents data and interpretation from only one source, a randomly pulled group of professors, all of whom attended the workshops. Although talking with this group would not constitute the entire performance analysis, you can see that what they say is important if you want professors to adopt BlackBoard.

The professor case would not have been solved by carrying on with the same or revised workshops. Notice how even these limited data from ten professors provide a much clearer picture of what ought to happen, and it makes a case for investing in the more comprehensive and expensive cross-functional approach. With data, it is easier to "sell" the administration on going beyond workshops to bring more players to the table. Note also that the performance analysis effort begins to define subsequent training, providing guidance for a lengthier training needs assessment as the technology professional develops workshops and just-in-time information for the faculty.

Another example was provided by Jim Harwood and Steve Bush from IBM. Their challenge was to improve IBM sales professionals' reliance on specified customer relationship processes and methodologies. After they determined exactly what salespeople were and were not doing, they asked a critical question about drivers. What was getting in the way? Their insight into drivers then enabled them to define their solution system. One interesting aspect of what Harwood and Bush did was that they systematically sought drivers and causes of the gaps and then gathered a group to help them devise solutions appropriate for those barriers. Table 3.8 presents selected gaps, drivers, and solutions provided by the analysts.

Table 3.6. Drivers Matched with Solutions.

Type of Driver	Description	Solutions
1. Lack of skills, knowledge, or information	People don't do it because they don't know how or didn't know it was expected or have forgotten.	Education and training, in classrooms or online, via instructors or coaches or e-coaches Job aids, documentation Performance support tools Knowledge bases Communication initiatives, including clear and updated expectations
2. Lack of motivation	People don't because they don't think they can or because they don't care much about it.	Selection of individuals who want to do it Participatory goal setting Education and training, coaching, mentoring Job aids, documentation Performance support tools Knowledge bases Communication initiatives, such as podcasts by leaders
3. Ineffective environment, tools, processes	People don't do it because the processes, setting, tools, or workspaces foil their efforts.	Job design, job enrichment Workspace design Reengineered processes New or improved tools
4. Ineffective or absent incentives	People don't do it because doing it does not appear to matter or other efforts are indicated.	New policies Revised performance management system Management development so that managers and supervisors advance key goals

Table 3.7. Drivers Matched with Solutions: An Example.

Findings	Drivers	Potential Solutions
Eight of ten profs could not say why the university was keen on a shift to BlackBoard	They are not motivated. They do not value BlackBoard and do not see it as a component in the strategic direction of the university.	Establish a strategy advanced by use of Blackboard. Determine benefits from peer users and share with colleagues. Communicate the benefits. Create a blog where professors talk about how their uses of BlackBoard benefit students and professors. Anticipate issues and problems and include fixes and support online.
One professor in the focus group was unsure about how to access or use the system, had lost relevant job aids and documentation distributed at the training.	This is not really a question of skills or knowledge.	Create an online resource center with job aids that answer basic and recurring how-to questions. Support a coach for neophyte users to help them find their resources, take a maiden spin with the system. Provide help desk support.
Four of the ten in the focus group thought that they probably would use the system sometime, but not this semester or even next.	They are not motivated. They do not value BlackBoard, at least not now and not much.	Determine benefits from peer users and share with colleagues. Conduct a larger review of the literature to determine why an LMS has potential benefits in higher education. Seek examples that link to core university courses and topics. Communicate benefits.
Half the group agreed or strongly agreed with the statement: the technology poses a threat to job security.	There are incentives to avoid BlackBoard, since there is general unease about job security and technology. They are unlikely to embrace an innovation if it threatens their positions.	Generate campus policies that provide protection. Create incentives for those willing to try the system.

Table 3.8. IBM Sales Solution System Defined by Drivers.

Sales Processes	Drivers	Solutions
Identify a sales opportunity	They do not know how, at least not well enough. They don't see it as the job they are supposed to do. Skills or knowledge and motivation are at issue here.	Redefine jobs and communicate identification and qualification as key aspects. Provide training, job aids, playbook. Provide online support, perhaps through a performance support tool, to help salespeople consider options. Develop sales managers to see the value here.
Enter and edit opportunity in the system	They do not know how, at least not well enough. They don't see it as the job they are supposed to do.	Conduct a process walk-through. Use software tools to demonstrate system. Provide help system within the software. Develop sales managers.
Enter all opportunities of a certain size in the automated tool	They do not know how. They lack authorizations.	Provide training, job aids, playbook, documentation. Revise requirements and authorizations. Communicate changes.
Use national standards tables, definitions, and trigger field	This is not yet required by the online tool. They do not know it is expected of them.	Alter the tool. Communicate about these changes. Create a podcast featuring executives who speak about the tool and the value of these elements.

Table 3.9. Summary for Chapter Three.

	Performance Analysis	*Training Needs Assessment*
Sources	Sponsor, work products, supervisors, customers, job incumbents	Sponsor, model performers, the published literature, documentation, subject matter experts
Kinds of information	Optimals and actuals (basis of directions for the effort), drivers (which enable the definition of solutions)	Optimals, current skills and knowledge (emphasis on optimals to be addressed through education, information, and coaching solutions)
Typical questions	What are you trying to accomplish? What are the important problems? Why isn't it happening? What might get in the way? Do they know how? Do they care?	How do you do it? How might you think about it? What must they know by heart? What can be provided through job aids or documentation?
Outcomes	A description of what it will take to realize the opportunity or solve the problem; a plan that involves individual growth and organizational change; both are handed off to HR siblings	The detailed specifications for the education, training, information, or whatever it will take to improve individual's capacity

---

A visual is a good way to reprise this chapter. Table 3.9 summarizes the points we discussed in this chapter and takes us back to the distinctions between performance analysis and needs assessment drawn in Chapter Two.

4

Opportunities for Performance Analysis

VP of sales: We're rolling out a brand-new system. I want all our salespeople up to speed on it ASAP, no matter what country they're in. When can we get a class planned and scheduled? We'll need to put instructors on the road.

Director of HR: Unsatisfactory is the only way I would describe the way they handle the appraisals. We've trained them. We've exhorted them. Heck, we even redesigned the forms last year. I don't know what-all to do about it. . . .

CEO: Everything is changing here, and we need a management cadre that is flex, adaptive, able to handle boom times and bust. I can't tell you what it will be, just that they must be ready and smart—for whatever.

Chief learning officer: I want to put a planning initiative in place. I want to meet with our key people to come together on direction for the future.

Focusing on Opportunities

Performance analysis is not always just the same. It varies. The nature of the request for assistance influences the nature of the performance analysis.

Different requirements tilt us toward different approaches and emphases during performance analysis. These requirements are not radically different. All revolve around the quest for information about how it ought to be, how it is, and what to do to make it happen. But doesn't it make sense that a study to enable a salesforce to sell a new product is different from what you do to contribute to strategic planning or to support the ongoing development of twenty-first-century managers, engineers, or school principals?

This chapter describes four kinds of opportunities and an approach to performance analysis associated with each. Here we'll talk about what the analyst seeks and present some kickoff questions and planning templates matched with each of the four opportunities. The four opportunities are summarized in Table 4.1, with an example of each.

1. *Rollout.* An organization is seeking to introduce something new. It might be a new product, such as software or a computer peripheral or numerical control lathes. Or it might be a new philosophy or perspective on the work, such as a commitment to continuous process improvement or the self-regulation required of mobile employees. The VP of sales at the beginning of the chapter is managing a rollout; other requests might sound like these:

> "We are moving our stores and inventory to RFID (radio frequency identification). That means some significant changes for the staff. How can we help them?"

> "One of the things that I want to bring to this position is my commitment to global outreach. I want us to move forward on supporting employees as they do short- and longer-term stints worldwide."

> "Since the beginning of the year, we've had an influx of families from Iraq and Afghanistan. I want to do something for teachers and principals that will help them understand and serve these children and their parents."

2. *Problem.* An organization wishes to do something about a performance problem. Perhaps it is a glitch in an ongoing situation, where once things were OK but now they are not, as indicated by a dip in sales or an increase in complaints. Or it might be a situation in which mandated training continues but isn't making a dent in the problem. Examples abound: sales drop; accidents

Table 4.1. Opportunities and Rationales.

"We're shifting the organization out of a UNIX environment, and there's going to be some significant need for support."	Rollout	The challenge here is to determine swiftly the essence of the change and what it will take to support it.
"I went to a dinner party, and the two women sitting next to me complained about the service they got from us. What's up here? Haven't we done training? What else should we do so I can eat dinner in peace?"	Problem	Something is wrong, and the executive needs to know two things: the nature of the problem and the drivers of each aspect of the problem, so that a cross-functional program can be launched.
"Our sales are down 11 percent while the industry trend is up 2 percent. We need to do something, and fast."	Problem	The focus here is on finding out why there is a problem, prior to figuring out what to do. What should that "something" be?
"Our hospital administrators must be able to thrive in an environment that is changing radically. How can we prepare them for the new competitive environment?"	People	The focus here is on the position and on developing the people who hold that position. The challenge is to determine current and future growth needs and to involve incumbents in the process.
"What I envision is HR helping us with a program to get everybody on the same page here. We need a shared vision."	Strategy	No specific problem. No new development technology or philosophy. No focus on one position or another. This is about bringing people and "smarts" together to plan.

increase; scrap production is up; a new leader is dissatisfied with order fulfillment; professors ignore a technology resource, even after several workshops on
the topic. The HR director at the beginning of the chapter is confronting this
dilemma with performance appraisals. He has tried to improve the situation,
but to no avail. Other requests for assistance might sound like these:

> "Do what it takes to get those sales numbers back where they were."

> "I reviewed the order fulfillment numbers and they don't come close to
> my goals. What can we do?"

> "Have you seen the complaints from customers? We put everybody
> through customer service training eighteen months ago. Let's retrain
> them, or something. Frankly, I'm stymied."

3. *People development.* Rather than a topic, product, or service, here the
focus is on a particular group of people. An organization is directing attention to a particular position, job, or what the military calls "billets." The
leadership is looking ahead in order to maximize the contributions of people
in these roles. The leaders also note that the world, customers, technology,
and products are changing and that they must ensure that their people will
be fit to contribute. The CEO in the opening dialogue is expressing the need
for this type of help. Other requests for assistance might sound like these:

> "Have you read what Prahalad and Krishnan wrote in their 2008 book
> about innovation? They see a convergence of sales and services. How
> can we begin to help our salespeople move in these directions? Do
> they know what they need to know in order to respond?"

> "Insurance companies will not pay for long-term psychodynamic ther-
> apy. We're going to have to find a way to support and develop our
> member therapists to cope with these changes."

> "I just finished reading Jeanne Meister's blog about JetBlue's attempt to
> collect and deliver expertise across the organization. She put it this
> way in the May 19, 2008 entry: 'while the training faculty might
> have good intentions about sharing best practices, they often lack an
> easy tool that allows them to collaborate with their peers. So, I can
> see how empowering faculty to be a community of blogger and wiki

champions can create excitement and even be a vehicle to reinvent and rebrand an entire learning organization.' Let's see if we can move our instructors in this direction."

4. *Strategy development.* Human resources and training professionals find themselves helping the organization or a particular unit to make decisions about direction, values, and alignment. Often this involves facilitating dialogue and process and ensuring that many voices are heard. Although the typical human resources specialist may not often handle such broad requests, shouldn't we play some part?

As organizations seek their strategy, they confront questions about what factors to weigh. The debate is often framed with the words *inside-out* and *outside-in.* What they are talking about is a focus on the strengths within, urged by Hamel and Prahalad (1994) in their famous work on the core competences in the organization. What are our strengths? What are our competitive advantages? On what should we build, moving forward?

The "outside-in" perspective emphasizes competitive and market forces. Michael Porter is the strategist most associated with that view. At its heart, Porter finds opportunities in the world that surrounds the organization. What are the new markets? Products? Technologies? Competitors?

The chief learning officer at the beginning of the chapter is looking for this contribution. Other requests for assistance might sound like these:

"We're not 100 percent certain about where we stand on this, but we need some help in establishing options and priorities."

"I think we've been so busy getting it done that we've not stepped back to make certain that we're going in the right direction. We'd like assistance on that process."

"I want to make sure that our people in far-flung locations are heard on this issue. They must be part of our strategic plans. I want you to fold them into this process."

"The budget situation is likely to force cuts on us. In order to make good decisions about people and programs, I'd like to revisit our strategy."

As director of enterprise learning for Ingersoll Rand University, Susan Guest manages an enterprise learning management system, e-learning, blended learning solutions, knowledge centers, communities of practice, and global deployment of learning.

Susan thinks that analysis can increase organizational support for a complex performance solution. She provided an example. Ingersoll Rand is currently acquiring a same-sized company, which will entail supporting enterprise learning for the combined organizations. Ingersoll Rand uses a learning management system (LMS); the new company does not. Susan organized a three-day Kaizen event regarding business processes related to the LMS. Kaizen is an action-oriented continuous-improvement activity that energizes people to obtain significant and measurable results in just a short amount of time. Susan, the LMS vendor, the Kaizen facilitator, and an external LMS expert led stakeholders from both learning groups through Kaizen techniques to map and analyze current processes in order to identify and mitigate gaps. Through the Kaizen analysis, the groups uncovered the need to improve documentation and functionality before training. According to Susan, "We realized that to prevent costly and embarrassing errors, we needed to totally redesign our training administration system permissions." They also redesigned the processes for e-learning course loading and for LMS administration problem tracking and resolution.

Through this analytic process, the group of twenty learning professionals recognized the need to define business requirements before jumping into a new initiative. In this instance, it was an LMS, but the lesson learned is applicable to any endeavor. Susan is proud that the group identified the need for governance and designed a learning technology council to represent their collective interests. They realized the need for common processes, for documentation, and for consistent training. "By taking a consultative approach and analyzing our current-state gaps," states Susan, "we gained stakeholder buy-in for systematic solutions. This will help us gain management support and the funding needed to expand the use and functionality of our LMS." This approach also increases business unit buy-in because the solutions are based on their unique business requirements and were developed by business unit representatives.

Analysis is used in ways both large and small at Ingersoll Rand. Susan reports that analysis is used on a larger scale as Ingersoll Rand acquires new companies.

CEO Herbert Henkel encourages using process analysis globally to determine how newly acquired companies operate and to then adopt the best solutions or design new processes to achieve business goals. "We emphasize that making incremental improvements today is better than waiting for the perfect solution to arrive."

On a smaller scale, Susan's group employs process analysis daily to improve customer service and efficiency. In addition to traditional course evaluations, they administer quarterly "voice of customer" surveys to understand the learner experience. Analyzed data from these surveys has led to improvements in participant communication, travel arrangements, catering, and other logistical aspects of learning and development.

Susan Guest began a career in learning and development more than twenty years ago as an instructional designer, and has worked as both an external and internal learning expert for a number of Fortune 500 companies. "This is an exciting time to be in our field," she asserts, especially now that having learning professionals at the table with business partners is common practice. She remains a fan of Robert Mager, whose "pragmatic approach is still relevant today." Her work in consulting as well as corporate learning led her to her current position as director of enterprise learning at Ingersoll Rand University. You may contact Susan at susan_guest@irco.com.

How Opportunities Structure Performance Analysis

In Chapter Three we looked at the kinds of information a performance analyst seeks, condensing the inquiry into two large buckets, directions and drivers. Thus far in Chapter Four we have introduced four kinds of recurring opportunities. Now let's put it all together. The remainder of this chapter provides some templates, shown in Tables 4.2 through 4.5, for handling each situation. In each, I focus on the kickoff meeting, assuming that the initial interaction with the sponsor is where we set the effort on a fruitful course. The templates include sample questions for that kickoff session. Tailor these queries to your particular situation and customer, of course.

Table 4.2. Rollout Focus.

Opportunity	Rollout
Example	"What I have in mind is something that will help our people understand our new commitment to empowerment. I see your eyebrows raising, and I want you to make sure we have a program that doesn't raise eyebrows, that sincerely helps our folks move in this important direction."
Focus	In a rollout, your emphasis is on figuring out what "it" is that the executive is attempting to bring forward and on anticipating what will drive success. You are looking for the beginning outlines of the vision, the optimals, of how performance and perspectives will shift if the rollout is successful. Top priority then is to seek the essence of optimals from sources, to compare those views of optimals, and to press leadership toward something resembling the beginnings of consensus on "empowerment" or "teaming" or "conversion to automated records management." The next priority during performance analysis for a rollout is to identify drivers, to anticipate what might get in the way. What obstacles will appear? What should be put in place to drive toward success?
To the executive:	How do you define empowerment? If we had empowered employees, what would they be doing? If we were in conversation, now, with an empowered employee, how might he or she be different? Do we have employees who are already that way? If so, what do you see them doing? May I work with them? Have we captured examples of their thoughts and actions? Is there a way we can begin to create a database of examples? What can I read to help me understand empowerment? What has influenced you? As we look a little further along, what might get in the way of our move in this direction? What will it take to successfully move your people this way? Do you think your employees will embrace this shift? Why? Where might there be resistance? Why?

Table 4.3. Problem Focus.

Opportunity	Problem
Example	"My patience with the performance appraisals is gone. Last year we redesigned the form. Two years ago we trained all the managers and supervisors. I'm at my wit's end now. Look at these. They're perfunctory. What are you going to do?"
Focus	When addressing a problem, you must do two things. First, it is critical to nail the problem. Where is it? Where isn't it? In this case, what you're attempting to discern is what's wrong and what's right with the appraisals. That involves comparing optimals with what is currently happening, looking at where we are versus where we want to be. Focus on key problem areas—in this case, the lines in the appraisals that are unsatisfactory. Second, you must answer the question, Why do we have these problems? What are the causes, forces, and drivers associated with each aspect of the problem? Answering this second question allows you to determine who needs to come to the table to solve the problem.
To the executive:	Why are you unhappy with the appraisals?
	What are the biggest problems with the appraisals?
	Where is there a clear statement of what constitutes a "proper" appraisal? What policy documents should we examine?
	Why do you want to tackle this issue now?
	Why do you think that past fixes haven't worked?
	If a supervisor wants to do a bang-up job, to what references and materials can she turn?
	Let's look at the primary problems you've mentioned. What will it take to fix each of them?
	What are the managers' perspectives on appraisals?
	What would job incumbents say we should do to improve the appraisals?
	If you could wave a magic wand over each problem, what would you do?

Table 4.4. People Development Focus.

Opportunity	People Development
Example	"I attended a technical training vendor conference last week, and 100 percent of the attendees are shifting some portion of their training to multimedia and distributed formats. Obviously, we will be going in that direction too. But what to do about our 190 instructors and 85 product development people?"
Focus	To facilitate professional development, you must assist the organization in getting a fix on the many directions that might be appropriate for this group of people. Then you must set priorities. There are many ways to conceive the role of the trainer (in this case), or the systems analyst, mental health professional, principal, or hospital administrator. Performance analysis here resembles a rollout, with an emphasis on optimals, but it is targeted at a broader and more strategic level. The effort will be dominated by casting an expansive net for rich optimals and creating a process to involve colleagues in selecting directions and priorities. Given the emphasis on speed, use PA to identify appropriate sources, scope the boundaries of the domain, and begin to envision an approach based on drivers.
To the executive:	What do you envision this group of people doing over the next five years? What will they do more of? Less of?
	What challenges do you imagine they will confront?
	How do you expect them to prioritize their work? What accomplishments should be most important to them?
	What shall I read to help me understand your vision?
	What professional associations and experts shall I consult?
	What changes in technology do you view as most significant?
	What changes in relationships do you see with customers? With colleagues across the organization? In the work site?
	How are you collecting examples of desirable practice and thought leadership? How are you making that knowledge available to many?
	Do we have employees who are already approximating good performances? If so, what do you see them doing?
	As you talk about electronic learning, I can't help but wonder how your people will respond. Do you have a sense of their eagerness to move in this direction?
	I anticipate a wide range of definitions for the professional of the future. Who in your organization should be involved in this defining process?

The first challenge, rollout, is pervasive today. Although we often work on rollouts related to new technology, note that the rollout in Table 4.2 focuses on the introduction of a new way of thinking about the work. When an organization attempts to change the ways salespeople sell, say to sell higher inside organizations, that too should be treated as a rollout.

Looking now at Table 4.3, note how different the emphasis is when the professional is charged with solving a problem in an ongoing situation. In the rollout, the sponsor is excited, worried, eager. When it is a problem, you are more often dealing with an impatient client. Often, it is not the first time that the organization has taken a whack at this issue.

The remaining two opportunities, people development and planning, are more strategic. Each involves helping the organization define where it intends to go, using broader questions, raising more issues, and entering into more gray areas. The topic is not set, or if it is set, it is very general.

Table 4.4 illustrates people development; here the emphasis is on nurturing a particular group of employees more than on any predetermined topic or direction.

Human resources and training professionals must help the organization plan for its future. They do this with a performance analysis that contributes to strategic planning and development. Table 4.5 presents one way of commencing such an effort.

Gearing Performance Analysis to the Opportunity

What follows are templates linked to the four opportunities. The templates provide suggestions for sources and the order in which you might tap them. They encourage a way of thinking about this early analysis but are certainly not the only way to do it. Customize your approaches with individuals and circumstances in mind. Consider the power of sampling, because many organizations have people and enterprises across the globe.

Stages in PA for a Rollout

Although a performance analysis for a rollout will focus primarily on defining optimals, its purpose is not to specify exactly what is involved, for example, in

Table 4.5. Strategy Development Focus.

Opportunity	Strategy Development
Example	"I'm eager to have our people go through a process that will establish a common understanding about directions. I need your help to engage our people with this planning process."
Focus	Strategic planning is about a quest for optimals. The focus during strategic planning is threefold. First, you must lead a process that collects, converges, and articulates perspectives on where the organization or unit is going. Second, that process must have a link to reality and to possibilities and dreams that participants might some day see enacted. It shouldn't be mundane, but it can't entirely be off the wall; that means you must engage in some discussion of drivers. Third, you must create and nurture a process that helps many to feel involved.
To the executive:	Why do you want to engage your organization in a planning process? How do you want to be involved in this?
	What are your priorities in the future?
	Whose opinions do you want sought during this process?
	What published literature or live sources from the outside do you want to involve in this effort?
	How do you want to be informed about the results as we move along?
	What challenges do you feel are most critical for the industry in general and for your organization in particular?
	What competitive advantages and core competencies do you wish to emphasize? To nurture?
	Are there any benchmarking organizations we should examine?
	To what listservs or online communities do you refer? Are there any that are particularly appropriate as we move forward?
	I anticipate a wide range of opinions. How do you want to inform your colleagues about these options? How do you want to move to establishing priorities?
	Your comments tend to center on a few critical trends in development. What do you see as likely to be essential to moving your people in those directions?
	Are you committed to the changes and support it will take?
	Do you think others in the organization share your eagerness regarding these directions?

Deborah Pettry customizes her approach to each new client or problem. The human resources VP for a mid-size aerospace-defense firm asked her to help the HR generalists move away from transactional responsibilities toward more consultative relationships with their internal clients. His initial request was that she conduct a seminar on consultation skills. Instead, Deborah worked with him and his senior staff to establish clear agreement and communications about what the required performance would be, and then helped them create and deliver blended learning opportunities that fit those requirements as needed.

She began with understanding the client's context—and thus helping the client to think about it too. Deborah asked focused questions and reviewed business documents to gather context for the request. She needed to find out about the company—especially its strategic challenges and objectives, the composition of the particular group from HR, how it would contribute to the company's strategic success, and prior performance problems and successes.

Only after obtaining context did Deborah begin to help the client think about specific performance. She asked her client, "What would you like these folks to *do* in their new roles?" She found that HR management had general ideas about the "new" HR, but no specific communications describing what performance might look like after the role transformation. Deborah led a brainstorming session to help HR management determine how their broad goals could translate to specific responsibilities and competencies. From those brainstormed ideas, she partnered with HR directors in creating a draft "responsibilities" description and sending it as a survey to collect feedback from the HR generalists and selected line managers. Deborah considered this part of the data-gathering phase but also an early intervention: people reading and responding to the survey gained an active understanding of the new expectations. Just as important, the process ensured that HR management had developed united expectations across the business unit.

After identifying the responsibilities for the newly renamed "HR Business Partners," the process continued with a fast method for identifying competencies. In just two months, the HR management team had developed detailed models of both responsibilities and competencies for the HRBPs. They had also gained involvement and ownership from the HRBPs and key clients. Tying the competencies to the company's 360-degree assessment process to gather data about group and individual strengths and development needs, they were immediately able to kick off a year of blended learning opportunities that accelerated HRBP growth in the most critical individual and group performance areas. As the year continues, the client will gather additional data to shape future learning opportunities.

Deborah remarks that the very first conversation with a client should be considered an intervention. Introducing a new client to the process of performance analysis is an intervention. Asking the right questions—and helping the client to think about the answers—is an intervention. Every action taken within the client organization can be a performance intervention.

What are the "right" questions? It's always important to get the client thinking about outcomes and performance, so Deborah makes sure to inquire about needed results, matching responsibilities, and necessary skills. Do the employees in question possess appropriate skills? Do they understand the strategic mission of the organization and how they can individually support that mission? How does the client measure such understanding, and how might they do that better than they do currently?

Deborah feels strongly about sharing both raw and analyzed data with the client. "It's their data," she states, and the solution will likely "stick" if the organization has a hand in figuring out what to do with those data, what they really mean. "And I always try to recommend solutions that clients can do themselves," Deborah asserts. "It's not just about me."

While working on her Ph.D. in educational psychology at Purdue University, **Deborah B. Pettry** discovered that her interests lay in adult learning and performance, especially in leadership and management. After positions with Purdue, Aerojet General, and the Center for Creative Leadership, Deborah established her own business in 1991. As ACL, Inc., she and her associates help organizations large and small to solve performance problems through leader development, executive coaching, and strategic facilitation solutions. You can reach Deborah at dpettry@creativeleaders.com.

operating the system or in doing the work of a customer service rep in a more empowered way. Rather, the performance analysis is meant to determine the key components of the domain. Detailed optimals should be gathered later, during training needs assessment, after the handoff, when those aspects that demand training and information support have been determined.

After you have scoped a view of what performance should look like, move on to find out what it will take to successfully shift the organization and its people in the selected directions. Drivers for performance? Table 4.6 describes suggested stages for a performance analysis appropriate to the rollout of a new system, technology, or way of doing business.

Stages in PA for a Problem

When you are attempting to solve a problem, the mission is to find out enough about the problem to target your questions about the cause or causes. Typically, a client expresses general, all-purpose pain about customer service or performance appraisals; your job then is to swiftly peel the skin off that problem. Where are the problems with customer service? How are the appraisals disappointing? What is not a problem with the appraisals? Subsequent questioning about drivers is then linked to the particular service complaints or appraisal failures. Table 4.7 describes suggested stages for a performance analysis appropriate to helping customers cure what ails the service they are receiving.

Examine stage two in the Table 4.7 template. You have a choice for that critical stage. You can define optimals through reviewing policies or by meeting with experts, or you can go immediately to an examination of work products or records, something tangible that will help parse the general problem into something more specific. If you can look at the records or products and infer the critical problem areas without formally establishing optimals, then choose that approach. It will save time. This would work for customer service and letters and calls of complaint, for example. In this case, you would likely know enough about expectations for employee performance to review records and define the problem.

Sometimes, however, you can't just look at the work products and describe key flaws. You might not be sufficiently certain about what the

Table 4.6. Stages for Rollout.

Stage	Sources	Some Suggested Questions
One	Customer, sponsor	Why? What will this do for the organization? Why have you decided to go in this direction? What are the essential elements of the shift? Are employees eager for the change? (See Table 4.2 for more suggestions.)
Two	Internal expert	What about this change is most promising? What can it do for the organization? What problems will it solve? What opportunities will it create? How do you want people to use it?
Three	Committee members involved in rollout decisions	What about this change appealed to the committee? To you? What is new here? Familiar? What will it do for the employee? The unit? What will it take for a successful rollout? Will your colleagues be enthusiastic about the change?
Four	Vendor, vendor materials and documentation	How does "it" work? How do effective users think about this? What examples do you have of it at work on critical opportunities and issues? When others have begun to use it, what helped make a successful rollout?
Five	The published literature	What does the literature say about rolling out hardware, software, or a new philosophy of leadership? What does it say about the most typical barriers to successful rollout?
Six	Job incumbents and their supervisors	Now that I've described the rollout to you, I'd like your reaction to it. Can you see why the organization is going this way? Do you see benefits for your work? For your unit? What will it help you do? Do you think you have the skills it will take to make the shift?

Table 4.7. Stages for a Problem.

Stage	Sources	Some Suggested Questions
One	Customer, sponsor	What is the problem? Why are you seeking help now? Why hasn't the problem been solved already? What have you done thus far? (See Table 4.3 for more questions.)
Two	Records, work products, examined with an expert (if you are not one) or with policies to which the work is compared	What information do we have that defines the problem, that compares what is happening with what ought to be happening? Where are the major problems in these work products? Where are the most costly errors or problems? What would the situation be like with no problem?
Three	Expert	What would it look like if there were no problem? What should we expect of excellent performance? Why aren't we getting it? Why have past efforts failed? What's in the way?
Four	Job incumbents	What's getting in the way? Why are employees having these problems? If you were king or queen, how would you solve it?
Five	The literature	What does the literature say about the most typical barriers to success in these areas?
Six	Supervisors	I've shared the major problem areas with you. Do they match your perceptions? Why does the organization have each of these problems? What are the causes? What can the organization do? If you ruled the organization, what would you do? Do you care about this problem? Is it one of your priorities?

Table 4.8. Stages for People Development.

Stage	Sources	Some Suggested Questions
One	Customer, sponsor	Why are you focusing on these employees now? What do you perceive as key skills for the future? What are the emergent challenges they will face? What are they doing now that will endure? In what ways are you collecting best practices? (See Table 4.4 for additional questions.)
Two	The literature, professional associations	What trends are identified? Emergent skills? Perspectives? Emergent challenges? New technologies? Where is the disagreement about emergent challenges and skills?
Three	Internal and external experts	What trends do you identify? Emergent skills? Perspectives? Emergent challenges? New technologies? From all these, what are the priorities that you associate with this organization and market?
Four	Model performers	What are you doing that strikes people as model? How are you approaching your work? How have you acquired new skills and knowledge? What support did you get from the organization? What do you think will be involved in redefining this role? Have you been asked to collect your perspectives and practices in any ways?
Five	Job incumbents	Do you see the value and benefit in these new roles and competencies? Do you feel ready? What do you think it will take to support your growth in these directions? What might drive or impede your development?

standards ought to be. Or there are several views of how it ought to be. Or you are working in an organization that has a murky picture of what it is seeking. Problems with performance appraisals or engineering reports are examples of these more messy and undefined situations. In those cases, stage two should be the swift collection of optimals from policies or models. Turn those optimals into a checklist to help in the examination of the work

Table 4.9. Stages for Strategy Development.

Stage	Sources	Some Suggested Questions
One	Customer, sponsor	Why do you want to engage in strategy development? What do you hope to achieve? How broadly do you want the process to extend? Who are the critical people that must be involved? (See Table 4.5 for additional questions.)
Two	Key managers and leaders	What are the things that distinguish this organization? What are your customers saying about you now? What new things do you want on their lips? What trends will affect your business? Emergent skills? Perspectives? Emergent challenges? New technologies?
Three	Internal and external experts	What will our people be learning about? In what new areas will our people need to develop? Emergent skills? Perspectives? Emergent challenges? New technologies? Emergent opportunities? From all these, what are the priorities?
Four	The literature	What are the current trends? New business opportunities? Emergent skills? Perspectives? Emergent challenges? New technologies? What are benchmark organizations doing to respond?
Five	Supervisors	What worries you? What business opportunities are most interesting? What are the emergent skills? Perspectives? Emergent challenges? New technologies? Do you feel ready? What do you think it will take to support your growth in these directions? To move the organization in these directions?
Six	Job incumbents	What worries you? What opportunities do you perceive? What emergent skills will be required? New technologies? Do you feel ready? What do you think it will take to support your growth in these directions? To move the organization in these directions?

products in stage three. That will nail down the details of the problem, also known as the "gaps."

Stages in PA for People Development

The challenge here is to define the future. It is critical to involve as many sources as possible, given your time constraints. If there is little time, the template in Table 4.8 will work for you. If you have more time, add more sources of optimals, including a deeper dip into the literature, and contacts with benchmark organizations. Technology can be enormously useful here. If you are worrying about opportunities for developing retirement specialists, it would be critical to join a professional association and engage online in their discussions about current opportunities and future trends in certification, for example. Use technology to help you see what people are thinking, reading, and worrying about. This is discussed in more detail in Chapter Seven.

Stages in PA for Strategy Development

In these situations, as in PA for people development, the focus is on defining the broad strokes of optimals and making certain that the process provides rich information and broad participation. Table 4.9 provides a template for strategy development. Once again, technology can help bolster the research for strategy development.

5

Putting the Speed in Performance Analysis

Mei: They put this sales skills project in my lap, the one about repeat business and customer focus. Jorge said it is similar to what they did on customer-oriented selling two years ago, but that it is also different. And they want the finished solution yesterday. I need to do some up-front study. I don't want to make a mistake with a program that everybody is scrutinizing.

Floyd: Been there. Of course I believe in study prior to action, but there's no time, none at all. Dagmar just emailed the specs from Germany for our new operating system and said that we had to have courses ready to go by the end of the quarter—this quarter. What do I do?

Mei: Prayer comes to mind. We both need to pray—and get busy.

In this chapter, we will focus on how to plan when there is precious little time for it, which is almost always the case.

Analysis-Paralysis

When teaching an analysis class at a global high-technology company, I asked each participant to share reasons for taking the class, especially reasons that related to a current project or priority. The sixteenth man in our class introduced himself as an engineer. This got everybody's attention, as this was a company that defined itself through its engineering, and he was the first in the room to identify as one. He said something along these lines: "I am responsible for the engineering needs assessment that you may have heard about. It's my job to figure out where we need to go with development for our large and varied engineering population." Everybody turned toward him. This was a very high-visibility task. (It's also a good example of a people development challenge, as described in Chapter Four.)

The engineer continued, "I don't know why, but recently I've felt like I'm losing support for this study. I've been at it for nearly thirteen months, really working to get it right . . . I guess I'd better find the answer pretty soon."

The people in the room gasped. He thought that finishing up soon would be a good idea after thirteen months. Imagine!

Why was there flagging interest in his study? The question is easy to answer. He was taking too long. He'd gotten caught up in the study and lost sight of the reasons the organization had asked him to do the study. This engineer had a case of analysis-paralysis, perhaps because he was on a quest for the "right" answer regarding engineers' needs. What he didn't realize is that there is no single right answer out there for the plucking and that his findings could and should change as conditions in the company, marketplace, and industry evolve. As Marguerite Foxon, then of Motorola, said in a 1997 personal communication, "The more thorough and laborious the needs assessment, the more likely it is to be out of date when completed. These things are works in progress." Marguerite was a harbinger of the kinds of analysis processes and products now characterized by Web 2.0 and discussed in Chapter Seven.

The engineer had turned an ongoing responsibility to scan, scope, plan, and deliver into a lengthy quest for the Holy Grail. While seeking finality and perfection, the engineer for the high-tech company was ignoring a greater priority: to create a system to capture needs and priorities and to report continuously on the implications of what he was learning.

In the eyes of those around him, he was disappointing. He promised the definitive word on engineering development needs and failed to deliver.

Speedy performance analysis could help this engineer. Table 5.1 presents how PA might work for his people development challenge. It is based loosely on Table 4.8, the people development template in Chapter Four. Note that I've changed it for these circumstances, as you would adapt the templates for your programs.

It is critical to report back to the customer throughout the stages of performance analysis. Consider the example in Table 5.1. It makes sense to brief after the literature review in stage two, engaging the sponsor in a discussion about what others are saying about engineering trends and opportunities. Which directions make the most sense? Are the leaders keen on any direction in particular? Are they skeptical about any? What are the priorities, given the inevitable conflicting messages found in the literature?

Then, after stages three and four, write a memo or short report based on interactions with a handful of internal and external experts and successful engineers. What were their priorities? What resonated for them in the literature? What did they add? Where did they disagree? Consider using a shared web space to post findings and encourage conversation about what the findings mean. NING, a marvelous free social networking development tool, is an excellent low-cost way to bring ideas and people together. Want to see how NING works? Visit pinotnet.ning.com. It is a networking site devoted to nontraining interventions.

The benefits of frequent reporting, through formal and informal means, are significant, even when the performance analysis is swift. Keep clients and sponsors informed so that they are learning as you are, increasing the likelihood that you will get support for subsequent recommendations.

Note that the proposed engineering PA in Table 5.1 didn't yield the details of any training or hiring. Rather, it is likely to generate broad outlines for where resources might be concentrated. A training needs assessment (see Rossett, 1987) would follow to plan instructional and information interventions, with emphasis on what these engineers need to know about computing in the cloud or information technology security, for example.

Table 5.1. Performance Analysis for Engineers.

Stage	Sources	Some Suggested Questions
One	Customer, sponsor	Why are you focusing on the development of engineers now? What do you hope to accomplish by developing engineers? Are all engineers of equal interest, or is it one group in particular? What do you see as key skills for the future? What are the emergent challenges? Have you established an online community that captures the ideas of thought leaders or enables collaboration between engineers, no matter their location? Which professional associations or thought leaders are most influential as you think about the engineer of the future? (See Table 4.4 for additional questions.)
Two	The literature, professional associations, sources of expertise	What new skills and knowledge are emergent? What are the emergent opportunities? Tasks? Tools? Technologies? What are people talking about in blogs and other online communities? What questions are they asking? What topics are beginning to be discussed at conferences?
Three	Internal and external experts	What trends do you see as most critical? Emergent skills? Perspectives? Emergent challenges? New technologies? From all these, what are the priorities that you associate with this organization and vertical market? Who are the people in this organization who already manifest some of these skills and perspectives? What explicit and tacit knowhow is key? Are there any records of this knowledge? How is it maintained? Shared? What questions are our people asking you? What do you anticipate they will ask? On what topics are you asked to speak, write, or offer webinars or podcasts?

Table 5.1. *(Continued)*

Stage	Sources	Some Suggested Questions
Four	Model engineers	You have been identified as possessing skills that are considered "model"; what do you think people are referring to? What strikes them as model about how you do the work? What do you know that has attracted attention? What do you read to stay up to date? What online sources are useful? Whose ideas are influential to you? How have you acquired new skills and knowledge? What support did you receive from the organization? Think about your colleagues. What needs to happen to ensure that our engineers are contemporary in their skills? That they are ready for the challenges to come?
Five	Randomly selected engineers	Over the past two weeks, we have created a list of emerging challenges and competencies for engineers in our organization. Would you read it, please? Do you agree with what you see here? What strikes you as true for the future in your unit? Do you see the value and benefit in these new roles and skills? Do you feel ready? What do you think it will take to support your growth in these directions? How might supervisors function differently, if engineers and the organization move in these directions?
Six	Engineering supervisors, also randomly selected	Over the past two weeks, we have created a list of emerging challenges and competencies for engineers in our organization. Would you read it, please? Do you agree with what you see here? What strikes you as true for the future in your unit? Do you see the value and benefit in these new roles and skills? Anything that you want to add? Do you feel ready? How might supervisors function differently, if engineers and the organization move in these directions?

When she worked at the Qualcomm Learning Center, Antonia Chan focused on projects involving blended learning, mobile learning, and management development initiatives. Management development in particular has great potential to affect the organization, so the Learning Center was eager to ensure that programs are oriented toward business results and utilized effectively. One analysis Antonia undertook within the past year involved Qualcomm Manager's Network. This one-stop-shop web site offers resources and information to support managers in their roles. "When I first saw this site," Antonia explains, "I knew that it could be better so I volunteered to give it a makeover. This was my first project."

She knew that she wanted the site to be more visually appealing, but she also wanted to focus on content and to explore whether the site was being used as intended. Was the content appropriate? Were there other sources of information that should be included? Antonia recognized a perfect opportunity for analysis.

She created a timeline that included an initial analysis and presented it to the project sponsors. Analysis wasn't a traditional approach for web site redesign, so the sponsors raised concerns about appropriate use of time and resources. Antonia agreed to perform a fast analysis with recommendations delivered within two weeks. She made best use of the time by interviewing the sponsors, the management development expert (who was also the web site owner), and Qualcomm managers, the intended targeted audience of this site. Antonia worked with the web site owner to learn more about the Manager's Network and explore ideas to increase its success. The site owner was concerned about how often the target audience used the site, which sections they considered useful, and ways to make the site more relevant for their work. Antonia also reviewed site usage reports offering details about the number of hits to the site and the number and type of documents downloaded.

Antonia was given permission to contact 53 managers out of a total potential population of more than 2,500. In addition to scheduled phone interviews, she created an online survey with the same interview questions to gather as much data as possible. Even with a low response rate, Antonia was able to identify opportunities for improvement. The first was an awareness issue. Some managers did not know about the Manager's Network, so their usage was absolutely zero. The second issue was that many managers mostly accessed the Network during performance reviews. A third problem was that even those managers who agreed the Network had valuable information thought they had little or no time to use it.

Antonia felt powerless to address the time barrier, so decided to tackle those comments related to information overload. Her recommended solution focused on finding ways to make the information less overwhelming. She removed, updated, and reorganized content; she categorized topics and improved the navigation; and she added delivery systems for the information, such as podcasts and wikis. She also recommended a marketing strategy as part of her solution system to increase exposure to the Network.

The findings and recommendations were also shared with the Employee Communication group that collaboratively generates some of the Manager's Network content. This group has incorporated the recommendations in order to better create and select articles for the Network and for the monthly newsletter to managers.

The recommendations were received well, particularly considering the small sample size on which they were based. Antonia says, "Part of the positive response occurred because the stakeholders already suspected some of the findings, and analysis confirmed them. I also think the stakeholders and site owner really did want to make things better."

"A good technique to increase acceptance of findings," shares Antonia, "is to present a report that focuses on solutions rather than problems or negative findings. Also, provide a wide range of solutions that go from quick fixes to long-term ones. That way, decision makers can create a prioritized actionable list."

Antonia feels that this little analysis facilitated a more positive outlook at Qualcomm toward analysis in general. "Before this," she asserts, "analysis was considered by some to be long and cumbersome and time not well spent. I feel my internal clients are more open to analysis now that they've seen the value of making decisions based on data."

Antonia Chan, a Fulbright scholar from Panama, received her MA in educational technology from San Diego State University in May, 2007. She also holds a BS in computer science from Universidad Santa Maria La Antigua, Panama. You can reach Antonia at antonia.chan.liu@gmail.com.

Shaving Time Off the Front End

A mantra in corporations and government today is the exhortation to reduce cycle time and increase speed to market. Whatever it is that is being done, operations managers are pressed to seek ways to shave time off the process. Why should learning and performance professionals be any different? The same concern for speed that is expected in design, manufacturing, and order fulfillment is reasonable to demand of training and development too. This chapter presents eight strategies for speeding up the planning process. We seek to avoid analysis-paralysis.

1. Clarify the Effort

The number one strategy for saving time is to know what you are doing. This idea harkens back to time-tested wisdom from Robert Mager, who reminded the profession that we are not likely to get where we want to go if we are not clear about where that is. Instead of wandering aimlessly in the land of analysis, gather defined kinds of information from sources like those included in the templates provided in Chapter Four. The nature of the requirements tilts us toward particular patterns of effort and levels of specificity in our questions. Note, for example, that even though the pattern of sources and stages in Table 5.1 and Table 5.2 (which we will see later) are similar, specificity varies. Each approach is influenced by the nature of the initial request and by how much is known at the get-go.

The conceptual framework in Chapter Three and the templates in Chapter Four provide guidance. Although you shouldn't follow the templates to the letter, they do suggest a path that you can modify, as I did with the engineering initiative in Table 5.1.

Let's look in on Floyd and Mei as they continue to discuss Floyd's project, the rollout of a new operating system across a large, global organization.

Floyd: I've got to do some kind of analysis before I roll out the operating system. I decided to do a survey. I am going to post it up online, on our portal, and use SurveyMonkey. They're pushing me hard to get this finished.

Mei: It's a good idea to get something out there, like an online survey. People want us to seek their opinions. Have you sent an email out yet, one that explains what you are up to and points them to the SurveyMonkey URL?

Table 5.2. Floyd's Operating System Rollout.

Stage	Sources	Some Suggested Questions
One	Customer, sponsor	What is unique about this operating system (OS)? Why have you decided to go in this direction? What are the essential elements and benefits associated with the shift? What do you want different employee groups to do with the system? What do you think must be done to make this a successful rollout here and globally? (See Table 4.2 for more questions.)
Two	Review of minutes associated with the OS decision	Examine minutes related to the decision to go with the new OS, the new technical specifications, how the new differs from the current OS, expectations for vendor performance, and any concerns associated with rollout. Find out why they've picked it; identify key elements, concerns, vendor promises.
Three	Internal expert or executive closest to the technical details associated with the new OS	What about this change is most promising? What can it do for the organization? What problems will it solve? How do you want people to use it? What are some of the costs and benefits? What is the anticipated impact on processes? As we think about introducing people to the OS, what will it take to increase their comfort and use?
Four	Vendor, vendor materials and documentation	This is Floyd's opportunity to capture details associated with the OS and to focus on lessons learned from rollouts in other organizations. How does it enable____? How does it work? When others have begun to use it, what helped make a successful rollout?
Five	Job incumbents— focus groups with employees randomly pulled from the organization	Now that I've described the new OS, I'd like your reaction to it. Can you see why the organization has made the switch? Do you see benefits? Do you think you have the skills it will take to make the shift? What questions and concerns do you have? What support would help you move in this direction?

Floyd: Uh oh. I don't know what questions to put on the survey. What if only a few respond? Maybe it would be better to run some focus groups? Whatever I do, it's got to be fast.

What is Floyd's problem? Floyd doesn't know what he's looking for. He is jabbering about his data-gathering strategy and is silent about WHY he is seeking data at all. He wants to do a study, but it appears to be a study for the study's sake, with little clarity about the substantive purposes. What questions is Floyd trying to answer? What information is he trying to gather? Remember the purposes discussed in Chapter Three. What does he already know? About what is he in doubt? What sources are critical? Beyond showing "people" that he "cares" about their opinions, and exerting effort during his hours at work, what is he likely to accomplish with an unfocused inquiry? Not much. And he produces cynicism in an organization that perceives no connection between his inquiry and the resulting programs.

How could Floyd sharpen his approach? Table 5.2 presents one possibility.

Because it is a rollout, Floyd should focus attention on a preliminary definition of "it," in this case, of the new operating system. Simultaneously, he must scan for performance drivers and anticipated obstacles. He can gather both kinds of information from the same sources, at the same time—a certain time-saver.

Floyd deviates from the rollout template in Table 4.6 in two ways. First, after meeting with the sponsor, he decides to review the minutes of the meeting of the internal committee charged with the leap to the new operating system. He will save time by not meeting individually with committee members; he's hoping that the minutes captured the issues about which he is most concerned—why they are switching to the new system, comparisons with the prior system, and priority uses for the operating system. If the minutes are sketchy or unclear, Floyd will contact members for explanations. He might also create a blog to encourage a conversation about the new system.

The other departure from the template is that Floyd skips the review of related literature. He's depending on the vendor for information about operating system rollouts, both those specific to their system and lessons from the operating system domain in general. If that's not forthcoming, then a quick trip to the literature will enhance planning.

The new and improved Floyd (in Table 5.2) knows what he is after and uses focused questions that reflect this clarity. He picks his techniques for gathering information on the basis of what he's looking for. And he's on target to complete the performance analysis speedily. Even assuming the usual bumps and glitches, Floyd could complete the planning shown in Table 5.2 in a few business days.

Let's think about Mei's comment, "People want us to seek their input." They do, but not so that they can experience the thrill of being asked. Most want their input to contribute to tangible recommendations, options, and suggestions. Making a show of interest doesn't substitute for authentic use of the data. In fact, conducting numerous surveys without distributing meaningful results to the respondents will eventually produce more cynicism than appreciation. That's how organizations find themselves suffering from "survey satiation."

2. Repurpose Existing Data

The following example is based on a phone call I once got from a human resources manager charged with developing a safety program for five manufacturing plants. Let's call her Emma. Moved by the importance of the effort, Emma had been studying the situation for months and had commandeered a room for the assembled materials and reports associated with safety in manufacturing. Her treasure trove was vast, overwhelming. It was difficult to move around the room, there were so many documents and boxes. She was awash in statements about the directions a safety program might take, including optimals, best practices, and actuals detailing where efforts have gone wrong in the past.

Emma, even though she possessed a torrent of information about directions, had failed to put it together. Should she assemble optimal safety performance expectations for all people, tools, equipment, and situations? That was the intended approach. It had frozen Emma and her colleagues.

It lacked focus. Which of these optimals had the most meaning to people and their units? This should have brought Emma to actuals, to where things weren't where they needed to be. Where were the different plants messing up on safety? Where were employees doing well and not so well? Where and when were the accidents and near-misses? What were the gaps in performance associated with the employees in and across plants? What might be causing the documented unsafe moments and actions? The detailed optimals would eventually prove useful, related to problems and accidents. Later, in training needs assessment, after having established the nature of the problems and their drivers, Emma could pluck targeted optimals from her room.

Table 5.3 details how Emma could have proceeded with this initiative. The suggestions are based on Table 4.7, the performance problem template in Chapter Four.

Although Table 4.7 was the jumping-off point for these recommendations, note that this PA was tailored to Emma's situation. For example, I suggested that she rely heavily on existing information. This enabled her to customize her study to her plants and circumstances. In the early stages of the analysis, Emma needed to swiftly find out where safety was an issue and where it wasn't. She did this by querying the sponsor and reviewing insurance claims and regulatory and accident reports. They told her where the problems, accidents, and weaknesses were. It was these extant documents that made her efforts meaningful to the organization and allowed her to save time. There are many kinds of data that one can repurpose in this way: accident reports like those Emma reviewed; exit interviews with employees; help desk logs; insurance claims; online conversations in blogs and wikis; and letters, voice mail, and emails from customers.

There was then little need for Emma to spend time studying optimals. She had already attempted that, to little avail. Optimals about safety, at the level of specificity she needed for a PA, were pretty obvious. Capturing the details of safe operations associated with particular gnarly tasks or machinery or error rates could happen later, during the training needs assessment.

Stage five in Table 5.3 is interesting. I recommended that Emma take some time to look into the literature on the causes associated with the manufacturing safety issues she unearthed in previous stages. What does the literature say about critical success factors for manufacturing safety? Although she'd done some prior examination of the literature, what she found was not what she needed. In a performance analysis, she would have wanted to know about recurring drivers for these kinds of safety challenges. That is where her attention was directed in stage five.

Table 5.3. Emma's Safety Challenge.

Stage	Sources	Some Suggested Questions
One	Customer, sponsor	Why do you want to focus on safety now? Why hasn't the problem been solved already? I looked at our current safety program and wonder what your thoughts are about it. What are our strengths and weaknesses in this area now? Where can we find the details about current safe and unsafe situations and actions? (See Table 4.3 for more questions.)
Two	Regulatory reports	Review the documents for answers to the following: What are we doing right? Wrong? What did outside evaluators pinpoint? What did they recommend? Where are the most grievous errors or problems?
Three	Accident reports, insurance claims, employee complaints	Review the documents for answers to the following: What are our problems? Where are employees getting hurt? What are the patterns? What situations and actions are unsafe?
Four	Job incumbents	What is causing the major problems (identified in stages one through three)? Why are employees having these problems? If you were king or queen, how would you solve each of them?
Five	The literature	What does the literature say about the most typical barriers to success in these areas? What are the recommendations? Why does safety training fail?
Six	Supervisors	I've shared the major problem areas with you, based on my review of reports and claims. Do they match your perceptions? Why does the organization have each of these problems? What are the causes? What can the organization do? If you ruled the organization, what would you do? How might the organization make safety a higher priority? Is it one of your priorities?

The real challenges in Emma's performance analysis were twofold: first, to swiftly find the major safety snafus and second, to determine why they existed. The first aspect didn't have to be that time consuming: she could use existing accident data and look at reports from regulatory visitors. The second critical part of the PA depended on getting answers to questions from several sources close to the work and danger—in this case, job incumbents, supervisors, and the literature. Once she knew why things went wrong, Emma would be able to figure out what the organization must do. She might then have contracted for training, job aids, and performance support tools in some areas; new equipment and gear in others; and supervisory development, enhanced recognition programs, and reengineered processes for still others.

3. Use "Straw," Not Tabula Rasa

The following dialogue is typical:

Mei: Thanks so much for being willing to talk to me about sales strategies for ensuring repeat business. You're pretty famous in the company for doing that yourself, so I wanted to be sure to talk to you.

Rick: No problem, Mei. What can I do for you?

Mei: Two things, really. I want to know how you do it, and I want to know why you think so many of our sales staff experience problems in this area. Let's start with what you do to ensure repeat business.

Rick: Never really thought about it much. Just seems a good thing to do, somehow easier to keep adding on to what you already have. I'm a little shy, so I prefer talking to people I know more than people I don't. Uh, sorry. Not sure, really.

Mei: What do you do that is different in the way you service accounts, perhaps?

Rick: Don't know that I do anything special . . . never thought about it, and not sure what everybody else does.

Mei: Why don't you describe what you typically do for the customers who are most likely to become repeat customers?

Rick: Just the usual. Lots of calls, of course, to make sure things are going OK. I send email messages, leave voice mail too, just to let them know I am thinking about them and ready to help, in case. Occasionally I point to a useful blog entry, if I think a customer will appreciate it. I just try to be me, and it seems to work.

Mei is having a devil of a time drawing details from Rick. When she eventually despairs of acquiring direction about optimals from him and switches to a question about why so many salespeople fail to create repeat business, he continues to be taciturn. The fact is that many sources, whether incumbents, sponsors, or experts, are less than eloquent about what it is they know and do. You can waste time here.

An effective strategy is to use "straw": give your sources something to which to respond. It might be an outline, a video interaction, a diagram, technical specifications, quotes from a wiki, a podcast posted on a web site, or a printed table of symptoms and recommended tests. What's important is that it provides detail to stimulate responses from the source. Many sources, such as Rick above, do not fare well with open-ended questions. Instead, provide specifics on a topic about which they know and have opinions. What often results is a flood of corrections, amendments, agreement, and disagreement. For example, a description of how one salesperson might approach securing repeated business is likely to stimulate Rick to describe how he does it, with specifics on what's similar to and different from the "straw."

Several professionals at Boeing, for example, described how they used video to elicit responses from experts, managers, and job incumbents. For a manufacturing challenge, they videotaped processes and asked their "talent" to talk about what they were doing and why. This generated useful comments and organizational support for the effort. It made the domain and challenge more tangible.

People often ask, where do we find this "straw?" It is not difficult. Imagine, for example, that you are charged with taking a fresh look at leadership development for the top fifty in your organization. You could go to "C" levels and ask them what they mean by great leaders. But I anticipate frustration from that kind of open-ended search. Instead I would use "straw" to structure their responses. And fortunately, just today (May 12, 2008), Elliot Masie is collecting expert opinions on leadership competencies at the Harvard Kennedy School of Government. As the conversation between Rosabeth Moss Kantor, Joe Klein, David Gergen, and Ken Blanchard proceeds, Masie is twittering (www.twitter.com) about all he is hearing. It's a speedy and pithy message to interested parties, through email, instant messaging, or cell phones. Those opinions, now readily available to you, and selected articles, provide a jumping-off point to tailor directions for the leadership effort. Your source may agree with Kantor, Klein, Gergen, and Blanchard—or not. What you seek to do is stimulate their contributions.

4. Establish Hypotheses and Test Them with Sources

Jim Harwood of IBM calls it fastpathing. I call it rearview validation. Either way, it is a slick way of saving time. Harwood and Ann Leon, also of IBM, were charged with the global rollout for an automated skills tool. They had a considerable change-management challenge on their hands and no time. What they did was to generate a massive amount of "straw," based on their experiences and brief and pointed discussions with the experts who had used the tool earlier, in Australia and in other pilots. Harwood and Leon guessed gaps, guestimated drivers and barriers, and then were so bold as to generate a solution system based on these hypotheses. They produced a report with so much "straw" that it was flammable.

Here is where it gets interesting. Harwood and Leon then gathered a group of irreverent and knowledgeable people from across the organization and charged these people with checking out their assumptions. With what did they agree and disagree? What had they forgotten? Did they see it the way that Harwood and Leon and their sources saw it? How realistic were the approaches they proposed and the drivers on which those approaches were predicated? What additional data should be collected? Basically, Harwood and Leon had gathered people to rewrite the report, to craft a better story about what needed to be done to support the rollout of the software, to inform them as to how much more data needed to be collected. Harwood reports that their hypotheses were mostly on point, that they saved time, and that this planning approach resulted in a sound rollout.

5. Establish a System for Virtual Analyses

Maybe the analysis process can be too customer driven. I know that those words are heresy, and perhaps they are a bit extreme, but there is an important theme here, relating to our role. Should we wait for requests from customers for the services that we provide? Should we perceive ourselves as dependent on customer initiatives for the genesis of performance improvement programs? Should our first reckoning of a new program take place only after our involvement is sought?

I don't think so. Although there will always be a significant number of programs that are born because an executive wants them, wouldn't the organization and its people be better off if those kinds of programs represented a dwindling percentage, if training and human resources development professionals were playing a more strategic role? Rather than wait, shouldn't we anticipate?

How do we do that? We do it by enjoying a seat at the table. We must often collect formal and informal data from key sources. We must participate in company blogs. We must review and initiate online communications. We must scrutinize the annual climate survey, salting it with questions that help us mitigate. We must chat in the cafeteria and when walking from the parking structure to the building. We must read the journals that the people in our organization read.

And we must ask questions like these: What do sources see as emergent trends, changes, new skill and knowledge areas, competitive arenas, emerging technology? Where are our current problems and successes? What is working? What isn't? What's getting in the way? How do employees perceive the current systems and the changes that lurk in the wings? As they look forward, what is keeping them up at night?

Virtual analysis collects information in the normal course of doing business, maintaining it at the ready, and saving time because the data are on hand when a need appears or a request for assistance is presented.

A program for a military contractor provides an example. The learning unit at the school is typically involved in collecting information about new directions, current performance, and obstacles and drivers. They do this in post-class evaluations, regularly scheduled focus groups with employees, regularly scheduled interviews with executives, online surveys, and participation in professional associations. These data are at the ready, no matter what comes up, such as a question about professional development priorities for engineers, or about readiness for the plunge into digital and away from analog, or about shifting expectations to rely upon team performance. The professionals are speedy at their work because they are already knowledgeable. Their performance analysis process is more one of confirming and extending than of generating anew.

So the press here is to establish a data-capture system to ensure ongoing collection of data. Do you regularly meet with leaders in the organization? Do you scan the literature associated with the business your organization is in? Do you read the annual report? Do you add items to corporate surveys and pore over survey results for their implications for performance improvement? Do you ask pointed questions about drivers when you find yourself at a luncheon table with associates? Do you have a system to capture these data and feed them back for additional reactions? Do you know who else in the organization is asking related questions and how to access their data, should you need it? Have you established a system to repurpose the virtual data? Chapter Seven is all about the implications of technology for virtual performance analysis.

6. Generalize

Another time-saving technique is to assume that what you discover through systematic study in one unit or location has implications for others. This information becomes the "straw" for presentation to other regions and groups of employees. Although you may be making a leap when you generalize this way, more often than not there are similarities in responses to a new operating system, for example, or in the causes of unsafe conditions in manufacturing plants. The important point is to use one source to frame up possibilities and then to validate the generalizations with other sources. Your early findings in one setting can serve as the "straw" to generate reactions in other locales.

Some colleagues at a computer company used this approach to plan skills development for their global sales organization. Initially, they focused their analysis energy in one part of the United States. When their findings from this region were presented to others across North America and even worldwide, the typical response was accord. There was more fit than not. And when the fit was off, their salespeople filled in descriptions more relevant to their terrain.

7. Collapse the Steps

Early in this book I emphasized the importance of systematic processes, in which data are gathered and the output of one phase turns into input for the next. This method is deliberate, desirable, and appropriate. But it is not always feasible.

One way to speed up the process is to bring key players together to answer critical questions right at the beginning. Peter Senge, in the handbook that supports his *Fifth Discipline* (1990), encourages just this kind of process. Put a potential solution system on the table and then do the kinds of hard querying that make certain the solution is pointed in the right directions and predicated on the true drivers. If we were talking about a rollout, we might ask the following questions:

Is this an apt description of the situation?

What problems might stump the employees?

If we ruled the universe around here, what are all the things we should do to ensure that this successfully contributes to performance?

What is likely to contribute to the employees' ability to handle this change?

One year from now, what will we wish they knew and did?

One year from now, what could have gotten in the way of their effective movement in this direction?

Now, as we look at the solution that is proposed, ask the following questions:

Will this system successfully introduce the change?

Does it touch all the bases?

What concerns you? Where are the risks here?

Will the programs we're proposing result in a successful rollout?

Do our plans match your understanding of what works in this culture?

8. Rely on Automation to Speed the Process

A decade ago, Mark Fulop, Kelly Loop-Bartick, and I published an article about automated analysis in *Performance Improvement* (July 1997). We told the story of constructing a site on the World Wide Web to do an analysis with university health educators across North America. In a nutshell, questions and responses were posted at a web site in order to encourage broad participation and comment. As new responses were generated, they too were posted. A gatekeeper monitored the process, making certain that things flowed smoothly and that comments were appropriate and advanced the goals of the effort. Once diverse and rich information had been collected, the team turned to expert health educators with experience on the web. They helped to focus and tame the abundant possibilities. The resulting web site surprised its developers, as it placed more emphasis on facilitating dialogue and research between institutions through chats and newsgroups and less on providing static health information. With hindsight, the effort was a harbinger of Web 2.0 approaches, more than the 1.0 initiatives that characterized the late 1990s. What's important here is that this approach worked and that many miles were leapfrogged and many people were involved—all in speedy fashion.

Recently, with different technology, I did just the same thing. We created a blog to query learning professionals across the globe about their approaches to evaluation. What do they now do? What writers or studies have influenced their approaches? What is working well in their settings? In what directions would they like to go? What system do they envision would help them elevate their efforts in this area?

Automation is a good way to save time. An example is the performance support tool associated with this book and available at the Pfeiffer web site, www.pfeiffer.com/go/allisonrossett. Its purpose is to help you do what you are reading about. I've done many front-end studies, but I still turn to an automated tool because it saves me time. It also encourages me to remember sources and queries that I might skip in haste. Chapters Seven and Eight discuss automated data collection, communications, and analysis.

Professional Hesitations About Quick-and-Dirty Analyses

The demands on a human resources and training professional can be contradictory; for example, to study prior to action and to provide speedy service to customers in need. The remainder of this chapter is a response to the concerns you might be having.

I Can't Be Certain

No, you can't. But when would you be 100 percent certain? It is the rare analytical technique—at least among those involving people in organizations, not laboratories—that results in absolute certainty, and even then, the certainty doesn't last very long. What you're seeking is to gather more information than you had when you began, to transcend habit and bias, to involve a wide array of sources, and to create a textured and convincing picture of the possibilities.

I Didn't Talk to Everybody

You shouldn't talk to everybody, not if you have any hopes of timely performance. Instead, use sampling; that is, randomly pull representatives of the larger population you are concerned about. Then you are able to generalize from their responses to the larger group that they represent. The power is in randomization, because every person in the group has an equal chance of being selected to provide a view of the situation.

Using sampling doesn't mean that you can't talk to a reflective person here, a renegade there, or an expert over there. They provide other kinds of perspectives. But if you wish to get a broader view of how the information security specialists or bank tellers or frontline supervisors or teachers see it, you will need to pull randomly from the larger population. Stop gathering data when the findings begin to be repetitive.

How Will I Sell This to a Skeptical Sponsor?

Most sponsors favor speed. Occasionally you'll come across a sponsor who demands large numbers. In that case, deliver on that request. This provides an opportunity to conduct interviews, and then to conclude with an online survey or a focused blog (see Chapters Seven and Eight). Usually, however, if you can point to the involvement of several worthy sources in interviews and focus groups, to randomization, triangulation, and, most important, answers to useful questions, the sponsor will appreciate what you are doing.

Interpretation is always tricky. An article in the *New Yorker* (Hertzberg, 1998) makes this point. The editors commissioned a broad opinion survey of the American public that they called "a fearless inquiry into whatever" (p. 27). Let's take their question "Do you believe in God?" Of the respondents in the group they dubbed Main Street, 92 percent answered in the affirmative; 61 percent of *New Yorker* readers, a well-educated group the editors called High Street, said they believe in God. The magazine then provides examples of the art of interpretation. One writer could take those numbers and note that High Street, a group many would describe as elitist and unlike Middle America, is really God fearing. Note the strong majority (61 percent) affirming their belief in God. Another writer could use the same numbers to point out the striking difference (92 percent versus 61 percent) between educated and middle America. Much can be accomplished with the same data, as you can see.

What's important is that you solicit and present opinions. It is up to you and the customer to discuss alternative interpretations.

Isn't There More I Could Do?

There's always more that could be done. Remember that this is the initial scoping of the effort, during which you set direction and determine who ought to be involved. As I've said before, the task during performance analysis is to determine, from the perspective of judiciously selected sources, what people ought to be doing and considering. Having done so, you can then marshal, direct, and even save resources for the subsequent training needs assessment and collaboration across units to follow.

You *can* shave time off the front end. Here's how you do it:

Get clear about where you're going. What kinds of information are you seeking? In what ways is this source likely to be most helpful? How can you enhance the political benefits of the interactions? Time is wasted in aimless meandering.

Repurpose existing data that reside in the organization. Look to exit interviews, sales records, help desk logs, customer feedback, work products. There is much there that gives you a quick picture of the current situation, often from several sources. It's always quicker and cheaper to repurpose existing data than to gather anew.

Capitalize on what you and other wise people know by putting "straw" out there for reactions and improvement. Most sources need assistance in being helpful to you. Provide outlines, hypotheses, schematics, suggested ways of handling challenges—your sources will have much to say about what you've proposed.

Engage in virtual performance analyses. Use technology to continuously gather trends, directions, problems, issues, and drivers so that you are never surprised when a request for assistance appears.

Use automation to reach out, to gather and analyze data.

Gather examples of successful analyses and use them to spread the benefits of this kind of thoughtful approach.

6

Communicating to Gather Information and Support

Axel: Remember I told you I was going out to the plants in Mexico City and Wuhan to interview foremen and engineers? It's a key part of the planning for the safety project. Well, it went really well—much to my surprise.

Ludmila: I remember that you were worried. I think you said you were thinking about not visiting the plants, and instead relying on an email survey.

Axel: I was worried. Once I had a focus group that ran amok—that's the only way I can describe it. I had a near mutiny on my hands. And a couple of times I've had experts who refused to tell me much of anything at all—and I had traveled halfway across the globe to meet with them. Now this didn't happen to me, but I heard about a human resources guy who sent out a survey that bounced back with nasty comments because he used the wrong terminology. There's more to this than just scheduling some meetings or posting up a survey.

In this chapter, we focus on the communications that underpin analysis. We'll start with a quick tour of the methods used to gather information: interviews and focus groups, observations, surveys, and examination of existing data and work products. Then we'll focus on general communications principles applicable to all methods.

Methods for Gathering Information and Support

There are four methods for gathering information and support during analysis. What I'll do here is briefly describe them and then make some comparisons, focusing particularly on how they can be helpful during a speedy PA. More detailed treatment of these methods is provided in my book *Training Needs Assessment* (1987). In Chapter Seven, I focus in particular on the implications of technology for interviews, groups, and surveys.

Interviews and Focus Groups

Interviews are the most typical way of gathering performance analysis data. Focus groups, though popular, occur less often. Table 6.1 is a brief comparison of interviews and focus groups.

Both focus groups and interviews depend on the ability to listen. As reported in Barwise and Meehan's 2008 article in the *Harvard Business Review,* listening is not automatic. They cite data from a Personnel Decisions International survey of more than four thousand U.S. companies. Managers typically rate themselves higher than their colleagues rate them, especially on measures of performance that involve listening.

During an interview, one individual asks questions of another in order to seek opinions. Not surprisingly, we tend to be interested in those factors that are not observable or obvious, such as expertise, feelings and opinions, and data often labeled as qualitative or tacit. Often we're interviewing or running a group to make manifest the skills, perspectives, performance drivers, and cultural forces of which respondents are not consciously aware. For example, we might ask an executive if her regional managers are confident about their abilities to manage now that the organization is using technology to distribute information more broadly. Or you might use an interview to ask individual doctors if they share executives' enthusiasm regarding the shift to hospital care teams headed by nurses. Or you might use interviews or

Table 6.1. Interviews and Focus Groups.

	Interviews	Focus Groups
Kinds of Information	Defines direction (optimals and actuals) and drivers. Very useful for establishing relationships and defining subsequent ways of working together.	Typically used for defining optimals and for seeking consensus across organizations and geographic areas.
Benefits	Shows commitment to opinions beyond your own or the executive's. Enables probing for the meaning behind statements.	More efficient way to involve many individuals and organizations in planning. Enable probing and follow-up queries.
Limitations	Costly in time and resources. Some respondents are hesitant to share opinions; they sometimes fear what you'll do with their views. There's no anonymity in an interview, of course. If your project isn't their priority, some sources hesitate.	Gathering disparate people and viewpoints can lead to chaos and to the hardening of positions instead of to consensus. People in groups may not offer honest opinions. Not everybody is adept at leading focus groups. Anonymity is nonexistent, and opinions can become public.
PA or TNA?	Used for gathering information during PA and TNA.	Although they are common as general kickoff sessions for both PA and TNA, focus groups are more often used in TNA, as they are appropriate for simultaneously gathering detailed information about skills and knowledge and encouraging buy-in.
Chronology	Use interviews at the beginning of the analysis, and throughout.	A focus group is not the best way to launch your quest for optimals (though some disagree). It's better to commence with interviews with experts and review of documents, and then, after you are familiar with likely views, assemble a group.

Table 6.2. Six Kinds of Questions for Interviews and Focus Groups.

Type of Question	Analyst Queries
Hypothetical questions ask how the respondent might want the situation handled. They use the words *how, might, what if, suppose.*	Suppose that the organization had hit a home run with the customer services program rolled out nearly two years ago. What would you be seeing in the organization now? How might things work differently?
Ideal position questions press the interviewee to describe what he or she wishes it would be.	Picture yourself in one of our stores. Imagine that you are witnessing stellar customer service. What's going on?
Devil's advocate questions press the interviewee to take a position he or she might not have considered or take the opposite position.	Customer service is like motherhood and apple pie. What if we didn't bother to tackle the issue? How would things be different? What if we did everything but training? What would that look like?
Flawed position questions press the interviewee to speculate on the opposite of the desired state.	Back to the store. But this time it's not a good customer service picture; in fact, it's very bad. You are upset about what you see. What's going on? Detail examples of flawed customer service.
Interpretive questions tie together some of what you've been hearing and ask the respondent for reactions.	Your references to training suggest that you think that employees aren't responding rapidly and well because they don't know how to do so. Is that accurate? Do you think they lack skills in this area? Is that the key factor?
Straw questions give the interviewee something to respond to. It might be a list, a visual, an audio interaction, or the like.	I want you to listen to this audio interaction and give me a sense of whether or not you think the supervisor is doing what's necessary to ensure good customer services. Please tell me what you like and don't like.

focus groups to seek examples of the strategies that contract negotiators use to successfully hold the line on costs.

Focus groups provide an opportunity to gather a group representing, for example, different perspectives, geographic regions, or organizational affiliations. The challenge is to garner diverse wisdom and views without creating or hardening chasms between constituencies.

The heart of interviews and focus groups is the questions. Interviews and group sessions should be driven by the purposes of the interaction and the desire to establish positive working relationships.

Strauss, Schatzman, Bucher, and Sabshin (1981) identify four kinds of questions: hypothetical, devil's advocate, ideal position, and interpretive. To their four, I add two: flawed position questions and straw questions. Table 6.2 presents each type with a sample question for an interview with Mick Reynolds, a senior executive for a large retail superstore. Mick, not his real name, is eager to launch yet another customer service initiative. (We'll meet Vicente Mata, one of his managers, later in this chapter.)

Another key aspect of communicating during interviews and focus groups is the use of probing questions. A probe is a follow-up question. Notice how the analyst uses two probes for drivers with Mick. The analyst is trying to understand how supervisors can contribute more to the customer service that their reps are delivering to customers.

Mick: . . . supervisors who understand the active role they must play in customer service. We've got some who do it and others who just don't, or won't, maybe. It involves a certain amount of engagement, when it's easier not to, I guess.

Analyst: What appears to be the difference between supervisors who do and those who do not play that proactive customer service role?

Mick: I'm not sure. Maybe they don't know how to do it, or fear that the reps will see it as an intrusion.

Analyst: Have you ever asked the reps how they perceive supervisors who play more active roles during customer service? When reps are trained, what messages are conveyed about roles?

Many of the benefits of interviews and focus groups are the same. Both can be employed to establish rapport and buy-in and to gather information from sources. Both allow a probing follow-up question. As you can see from the interaction with Mick, questions move the effort forward, as the professional drills deeper.

Focus groups can be particularly tricky, however. First of all, there's usually one of you and several of them. Managing several people with diverse and occasionally parochial perspectives, and keeping track of progress, can be daunting. Some have described it as a little like trying to ride herd on a group of frogs.

Use interviews and review of related documents to set the stage for focus groups. Visit or call key participants prior to the gathering. Determine ahead of time what they know and care about. Seek commonalties and distinctions. Look for hot buttons. When you commence with a group meeting, there is a tendency for individuals to swiftly home in on those areas in which they disagree. You don't want to be surprised by deeply rooted positions. It's far better to be aware and prepared for the inevitable abrasions that arise when varied constituencies are represented. It makes sense to send emails in advance of every meeting, including details about the why, when, where, and how for the group.

Observations

There's much to be gained from being vigilant in the field. Two forms of observation are useful. Observing people at work is one type; scrutinizing work products is the other.

Watching people at work will provide information about the nature of the work and what might be driving or impeding effective performance. For example, if you were asked to improve the performance of hotel employees during check-in, observations would be very useful. Table 6.3 presents possible stages for attacking check-in problems.

When you are in the hotel, situated near the front desk, you would want to take controlled snapshots of the situation, with your attention focused by what you had learned in the earlier stages of the performance analysis. Examine those areas mentioned by the executive and customers. What do you see?

Table 6.3. Stages in Analysis for Hotel Check-In.

Stage	Sources	What to Seek
One	Sponsor	Why address check-in now? What's the problem? What is the sponsor hoping to accomplish? Does she have any sense of the driver(s) of the problems?
Two	Customer complaints	Examine documents that reflect the concerns of customers and the sponsor. What are they emphasizing? Around what problems do they cluster?
Three	Observation of desk personnel	Do you see the issues that were noted in customer comments? Can you see trends in drivers of these problems?
Four	Interviews with desk personnel and supervisors	Seek the drivers of the problems identified in customer letters and calls.
Five	Review of training materials	Seek the details of what people are taught about issues related to the identified problems.
Six	Review of policies	What does the organization tell its people is required?

You're seeking the drivers of the situation. There are limited possibilities. Might the employees not know what to do? Do they know enough about the Internet connections in the rooms to answer questions to the satisfaction of guests? Might the computer system be foiling them during registration? Might their training or policies lead them to behave in ways that aren't congruent with current customer preferences? For example, are they engaging in friendly, exact explications about hotel amenities when business travelers are longing to be away from the desk and lounging in their rooms?

If you can watch unobserved and without influencing performance, you'll gather important information about drivers. It also makes sense to use "secret shoppers" to act like guests to see what really happens during this process.

Work patterns and assignments will be obvious. Missing information or clunky computer systems will be obvious too. If you decide to inform sources that you will be observing them, at first you will witness their attempts at engaging in optimal check-in activities. If they perform in ways that avoid the customer complaint areas when you're there and they're exerting special effort, then it is obvious that skill and knowledge are not the barriers and that training will not solve this problem. Look to the other possibilities, such as supervision, computer software, errant processes, or a new population of guests with different priorities and questions.

You can use observations of people at work to gather data about current or desired performance too, but it is a time-consuming method, perhaps best saved for training needs assessment, when you know that you will be rolling out training or information to support improved performance. For example, if you discovered during analysis that a problem was caused by an absence of knowledge about troubleshooting the computer check-in system, then during training needs assessment you might return to interview and watch effective performers in order to specify the details of optimal effort.

Documents and work products are important objects for our visual attention. They are a rich, bargain-priced source of information about what is currently going on and what we might want to review and consider. As you can see in Table 6.3, feedback from customers, captured in the record of their comments and complaints, is an early, relevant source for targeting the effort to where the pain resides.

Occasionally, you'll be able to infer causes from a pattern in this extant data; for example, if insurance claims are limited to one piece of equipment in a factory, you might begin to infer a cause associated with the equipment itself or skill regarding operation of the equipment.

When you are looking at documents and work products, you are examining the "stuff" of the organization. Examples abound and are limited only by imagination and access. Let's look at some possibilities for tangible sources in Table 6.4.

Table 6.4. Challenges and Suggested Sources.

Sample Challenge	Tangible Sources
The vice-president for global learning and development for a petrochemical company commits to the development of in-country talent. She wants local people, often in the developing world, to be able to contribute and rise in the organization.	Review job descriptions. Examine records from the learning management system. Review competencies published by professional associations. Examine and update self-assessments. Examine requests, kudos, and complaints. Examine available development assets, programs, and opportunities in far-flung locations in which the company works.
An executive for an aerospace company is eager to improve safety.	Review accident report. Review insurance claims. Review supervisor reports. Review state and federal inspections and reports. Review corporate response documents after government audits. Review employee comments collected via the online form that solicits concerns.

(Continued)

Table 6.4. Challenges and Suggested Sources. *(Continued)*

Sample Challenge	Tangible Sources
The leadership requests a course that will help employees write more appropriate emails.	Review existing, unsuccessful class.
	Review the literature to find standards for appropriate, successful email messages.
	Review emails identified as "optimal."
	Review randomly pulled email in light of standards.
	Review customer complaints.

There are many other possible sources, such as exit interviews, performance appraisals, and annual reports. Although nobody would deny you access to the annual report, it is not unusual to have roadblocks pop up when you seek to examine appraisals, exit interviews, or emails. Because it is not necessary to associate individuals' names with their output, tell the holders of the documents that they may mask identities prior to providing these sources.

Documents and work products should not be used in isolation from other sources. After you have determined patterns in performance or customer reaction or exit interviews, it is critical to talk to those who are involved or implicated. You will likely turn to interviews or focus groups as follow-up.

Surveys

In many organizations, surveys aren't popular with employees. There are two reasons for the low esteem in which they are held. The first is that there are too many surveys. The second is that too little happens as a result of the surveys, at least as far as they know. If you want results and want to avoid contributing to cynicism in the organization, survey judiciously and provide value to participants as a result of their efforts. Summarize the results for them. That's a good use of email. Or post results online. Describe the shift in program emphases that resulted. Detail a course of action that might not have been taken or that an executive might not have pursued without the data derived from the surveys.

My focus here is on surveys used for performance analysis. As you know, in PA we are concerned about quickly figuring out what to do. Surveys serve that effort in a particular way, enabling us to reach out to large numbers for their priorities and opinions—in ways that enable them to remain anonymous.

On the basis of what is learned in earlier stages of the PA, and tapping into opinions from leaders, documents, benchmarks, and experts, a survey places options in front of the people doing and supervising the work. The Internet, of course, makes it easy to serve up, collect, and crunch responses.

Don't wait until the effort is requested. Anticipate that wise executives will want to know of the major development needs within their organizations. Here is the opportunity for virtual analysis, in this case through surveys, as you look for direction regarding development for the engineers or hospital administrators or loan officers or training and development professionals of the future. While seeking priorities, we can also ask respondents to speculate on forces that block or impede their development and performance. Let's look at an example.

Table 6.5 represents the stages in a performance analysis associated with professional growth for training and development professionals in a global corporation. The task was presented like this: "We want to move our training and development professionals in some distinct ways. We're interested in performance, consultation, and technology. What we don't know is where these professionals are on all this." Table 6.5 presents stages associated with the entire PA effort; the survey (stage six), comprising the forced-choice options you see in Tables 6.6a and 6.6b, was based on what was learned early in the performance analysis. It's a system, as you know.

Table 6.5. Stages in Analysis for Global Training and Development Professionals.

Stage	Sources	What to Seek
One	Sponsor(s)	Why now? What are they hoping to accomplish? What are the priority directions for their training and development professionals? Any problems they're seeking to solve? Any models or benchmarks? Any literature that is influential?
Two	The literature or an expert or consultant	Examine articles, books, and contributions to professional associations for emergent competencies. What are they emphasizing? Around what topics and concerns do authorities' opinions cluster?
Three	Internal experts	What are the top-priority trends for competencies? What are they reading and scanning to influence their thoughts? What challenges will dominate here? What are the emergent problems and opportunities? Are there online collections of knowledge and wisdom that could serve as models? If so, are they relied on? Refreshed?
Four	Sponsor(s)	Report on stages one through three. Seek priorities.
Five	Job incumbents	What are the top-priority trends for competencies? What obstacles do they perceive? What will help them move in these directions?
Six	Survey	What are respondents' top priorities for growth, given what we have learned in prior stages? What obstacles do they perceive for their growth? What will help them move in these directions? See Table 6.6a, which represents the quest for priorities, and Table 6.6b, which seeks drivers.

Table 6.6a. Partial Survey for Training and Development Professionals.

Please rate priorities for your own professional development. For each item, circle the number that best reflects your priorities.

2 = Top priority
1 = A priority
0 = Not a priority

	Description of Capabilities	Your Priority		
Serve the client and the organization	1. Know where to go for information about what the customer needs.	2	1	0
	2. Know what questions to ask and what materials to examine.	2	1	0
	3. Know how to explain the analysis to ensure organizational access and support.	2	1	0
	4. Know how to use interviews, focus groups, and surveys to gather data.	2	1	0
	5. Know what the data mean and how to explain them to the customer.	2	1	0
	6. Know about the many ways that human performance can be improved.	2	1	0
	7. Know how to explain the impact of individual and organizational root causes on human performance.	2	1	0
Develop and deliver solutions	8. Know the attributes of effective instructor-led and independent learning programs.	2	1	0
	9. Know how to develop effective training materials, for example, instructor guides, student guides, cases, and practices.	2	1	0
	10. Know how to use a variety of learning technologies, for example, World Wide Web, CD-ROM, satellite, multimedia, blogs, and distance learning.	2	1	0
Measure impact	11. Know how to build and pilot prototypes prior to rolling out the finished solution systems.	2	1	0
	12. Know how to report results and revisions.	2	1	0

Table 6.6b. Partial Survey to Measure Priority Needs and Anticipated Barriers.

Do the following statements reflect your situation, thoughts, or beliefs? For each item, circle the number that best reflects your thoughts.

2 = Agree
1 = Neutral or Don't know
0 = Disagree

Statement	Your Rating		
1. I am in favor of the increased emphasis on technology-based delivery.	2	1	0
2. I need to know more about performance improvement strategies that go beyond instruction.	2	1	0
3. I possess a computer that I use in my work.	2	1	0
4. I see benefits in moving toward more collaboration with cross-functional colleagues.	2	1	0
5. My manager is eager for me to demonstrate the skills, knowledge, and perspectives emphasized in this survey.	2	1	0
6. I think I'll be good at moving in these directions.	2	1	0
7. I am eager to learn more about the topics that are described in this survey.	2	1	0
8. If I begin doing the things on this survey, I will be recognized for these efforts.	2	1	0
9. I am willing to make the time necessary to develop my skills and knowledge in these areas.	2	1	0
10. My customers are eager for us to shift in these directions.	2	1	0

This partial survey would be distributed anonymously, perhaps at a meeting, or posted online. Note that the questions in Table 6.6a seek perspectives and priorities. Table 6.6b asks training professionals to anticipate performance drivers associated with their transformation.

Effective Communications

Four principles should drive the way you communicate during performance analysis:

1. Understand your sources.

2. Be authentic.

3. Remember that performance analysis might be perceived as threatening, controversial, and intrusive—and deal with it.

4. Emphasize planning. It is at the heart of effective communications.

Understand Your Sources

No surprise here, but still a challenge. Before you go out in the field, consider the following questions:

Who are the sources, and what are their perspectives?

Are they delighted to participate? Are they hesitant? Why?

Where are their managers on this topic?

Will this effort influence the status quo? How?

How is the source invested in the status quo?

If things change, how might their world be altered?

Have the sources been properly briefed by their leaders? By you?

Do they know why you're there and why they are being tapped for information, opinions, and access to materials?

What related efforts have occurred in the organization? How do they muddy the waters?

Tables 6.7 through 6.11 offer the perspectives of typical performance analysis sources and make some assumptions about what their questions and concerns might be. I'm not suggesting that each of your sources will possess all of these views and perspectives. What I do know is that some probably will. Be ready for these questions and address them at the get-go. It will improve both your relationship with the source and the quality of data derived from the interactions.

Table 6.7 illustrates some key concerns of job incumbents during performance analysis. Job incumbents are the focus of the effort. Anybody could be a job incumbent. Engineers might be; so could maintenance workers, human resources professionals, teachers, and executives. When you hear, "Our IT consultants need a boost in their skills and knowledge regarding security," then IT consultants are the job incumbents.

Table 6.8 describes the perspectives that some experts bring into the interaction. I've included suggestions that are matched to those views.

Table 6.9 describes the perspectives that managers might bring into a performance analysis. Note the similarities with the hesitancies of the job incumbents.

Solution partners are colleagues across the organization or working as vendors from outside the organization with whom you might cooperate to ensure performance improvement. Compensation specialists, organizational developers, organizational effectiveness experts, business process engineers, and information technologists might be solution partners. Their concerns would emerge after data about drivers have been gathered and you are attempting to bring them to the table to collaborate. Table 6.10 presents some of the perspectives that such partners might bring into an initiative.

Executives come to the table with different issues. Table 6.11 presents some views executives might hold and offers suggestions for addressing their concerns.

Be Authentic

My trusty dictionary defines *authentic* as "genuine, true, reliable." Graduate students will often ask how they should handle one situation or another. Although specific suggestions vary with the circumstances, I always urge them to be authentic.

Table 6.7. Job Incumbents' Perspectives.

Incumbents' Perspectives	Analyst Strategies
The employee doesn't want to participate. Perhaps he avoids meetings. Or comes late. Or is unwilling to utter anything except monosyllables.	Remind him about the importance of the project. Describe positive effects on him, his unit, the work. Answer questions about who was selected, who you are, and confidentiality.
The employee wants to know why she has been chosen for these inquiries.	You can tell her one of three things: (1) she was randomly selected; (2) she was identified as a model performer (truth is important here—employees know if they're that kind of performer); (3) she was identified by X as having some important views on this matter.
The employee wants to know your credentials.	Share them. Note those elements with which the incumbent will identify. If he is an insurance agent, describe your years in the field selling insurance prior to this assignment. (No lies, of course.) Take a little time to explain your role, what you are seeking, the reasons you need him and others in that role.
The employee is unimpressed by your credentials.	Acknowledge that you haven't been an insurance agent or whatever. Describe how you've prepared for this conversation, indicating what you've read and with whom you've talked. Emphasize that you've come to her and other agents for their significant practical experience, which you admittedly lack.
The employee is concerned about being involved.	Why is he concerned? What might that suggest about the organization? This is where you make further assurances about the confidentiality of data and tailor your responses to the concern(s).
The employee isn't interested in helping out.	Why? If it isn't because of the issues already raised, then it might be that the employee hasn't been properly prepared to participate. Has the supervisor encouraged participation? Have you oriented the employee ahead of time and then again at the commencement of the meeting?

Table 6.8. Subject Matter Experts' Perspectives.

Experts' Perspectives	*Analyst Strategies*
The expert enjoys the distinction and job security that comes from being the only one (or one of the very few) who knows. She doesn't see good reasons to share, as that will erode the monopoly.	Reiterate the importance of the effort. Explain how she will be credited in the effort. Detail ongoing relationships and expectations regarding her continued involvement with the effort.
This issue is a low priority for this expert. Maybe he's moved on to another project. Maybe he's never been very interested in the domain to begin with. Maybe he's turned off by past experiences, where he failed to receive credit for contributions.	Reiterate the importance of the effort. If the expert persists in avoiding contact or fails to provide necessary information, ask why. There are many possible reasons. Target your responses to the particular concern—for example, by defining credit issues or assuring him there will be follow-through. In a pinch, make certain that an executive sponsor has weighed in on the importance of this project.
The expert is so enthusiastic that she is ready to devote energy that far exceeds your plans for her.	Express appreciation for that enthusiasm. Identify how you hope to involve the expert, using tangible examples about meetings or briefings or reviews. If the expert is disappointed by the role, explain why it is defined as it is—for example, by explaining that engineers from other geographic areas need to be involved in order for the program to be widely accepted. Consider increasing her role. Why not?
The expert is concerned that *other* experts are going to be involved in defining the outcomes and subject matter.	Describe the many sources who are involved in defining any effective program: internal and external experts, the literature, model performers, and so on. Explain why broad participation in definition is beneficial if the program is to be widely accepted.

Table 6.9. Managers' and Supervisors' Perspectives.

Managers' Perspectives	Analyst Strategies
The manager is acting uninterested in the effort. Perhaps she avoids meetings. Or comes late. Or is unwilling to utter anything except monosyllables.	Remind her about the importance of the project. Describe the benefits to her, her unit, the work. Note the priority that a sponsoring executive has attached to the effort. Answer the questions she has about who was selected, who you are, and confidentiality. (Also see below.)
The manager wants to know why he has been chosen for these inquiries.	You can tell him one of three things: (1) he was randomly selected; (2) he was identified as a model performer (truth is important here—employees know if they're that kind of performer); (3) he was identified by X as having some important views on this matter.
The manager wants to know your credentials.	Share them. Note those elements with which the manager will identify. If she is a regional manager, describe your years in the field and note any management experiences. (No lies, of course.) Explain why managers' and supervisors' perspectives are critical here.
The manager is unimpressed by your credentials.	Acknowledge that you haven't been a manager in the field. Describe how you've prepared for this conversation, indicating what you've read and with whom you've talked. Emphasize that you've come to him and other managers for their significant experience, which you admittedly lack.
The manager is obviously concerned about being involved.	Why is she concerned? What might that suggest about the organization? This is where you repeat assurances about the confidentiality of data.
The manager doesn't approve of the direction in which your effort is taking the organization.	Why? Solicit his opinions. Don't debate. Capture his views. Report those views back to the sponsors without attribution.

Table 6.10. Solution Partners' Perspectives.

Solution Partners' Perspectives	Analyst Strategies
"You're who? This is novel. Why is somebody from _____asking me to come to a meeting?"	Say something about the project and why it is a priority. Name the client or sponsor for the effort. Share the data that indicated it was important to involve this person (his skills, perspectives) in the effort. Seek participation. Sell a systemic approach to the initiative.
"Why is a 'training' person doing something other than training?"	Explain that before you could do any training, it was important to find out what training was appropriate. In that process, you found that there were other things that had to be done to fertilize the organization, or the training wouldn't matter.
"What's your role here?"	Explain that you're attempting to put the necessary people together. You're not the boss, just somebody who is attempting to make sure that the effort moves forward in all the necessary places.
"Does my manager know that I would be working on your project?"	Prior to inviting this person, make certain that his leaders are willing to play a part in this effort. It's possible that the sponsor or your manager will need to smooth the path here. Communication with leaders across the organization is important preparation for successful cross-functional collaboration.
"We're billable, as you know. Have you got the money for me to get involved?"	Use the same strategies as those immediately above. You know if the organization operates like this. Will you need to arrange to "buy" internal or external expertise? Seek that support ahead of time.

Table 6.11. Executives' Perspectives.

Executives' Perspectives	Analyst Strategies
"Thank goodness you're here. I've got to go to Singapore, and I need you to bring this one to fruition while I'm on the road."	If the executive is disappearing, who will play her role on this project? Your work as analyst needs to occur under the aegis of an executive or sponsor. Push back. The executive or another leader must be involved. The trick is to define a "reasonable" amount of executive involvement or to find a substitute sponsor.
"This is a tough one, and I'll want to see everything before it goes out. In fact, maybe we should meet daily."	This is the micromanaging executive. Why is he concerned? What's tough? Put some energy into gathering data on his views of the situation and then negotiating a close relationship that isn't oppressive.
"I'm concerned that your interactions with employees will stir things up in the field."	You are asking about drivers and barriers, about organizational consistency and messages. Explain why it is important to raise these issues and how you're going to use the data. Cite past efforts that were unitary and thus unsuccessful. Brief her regarding the solution system that will emerge. Offer the opportunity to review questions prior to your meeting with people in the field.
"Why is a human resources gal [or a training guy] talking about processes and software and organizational climate?"	Explain that you expect to be doing some training but that you want to customize and tailor the effort, which involves getting out into the organization. Does the executive want training events or the improvements in performance that he was talking about earlier?
"What role do you expect me to play?"	This is a good opportunity to make certain that the executive understands what it's going to take to be successful on this project. How can she help? What sources must be contacted? Will you draft a letter for her? What solution partners might be involved? How can the executive prepare people for collaboration on solution systems?

Tracey Benettolo takes a global view of human performance improvement. She has worked in both Africa and Southeast Asia in many roles, all devoted to leveraging performance in order to foster long-term business success.

Tracey faces numerous labor-related challenges in her current work in South Africa. "Many firms have lost skills in the last decade due to emigration and poaching by competitors," she explains," and coupled with that is the inconsistent access to quality education."

Three challenges hold particular significance for Tracey's work:

1. The shortage of skilled craftspeople and other technical workers, such as electricians and mechanics, engineers, computer technicians, and scientists.

2. The shortage of middle and upper managers within all industries.

3. The quality of graduates coming out of the educational system. This is a deficit rather than a shortage since it is a question of skills, not numbers.

The skills deficits and management shortages are so pronounced that the South African government passed a Skills Development Act designed to improve skills and increase global competitiveness. Unfortunately, some of the nationally registered qualifications are sometimes poorly articulated, and the learning strategies may not tie into existing business needs and competencies.

For instance, Tracey recently worked with a South African car manufacturer who wanted to increase productivity in order to compete with international auto companies. Lower labor costs in many countries make competing in a global export market very difficult. Tracey's client initially wanted to improve learning in hopes of improving productivity. But with employees financially rewarded for learning, more learning equals higher labor costs and higher labor costs offset increases in productivity. "Talk about a double-edged sword!" exclaimed Tracey.

Tracey aligned the learning program with clearly defined business results. The approach she adopted was as follows. She

1. Identified organizational performance goals.

2. Benchmarked related companies in the industry both locally and globally.

3. Translated the organizational goals and industry best practices into learning paths and programs, including the creation of a nationally recognized qualification.

4. Defined the measures of business success on which the learning programs would be evaluated.

5. Determined which existing business tools could be used to measure behavior change and thus business success.

Tracey happily reports that the manufacturer implemented a program based on its impact on business results. Learning now emphasizes the line manager and the importance of that managerial role in continued workplace behavior change.

But from beginning to end of the learning program design, Tracey focused on business success. "Don't get too technical with a client regarding learning theories and learning terminology," she recommends. "Ask the questions needed to make your recommendation, and ensure that you articulate that recommendation simply." Tracey emphasizes to each client that she must sometimes ask "silly questions" since she is a learning expert, not an expert in the client's particular subject area. "I can't make assumptions," she asserts, "and let them know that up front so that I can harness their specialized intellectual capital."

Tracey provides all of her recommendations in presentation slides that can be shown to anybody throughout the organization. She accompanies the slides with a more detailed blueprint document, but leaders can glean what they need to know to make the necessary learning- and performance-related decisions from the presentation.

> **Tracey Benettolo** has been involved in performance-based education and human performance improvement initiatives for twelve years. She currently serves as a learning strategist with the LR Group, an organizational effectiveness consulting firm with offices in Cape Town, Johannesburg, and Durban, South Africa. You can reach Tracey at TraceyB@lr.co.za.

Why am I fussing about authenticity? The reason is that there is a tendency for fledgling analysts to think that there is one correct way to execute the stages and deliver the questions and dialogues presented in this book. There is not. The words presented here are suggestions. They must be tailored to you and your situation. If you're effusive and enthusiastic, be that way. If you're quiet and measured, that is fine too. The key is to be prepared and consistent, and if your style and proclivities are causing problems in communications, to discuss them with the source.

The source gets to decide, if there is an issue. An example is the methods used to communicate. Imagine that you prefer email. Your two subject matter experts do not. They like the phone or face-to-face meetings. Honor their preferences.

Here is an example. A colleague in the software business often drew quizzical looks from engineers. He is perky, eager, and emotional about projects. Most of his sources were less so and didn't immediately trust his enthusiasms. After my associate noted the difference between his style and that of his sources, allowed that his manner can take some getting accustomed to, and began to spice his conversation with citations and numbers, communication improved. He didn't stop being himself, but he toned his presentation down a tad, to give them a little more of what they expected.

Here's an approach to more authentic communications. First, I suggest that you take a reading on your reactions, and monitor feelings and thoughts. It is easy to get swept away in the moment, when the expert refuses to help out. Start by getting a handle on what you're thinking and feeling. For example, one of my students put it like this:

> Well, I was coming off overly emotional on this. And I didn't want to do that. It makes me sound young and inexperienced. I calmed down and took my pulse on the situation. I really like this project, but I am getting a little resentful. I feel that my client ought to be more generous about letting me use this project afterwards. I'll put many hours into this effort, and I'm getting paid a pittance. OK, I'm overreacting. I want to be able to present at conferences, and this would be a great example. Shouldn't I be able to add this to my portfolio to strengthen my case for positions in the future?

Next, ask yourself about those feelings and thoughts. Are they reasonable? Can they be understood by the client or expert or colleague? How do your perspectives conflict or mesh with the other person's view? My student said, "[My client] could hear all of that—the parts about the effort and time and small remuneration. And I think he'll resonate to the part about my portfolio. Not sure about the conference thing. Might be a concern there. They're very serious about holding their examples and cases confidential."

Third, make your case based on what you were thinking and feeling and your rational assessment of the other's perspectives. Be willing to reveal concerns and priorities that are unique to you, mentioning your job hunt, for example, or your desire to show off your work at a conference. Rather than taking a general stand, such as, "I will work my fingers to the bone on this one and should be able to do with it what I want, especially since you're paying me so little," approach it more specifically and tangibly. Try, "As you know, I graduate in December, and I'm eager to be able to show prospective employers what I've done in graduate school. I want to do that at conferences and in interviews when I show my portfolio. I will be proud of the work done for you and want to include it."

Finally, ask for help. "How can we work this out so that I can use this effort for my job search and so you and your organization will wind up with a great project and be fully comfortable with our agreement?" (A note: the student succeeded in convincing her client to allow limited sharing of her efforts on the project.)

This approach would work just as well for an internal human performance professional who is trying to tempt a difficult expert into cooperation. Table 6.12 presents a similar example of authentic communications that highlights these four steps.

Remember That Performance Analysis Might Be Perceived as Threatening, Controversial, and Intrusive

Why would that be? The question takes us back to the kinds of information we gather during performance analysis. Let's start with a situation in which you are attempting to capture a picture of directions, including optimal performance and perspectives, and of what's currently going on. If we are

Table 6.12. Authentic Communications.

Steps to Authentic Communications	What You Might Think or Say
Monitor what you're thinking and feeling. Ask yourself what you're thinking, how you feel, why you feel that way, and what else might be going on.	I'm incredulous. This woman was assigned to talk with me about team nursing and nurse leadership. Now she's stonewalling, or I think she's stonewalling. Dr. Isaacs said he'd set it up. I presume he did. I can't believe this. It's close to rude. And I hate to beg for information. This is awful. Get me out of here.
Take a tour of your ideas and feelings. Are they reasonable? How would the other person respond to your inquiries? Why might they see your questions differently?	Maybe I'm overreacting to her lack of enthusiasm. Has Dr. Isaacs gotten around to explaining the effort to her and why she is important to it? Did he explain my role? Is she stonewalling, or does it just feel that way to me? She might perceive me as meddling in her ongoing project, whereas I see myself as helping to spread her view of the approach throughout the hospital. Could she be concerned that I won't give her credit for her work?
Make a case that includes your perspective and hers. Tell her why this matters to you; include carefully selected elements that reveal your priorities.	"Why don't we back up a bit? Did Dr. Isaacs tell you about this project? I get the sense that maybe you haven't been included up front in all of this, that you need for me to start from the beginning. You are one of the nurses who is heading up the hospital team leadership concept. You're actually doing it, and from what Isaacs says, you're doing it in a way that they want to spread across the organization. I'm here to learn from you. I'm hoping that you will provide key definitions for us and a clear view of where the barriers might be. I'm not a nurse, but I've done quite a bit of work on teaming and team leadership. We might have a lot to offer each other."
Ask for help on this.	"Can I answer any questions you have? I want us to work together on this. Without you, it's hard for us to tailor this important program to our hospital."

seeking to know what excellence looks like in a "broad stroke" kind of way, some experts or model performers might hesitate about sharing their secrets or views. If they reveal what they know to you, what impact might that have on their unique status within the organization? And if you turn around and package their wisdom for wider dissemination, wouldn't their contribution become less rare and valuable? Whereas you as a training and development professional may be participating in the current thrust toward organizational learning and sharing, some employees are more compelled by the waves of workforce reductions.

What else could threaten? Maybe the expert does not see herself as expert. Maybe she does not like to be distinguished from her colleagues and to receive recognition for distinction. Maybe the expert does not want to share good ideas. Or maybe the expert is unwilling to invest time in collaborating with other experts from elsewhere. Or perhaps the expert prefers to talk to other experts and recognizes that you are not one.

Your work as a performance analyst also involves capturing a view of current performance. That might concern people in the organization. If you're reviewing sales figures, scrap production, and customer feedback, somebody is going to worry about what you are finding out about individual contributors. If you are asking people what they do, how they carry out processes, about their successes and failures, this too might evoke concern. They will wonder, why are you asking? Why are you asking *me*? Why are we talking about *my* unit and people?

The same concerns arise when you get into the quest for drivers and barriers, only more intensely. Here you are going beyond documenting what's happening to inquiring about underlying causes. This rivets attention in a big way. The concerns frame up like this: Did somebody suggest that I'm responsible or that our group is responsible? Is there some perception that we're not getting it done? Why would you be talking to *me* about this? Will what I say be repeated? What are other people saying about this?

There are no simple solutions here. Find out what's causing the glitch in communications and tailor your responses. Which human and organizational concerns are pricked by your appearance? Table 6.13 presents some suggestions for addressing your sources' most loaded concerns.

Table 6.13. Threats to Communication.

Type of Concern	Suggested Approaches
Concerns relating to optimals: ownership of expertise, willingness to share, job security, collaboration with other experts, exposure of the absence of expertise, and so on.	Focus efforts on defining the relationship, including the expert's or model performer's ongoing relationship with the effort. Note credit that will be received. Note executive sponsorship. Acknowledge the concerns of the expert. Match your approach to the particular concerns.
Concerns about outsiders knowing what is going on and about who or what might be factors driving the situation.	Acknowledge reasonable concerns about revealing this information to others. Explain why you have been assigned to this project. Describe similar past efforts and how you have in the past and will in the future maintain total discretion regarding the data.
Concern about confidentiality.	Acknowledge legitimate concern about confidentiality. Focus on how the data will benefit this source. Detail strategies you will use to maintain confidentiality. Explain that you will never attribute quotes and opinions. Identify similar past projects in which you have successfully maintained confidentiality and individual privacy.
Concern about your lack of expertise.	Admit that you aren't an expert (unless you are). Explain that you are talking to this person or this group for that very reason. You need their wisdom about the topic or the context. Detail the methods you've used to prepare yourself to make good use of the time your sources are giving to this effort. Review documents and literature in advance so that you can cite your preparatory efforts. Revisit how you will credit their contributions.

Ask your source about these concerns. Identify and articulate them. Admit that you empathize with that perspective and hesitations, and then offer rejoinders matched to those concerns. Base your case for participation on past efforts and projects. Invest in the relationship.

Emphasize Planning

Take nothing for granted. Assume that every interaction, from an interview to a focus group to a survey, requires preparation.

Be certain that you know why you are inquiring. Be clear about your purposes. Are you seeking directions through inquiries about optimals? Are you looking for a fix on what is currently going on? Are you seeking opinions on drivers for performance? Note that these purposes then serve as the generators for your questions. The early chapters of this book and Tables 6.2 and 6.5 detail sample purposes and questions.

In addition to such substantive purposes, you are attempting to win friends for your organization and for this effort, in particular. That's a critical aspect of any and all front-end work. You're looking for both information and allies. You cannot do it alone. You want executives who understand and sponsor the mission; incumbents and supervisors who know where the organization is heading; experts who leave their fingerprints all over your plan; and colleagues from sibling organizations who will unite with you to mount a performance improvement system.

Review appropriate materials. What publications or documentation can you read prior to interacting with this expert engineer or developing this survey? What web sites might help you review various approaches to nurturing high-potential executives or understanding alternatives for security for mobile devices? You should not only read in advance, but also make certain that what you learn shapes and enlightens your efforts. You might say, for instance, "As you know, I'm not a software engineer, but I am fluent on the prior system and spent a couple of hours reviewing the technical specifications for the new one. I have a pretty good idea of where we're going in this version. What I need at this point is your view of the prior rollout and your ideas about what we can do to ensure more success in the future."

The cover letter or opening paragraph for a survey might include the following: "As you look at the list below, you might wonder about where we got this list of competencies. Recently I've interviewed people in our organization and reviewed reports provided by the two major engineering professional associations located in Washington, D.C. We have combined the information derived from those sources to create what you find here. Now we want your reactions to possible directions for the future."

Consider the likely perspective that sources will bring to the table. This chapter posits many outlooks that sources might hold (as detailed in Tables 6.7 through 6.11). Don't be surprised by what you find. Preparation includes reflecting on the viewpoints of the people you are asking to help with the effort and planning how you will respond to their concerns.

Establish a plan for each interaction, including introductory communications, agenda, and follow-up. Let's take a look at these sample communications.

A voice mail message to an external expert might sound like this: "Agatha, this is Jamilla Stone in human resources at North American Technologies. We met a few years ago when I was working on our call center customer service project. Well, we want to revisit that effort and would like to get you involved. It wouldn't entail huge amounts of time from you, maybe six to eight hours over the next month, but we'd need at least two hours in the next week. Our questions focus on new approaches to customer service and strategies to put those programs in place. We know quite a bit already, but we'd like to get your view, a view that we hope includes what other state-of-the-art efforts look like. Can we work that into your schedule?"

An email message to an internal expert might look like this:

Dear Vicente,

Mick told me he discussed the customer service project with you and that you're expecting this email.

What I want to do here is to give you a little background on the project and to get your thinking about what we'll be discussing on Tuesday at 3, in your office. By the way, I really appreciate your involvement in this. You've been very successful with moving your group in this direction, and the whole organization needs to learn from what you're doing.

We're going to ask you what you're doing, in some detail. How did you influence customer service improvements? Your organization had the same training everybody else did. Why did it result in so much change for the better?

If you've got any memos or policies that you wrapped around that training effort, will you please bring them to the meeting? There's some thought that the supervisors are key players in this initiative. Will you please think about their roles at your site?

Mick and the Council decided to take on the topic of customer service because we continue to get a steady stream of complaints and lukewarm opinions. Except from your region. That's why I need to know more about how you and your folks are handling it.

Again, thank you very much. See you Tuesday at 3. I will come to your office.

The agenda for the meeting with Vicente should be emailed to him in advance of the meeting—or if that's not possible, it can be presented when you arrive. An agenda is important because it establishes your leadership and keeps the discussion on task. Exhibit 6.1 is a sample agenda for the session with Vicente. Note the use of time-certains.

Exhibit 6.1. Agenda for a Meeting with an Expert.

Agenda
    Customer Service Initiative
    February 9, 2009
    Participants: Vicente Mata, Mesa Superstore; Nosilla Stone, Human Resources and Training
    Goals: (1) To familiarize Vicente Mata with the project; (2) To provide background about the effort; (3) To learn about the current successful effort at the Mesa Superstore.
    3:05 Describe the background of this project, including data on the prior service effort and results.

(Continued)

> **Exhibit 6.1. Agenda for a Meeting with an Expert.** *(Continued)*
>
> 3:20 Discuss potential roles for Mr. Mata in the upcoming customer service effort.
>
> 3:30 Discuss the following questions: What did the Mesa Superstore do prior to and as follow-up to past customer service training? What does Mr. Mata perceive to be the supervisor's role in this effort? What are he and the store doing now to ensure continued performance? In what ways might their efforts be strengthened? To which employees should Ms. Stone speak for their perspectives on effective customer service? What are the logistics for arranging to meet with employees?
>
> 4:00 Discuss future collaboration and next steps.

Some follow-up is appropriate. It can be as slight as a thank-you email or as grand as a letter, with a copy sent to Mick, and a set of minutes from the meeting. Let's look at what might be sent to Vicente by email. The minutes or a note that documents the interaction are valuable as a tool to revisit what occurred, to prod promised actions, and to serve as a record of the event.

Hi, Vicente,

Thanks for the time you spent on the customer service project last week. I think we made good progress. I hope you agree.

We decided that you would serve as an ongoing member of the Planning Committee, a group that will meet three more times over the next eight weeks. We also agreed that you would play some role in the work that we do with managers and supervisors. It might be briefing, training, or even appearing as an expert in video clips we might produce. One good possibility is for you to serve as an online coach for chats and discussion groups that we think we might be rolling out with the project. As you can see, our exact plans are still being hatched. We are eager to have you involved as we design the program.

You promised to dig out the supervisor checklists that you distributed to your people after the workshop. Please send them to me as soon as possible. We're going to consider adapting them for the entire organization.

I'm still working on a document that details the four key components of your customer service effort. I'm putting the description and the materials you provided together into a comprehensive package; I'll send it to you before I forward it to other committee members. I want to make sure it reflects your views.

As I promised at the meeting, I discussed your ongoing involvement with Mick. He was delighted, and appreciative. I am too.

I'll be back to you about subsequent meetings. Now, I'm off to meet with that external expert I told you about. Tomorrow, I meet with four of the supervisors. And thanks for setting that up.

7

What Technology Contributes

Ayesha: Did you get this email? Look at this—it's a survey about our parking policies. They are pointing us to a web site where we go to answer questions. I think we might use something like this to plan the customer service program, maybe for the up-front study with the reps and their supervisors.

Gus: But don't you think our people would resist? They prefer face time. That's what we have done in the past.

Wendy: This company is all about high technology. Look at our products and where our profits come from. I think we ought to be looking for ways to reach out to people through technologies. And more of our employees, and customers too, are all over the world. There are downsides to the technology, but I know there are more pluses.

Technology has always served the performance analyst, but never more so than today. Thanks in large part to growing access to the Internet and inexpensive products, we see new software and hardware that can be

---

Joe Williams, a performance consultant for twenty-five years, was a coauthor of this chapter.

summoned to gather and analyze data. What follows is a discussion of technologies linked to the priorities and concerns of colleagues like Ayesha, Gus, and Wendy.

In this chapter, we'll tour the ways that technology can contribute to analysis, looking in particular at how to use technology to collect data.

Using Technology to Collect Data

The theme woven through each chapter of this book is how to do analysis *fast*. Technology can provide the speed we crave. What once was a resource-intensive process (think people and paper and snail mail) can now be accomplished for many, everywhere, quickly and online.

In addition to the repurposing of data discussed in earlier chapters, analysts have four major techniques at their disposal for collecting data: interviews, surveys, focus groups, and data mining. Let's look at each in light of how technology enables them.

Interviews

When we want to gather data about actual and optimal performance, one of the most direct ways to do this is to talk to those with a stake in the outcomes. This includes the performers themselves, of course, but also managers, associates, experts, and customers.

Email

The dominant use of email in performance analysis stems largely from the fact that it is omnipresent in organizations and allows one-to-one asynchronous communication at very low cost with performers and stakeholders anywhere in the world. The analyst can ask structured questions or engage in a dialogue, asking opinions about how experts handle a situation, what a policy is, the reasons for a new approach, key areas of pain and gain, and how a customer perceives the effectiveness of a salesperson.

Consider this example: Via email, Mark Fulop, an experienced health educator, interviewed a VP for marketing at a software and consulting firm about the VP's uses of email. Mark reported, "Over the course of three email messages and a 'hard copy' postal mailing, I was able to build an understanding of how technology could better match individual employees with work challenges and how it could be used to track performance improvement. My . . . access to the VP of a company on three occasions was made possible by email."

The global reach of email is another advantage. You require that reach if your expert on security or disaster mitigation is in Singapore or London and you're in Frankfurt or Foxboro. Another clear advantage is speed, especially compared with snail mail. There is also the electronic record of the interaction, available for subsequent review and analysis.

The asynchronous nature of email offers the respondent an opportunity to reflect and respond when convenient. Late night? No problem. Dawn? No problem. Holiday break? Again, no problem. The flexibility that email offers overcomes the vexing challenges of getting calendars together to schedule a meeting, often across distances and time zones.

Are there downsides to email for PA? In fact, the respondent's control over how and when to respond is a double-edged sword. Respondents reached via email may never respond. Most in-boxes are clogged with routine business messages and spam—getting yours to attract a thoughtful reply requires both an artfully constructed message and some insight into what motivates your sources.

Another concern is that respondents may decide to hatch responses they think will please the analyst or others, and they tend to do so because they know that their "signed" responses are a record others might see. Email users know it is easy to forward and store messages. Would you share your feelings about the causes of current performance problems if you thought they might end up in the in-box of the very person you identified as being some portion of the problem?

There are no simple answers to these challenges, but it will help to develop a protocol for communicating via email. Be very clear about why this effort is worthy of attention. Send an initiating email that informs about the purposes of the query, along with what to expect and when you will be sending the inquiry. Even better would be for the project sponsor to send out that first email. Anticipate objections and concerns and invite sources to contact you via email or phone about anything you failed to cover. Assure sources that their responses will be kept confidential and remind them why the information they provide is important. Finally, work diligently to establish relationships and a reputation for honoring confidentiality and making good use of contributions.

Asynchronous Interviews

Although email is a dominant technology for asynchronous communication, there are other important technologies appropriate to the interview process. Web forums, blogs, and discussion groups offer sources the opportunity to respond to interview questions online. Unlike anonymous online surveys through tools such as SurveyMonkey or Zoomerang, when you use wikis and blogs to query asynchronously, you can follow up on responses by asking for clarification or for an example. Others in the group can also weigh in.

Wikis and blogs offer some of the functionality of web forums in that they too allow for threaded discussions. In general, however, they are designed for collaborative work, which also has its place in performance analysis, as we shall see later in this chapter.

Synchronous Interviews

For all the benefits that email and other asynchronous technologies provide, there are reasons to talk to people in real time via an interview or focus group. What is the tone of the response? Is the subject enthusiastic? Hesitant? Evasive? Your interview is likely to include open-ended questions that would benefit from follow-up. You might be dealing with a topic that is complex or controversial, one that will require elaborations and explanation beyond what you can provide online. You might want to ask unplanned questions based on an unexpected response. You might want to interview a group of people at once to gain the benefit of idea interchange or because of scheduling constraints. For all these reasons, technology that enables synchronous interviews is a useful addition to the analyst's toolkit.

Synchronous interviews can occur using technology as commonplace as a telephone or as specialized as a videoconference. To determine the optimal approach, the wise performance analyst will consider benefits and trade-offs associated with the technologies. The telephone, for example, long a mainstay of interviewing, provides simple, immediate access to almost anyone, anywhere in the world. However, a major disadvantage is the inability to see the interviewee. Are they stressed? Are they chipper? Are they doing email as they are talking to you?

Interviewing groups can be difficult. Even with a high-quality speaker-phone, it is not easy to achieve high-fidelity communication when all parties are in the same room. It is not unusual to struggle to identify which individual said what. There are also occasions when a few dominate the group, while the fourth source says nothing at all.

Internet-based synchronous meetings, driven by software such as Adobe Connect, GoToMeeting, Live Meeting, and WebEx, offer nearly the fidelity of videoconferencing at a fraction of the cost—and with more flexibility. Anyone with a computer, webcam, telephone or microphone, and a reasonably fast Internet connection, can participate. Analysis will grow increasingly reliant on these online systems, as access increases and costs diminish.

Surveys

The Internet has spawned a cultural shift from doing things on paper to doing them online, and surveys are no different. This has been a boon to analysts intent on speeding up the data-gathering process. From email to web-based surveys, research shows that there are many benefits to conducting surveys online.

Email

An important benefit of email surveys is rapid dissemination to a given group; you don't have to spend time and resources reproducing surveys, stuffing and addressing envelopes, and waiting and hoping for responses using global or national postal services. Researchers (for example, Thach, 1995; Mehta & Sivadas, 1995) identified a bonus in the quality of responses to email. Email surveys, they believe, tend to result in more insightful and candid responses. Although the reasons for this are unclear, Thach posits that survey respondents might perceive more social distance than in traditional communication situations and offer less-guarded opinions.

In 1995, two researchers at the University of Cincinnati, Raj Mehta and Eugene Sivadas, surveyed hundreds of users of twenty popular Internet discussion groups. Five random groups were established; two received traditional mailed surveys, three received email surveys. The survey methodology for the five groups differed in other ways as well, because the researchers were also attempting to examine the importance of incentives and pre- and post-survey notification. The group that was offered a $1 incentive to complete a mail survey had the highest response rate (83 percent), followed by the two email groups (one with no incentive, the other with pre-survey notification).

Mehta and Sivadas's study demonstrated that the costs were lower and the response time faster for the email group surveys. And the survey responses were similar across groups for completeness and response substance. The researchers found that email groups wrote significantly more than the snail mail groups, leading them to suggest that the quality of email response provides a compelling reason to use technology for open-ended inquiries.

Unlike people responding to printed surveys—or online surveys, for that matter—that benefit from anonymity, email respondents are sometimes concerned about the traceable trail of email.

The best solution here is prior notification, a topic touched on earlier. Intruding into a person's email with a survey that has not been preceded by an explanation is not a good idea. Mehta and Sivadas (1995) tangled with this barrier in their research. One of the groups in their study received surveys without warning, and because of the number of complaints from this group, the researchers aborted their participation.

A supportive strategy is to use "stripper" boxes. Electronic responses are sent to a neutral box that provides the automated service of removing all identifiers. Then the "stripped" version is forwarded to the person conducting the electronic survey, with a copy to the respondent that demonstrates how all designations have been removed. Again, prior communication is critical here, with respondents and the technical team supporting and explaining the effort.

This is particularly true today, in an era that Joseph Turow characterizes as a "culture of suspicion." As long as web users do not get how it all works, their concerns depress participation.

The issues surrounding confidentiality and privacy are intensifying. In May 2008, L. Gordon Crovitz wrote in the *Wall Street Journal* about cookies, the small files placed on computers that track online activity. Crovitz commented, "Web sites do a poor job of explaining how and why this information is used, even as details about our lives are increasingly knowable online. Risks to privacy make this a race between smarter self-regulation on the Web and threatened new regulation by the Federal Trade Commission."

Crovitz understands concerns about using the web to gather data: "The cookie debate reflects the tension between what technology will allow and what privacy we expect. One problem is that Web sites and marketers have failed to explain why cookies are harmless. Cookies simply indicate where users have been and do not include sensitive information like credit cards or Social Security numbers."

As we rely more on technology to gather data, more information must be provided to sources. What are we doing? Why are we doing it? What uses will we make of their contributions? Are they anonymous? How are we protecting their anonymity? The analyst often focuses on the questions to be asked. Attention must also be directed to the communication that surrounds data-gathering efforts and questions. If they wonder, and if they worry, they will choose not to participate.

Web Surveys

A more recent addition to the analyst's toolkit, web surveys (Zoomerang and SurveyMonkey are two examples) offer all the capabilities of email surveys, plus more. Consider these additional features:

- *Easy deployment.* The survey is created and hosted in a central location either externally or in-house.

- *Size and dispersion.* Many, everywhere, can respond and at no additional cost.

- *Anonymity.* Respondents' concerns about disclosing their identity are more easily mitigated using anonymous login.

- *Response sophistication.* Survey response types, such as true-false, open ended, and Likert scale items, are quickly created and easy to respond to. Both vendors mentioned above provide templates and samples to facilitate rapid instrument development—and a good look. No training is required.

- *Data analysis.* Data analysis is typically part of the back end of a web survey package.

- *Reporting.* Real-time reporting of survey results allows the surveyor to get a snapshot of how users are responding. Batch reports are also available, or you can export the data to Excel or a statistical software package to facilitate further analysis.

Businessweek magazine (Helm, 2008) took on a critical question: How good are online polls? Bud Helm notes that political pollsters continue to rely on the phone, while most businesses have shifted to online polling for market information. Helm raises concerns. He quotes a Stanford political scientist, Jon A. Krosnick: "Companies who buy this research are saying to themselves, 'The price is good and the firm tells me it's representative.'"

While Krosnick has his doubts, others are countering concerns with stricter guidelines and attention to the nature of the audience, even going so far as to count the responses of underrepresented groups twice. If the population is seniors, one pollster avoids the web. This is the main concern mentioned in the Helm article. Although the response rate can be massive, it would not represent the larger population. Respondents are rarely randomly selected, violating a tenet of probability-based research. Does this approach skew the sample in favor of people with access to technology or people with strong opinions, because they are most likely to respond?

What to do? First, consider the options. If your supervisors or new hires are everywhere, what better way to cast a wide net? Randomize your responses by randomly inviting a subset of the new hires or supervisors. The online survey should not be your only method. Add focus groups. Review the literature and work products. Check back with your sponsor. Situate the online survey as one powerful method, but not the only approach to data gathering.

Email Versus Web: Which Should You Use?

With all of the capabilities that online surveys offer, it is reasonable to ask why one would ever use email-only surveys. One major benefit to using email is that it can be put together and sent out very quickly, especially if the target audience is small. Also, if the survey is short, respondents can answer the questions quickly in the body of the message and hit reply. However, once the number of respondents grows, the case for the email survey weakens. Few analysts are eager to receive twenty-five lengthy responses. You have to make sense of all that they have said.

Focus Groups

While interviews provide the benefit of one-on-one communication and surveys allow us to gather data from large groups in a single gulp, focus groups offer the benefits of both approaches, plus some not offered by either. Focus groups by nature encourage group interaction. The interchange of ideas and opinions can help the analyst.

Email

Though more typically used in one-to-one or one-to-many communication, email can also be used to gather many perspectives. You can use email software to build group distribution lists for memos, newsletters, and other correspondence simultaneously directed at multiple recipients. Although not primarily designed for collaboration, with a little ingenuity, email groups can be used for this purpose. By carefully constructing and managing distribution lists and setting ground rules for etiquette, you can develop habits and, eventually, a rich repository of data. Email lists are appropriate for gathering perspectives on priority goals, what is going on currently, and performance drivers.

Performance analysis questions (for example, Which of the following do you see as contributing to the error rate?) can be widely distributed, with speed and at low cost. Distributing questions and receiving responses, both of which might take weeks using conventional mail or days using phone or fax, can be hastened with an email distribution network. Members of the group can react to what others have to say, adding nuance and color.

Will the members of an electronic group provide honest responses? That depends on the nature of the questions. My experience is that they will happily talk about their vision of optimals. Questions that touch on current performance and performance drivers are touchier.

Online

The past few years have seen the maturation of meeting tools that allow the performance analyst unprecedented opportunities to leverage—in real time—the benefits of focus groups, no matter where in the world participants are located.

Anyone who can connect to the Internet can attend or host a meeting with several or even hundreds of others. The meeting space becomes a virtual conference room, with a projector to show PowerPoint slides or other shared software applications, including the desktop, a whiteboard to make notes or annotate existing documents, and audio and video, if attendees are equipped with a microphone, a webcam, or both. Even without a microphone, telephone conference provides an audio link.

The meeting space is extended beyond the conference room paradigm with tools such as chat, file sharing, and interactive polls. Think of the ways to use meeting polls for PA. In many ways, these online meeting tools have equaled and surpassed the more traditional in-person focus group.

Some examples of tools with these capabilities are Adobe Connect, GoToMeeting, Live Meeting, Wimba, and WebEx. Some specialized products designed specifically for focus groups, such as Artafact's online focus group software, allow for both synchronous and asynchronous focus groups, with analysis tools built in.

For the highest fidelity in virtual meetings, dedicated videoconferencing is still the technology of choice. The high bandwidth and sophisticated hardware offer the greatest sense of presence—the perception that others are there with you, in the same location.

Of course, there are limitations to videoconference systems. The systems are costly. They require maintenance. Time zones create inconvenience. And some individuals are not yet accustomed to the experience of being in a meeting with distant others. In spite of the limitations, these technologies are powerful tools that allow groups to enjoy high-fidelity collaboration in real time across geographic distances.

In the mid 1990s, I was involved in the use of videoconferencing as part of the front end for a management development project for a medical equipment company. Although it enabled us to keep participants on both coasts involved in the effort and briefed about analysis results and future plans, the experience wasn't as smooth as silk. We suffered technology glitches that mucked up free-flowing communication. And back then there was always concern that the meter was running on long-distance phone charges. Today, it is different—and better. As you can see in the table at the end of the chapter, there are many choices. Voice over Internet Protocol (VoIP) and the web-based options listed throughout this chapter create new possibilities.

More than a decade has passed. Google, in 2008, announced its acquisition of Marratech, a videoconferencing and collaboration company, enabling it to compete with WebEx, recently acquired by Cisco. But there are many more choices, in various sizes and configurations, from Adobe Connect to Wimba to e/pop to Yugma to Vyew to iLink to Illuminate. What you see here is the shift from big systems installed in rooms to growing personal desktop functionality online.

Data Mining

So far, we have considered the technology from the standpoint of gathering new data. Often, however, one of the most cost-effective ways to understand needs and drivers is to analyze information that the organization already possesses. At the very least it can verify what is known and focus the subsequent investigation. And it saves time.

Customer emails, blogs, exit interviews, tech support log files, marketing and business plans, business requirements, documents, and vision statements are just a few gems with potential to yield invaluable data for performance analysis. What do we do with these riches?

There are tools that allow us to quantitatively and qualitatively analyze extant data. For example, a small yet important question is the number of errors repair people are making when they install cable systems. You can find out the kinds of errors by examining repair and call logs. For what kind of repair problems do customers call back to report that their systems remain broken?

Or imagine that managers of a global pharmaceutical company are eager to support their chemists worldwide in continuous professional growth and collaboration with colleagues from other, related disciplines. How do they accomplish that? How do they contribute to increasing interdisciplinary communities and reducing organizational silos? What can be done to turn experiences with customers, clients, products, and the literature into archives of lessons for their associates from other disciplines? How can they use existing messages to get a handle on relationships and habits that can be extended?

A particularly interesting example of a qualitative research tool is QSR's NVIVO (see Figure 7.1). The software takes on the gnarly challenge of analyzing rich data sources, including videos, interview recordings, documents, photos, media clips, and podcasts. Notice that the video of the interview can

Figure 7.1. NVIVO.

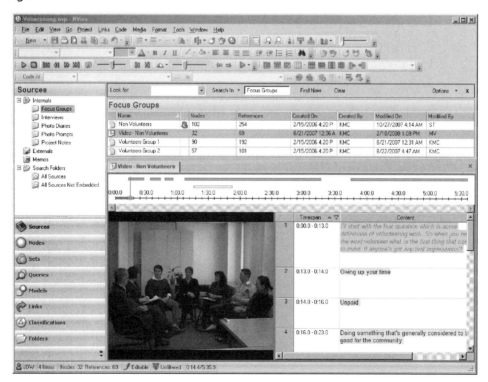

be examined for visual cues such as body language while one also analyzes the written transcript of the interview shown at right.

A companion product, XSight, offers a way to query data, highlight key information, and present results.

The Institute for Corporate Productivity (i4cp), in conjunction with HR.com, conducted a survey in May 2008 of 118 organizations and asked what they have done or plan to do about tapping into the knowledge and experience of Baby Boomers as they approach retirement. Seventy-one percent of respondents said that they were not doing anything to facilitate the transfer of knowledge from retirees to the workforce. The situation is even worse in small organizations. Technology in the hands of human resources and training professionals has much to offer here. Use it to encourage conversation, capture, and sharing. An organization that fails to do so, for auditors, sellers, or tech support staff, perhaps especially for its likely retirees, would be seen as remiss. Why ignore that opportunity?

Those conversations are rich sources of ideas about what is on the minds of the workforce. When something is working well, often it will be shared. When a concern is emerging, it most certainly will be included. A colleague who manages learning in the automotive industry said that he reads external customer blogs in order to anticipate the needs of his workforce. If customers are bemoaning pressured sales when they visit dealers or that their tires require replacement, there are implications for services provided to the workforce.

Mining Email and Instant Messaging.

We considered email earlier in this chapter, but like any good tool, it has multiple uses. Looking back over an email trail can provide answers to critical questions as programs take shape.

Instant messaging (IM) is a faster form of email. It has grown out of our need to communicate even more immediately than email allows. People in our universe of colleagues and friends can be aware of our "presence" (in the office, out to lunch, on the phone, in a meeting) and even our "mood" (happy, sad, frantic). Short of being face to face, IM is the most personal tool we have for collaboration. IM generally works best between individuals and small groups. Although IM is typically used for spontaneous conversation that "vaporizes" when the session is over, it is possible to keep records of the conversation, thus increasing the value of IM for substantive collaboration. Transcripts of these spontaneous conversations can be mined for key ideas, points of agreement, points for further discussion, or opportunities for additional research. This works best, of course, when planned in advance and with participants who are aware that you intend to do this.

Mining Blogs

Blogs (short for weblogs) have become a dominant force in web-based collaboration. Anyone from the CEO of a Fortune 500 company to your Aunt Guadalupe can have one—a testament to their simplicity and effectiveness.

Using a one-to-many communication model, the blog owner starts the discussion on any topic, the value of rapid e-learning development, for example, and anyone who is aware that the blog exists can respond with comments, or comment on others' comments. You can search for relevant blogs the same way you search for the best price on a Mini Cooper Clubman car. Google, Yahoo, and others offer search engines tailored to finding blogs based on your interests. See the latest posts or refine your search by key word, or date. When you find a blog you'd like to follow, RSS (Real Simple Subscription) lets you stay current using an RSS reader.

After a teleconference that did not allow sufficient time to discuss all relevant matters, we decided to move the analysis conversation online. Time zones were also a factor here. The shared phone calls were a trial for those who had to rise at 4 A.M. to participate. In this study for a large international accounting firm, the blog worked like a charm. We posed a few questions on our blog. Members responded, then others responded to them. It was interactive, substantive, and archived. Our software was WordPress. But it could have been Blogger, TypePad, or LiveJournal.

What a blogger says is meant to be read, even though it can be a shock that it is actually being read. *The New York Times* (Stelter, 2008) included a front-page story by Brian Stelter about a University of Washington student who was stunned that his blogged complaints about Comcast found their way to the company. Comcast emailed that they were producing a new document that might "illuminate the issues that you are experiencing." Comcast's Frank Eliason uses available online tools to monitor blogs, message boards, and social networks to read what is said about Comcast. He then attempts to make contact to resolve issues. Of course, Comcast is not the only company engaged in gathering intelligence online. Many are.

Mining Discussion Groups

Discussion-group software anticipates the challenges of knowledge management through discussion groups and automated distribution lists. These software packages are referred to as listservs, majordomos, or listprocs. In a sense they create a virtual post office that distributes email to the addresses of participants in a defined group. The group might be engineering managers, affirmative action officers, members of the customer service unit, people passionate about distance learning or Dalmatians, or customers who have purchased a particular printer. Routine administrative tasks are automated, and the software archives messages for future reference. The software typically enables a moderated group, in which messages are screened prior to distribution, or an unmoderated approach, with no prior screening.

Anticipate the challenges of the future and begin structured dialogues on those topics. What skills will people need to adjust to global teaming? What issues and opportunities are emerging for lawyers who are struggling to negotiate contracts in the developing world? What are the implications of the mobile workforce for supervisors? For supervisory development and support? How can the top two hundred executives in a large global organization better use the web to gather business intelligence? What are the current barriers to integration of technology into the sales process? How are training organizations operating more efficiently in these difficult economic times? Post questions like these within electronic discussion groups and watch the fun begin. Then initiate programs to address the concerns and opportunities that emerge, or hold the data for when a request is presented.

Mining Social Networks and Professional Alliances

Social networks of every sort offer the performance analyst an opportunity to develop and nurture relationships that might advance current projects or long-term professional development.

One of the first online communities devoted to our field was the Discussion Group for Training and Development (TRDEV-L). Approximately six thousand subscribers from sixty different countries exchanged information on training and development. In 2000, the group renamed itself TRDEV to continue to actively discuss matters related to the field. Real problems and people populated the listserv. "How do I prepare managers to receive their first dose of 360-degree feedback?" "How do I bring automation to salespeople?" "How do I learn more about electronic performance support?" "Has anybody read anything good on the subject of performance analysis?" Many fruitful responses resulted from these kinds of queries. One caution, however. This group, in fact, most groups, is open to anyone who wants to join. You can imagine that someone who has written a book about performance analysis—or 360-degree feedback—might have nice things to say about their product. Alas, in early 2008, TRDEV ended.

Growing ever more popular are web sites with far more functionality. Networking sites, such as LinkedIn, Plaxo, LearningTown, or Google Groups, offer those with similar interests the ability to create online shared spaces where they can point to resources, contribute ideas, and stay connected beyond the bounds of a particular project or initiative. There is value for those who want to know more about current thinking and real-world experiences. If you are working on an initiative for your organization, part of the quest for directions can come from a review of related literature and best practices readily available through such networks.

Imagine it for our world. I decided to take a look, in mid-2008, at the online conversations going on at Elliot Masie's LearningTown, a social networking site for learning professionals. At that time, the mobile learning group had attracted 217 registrants. Rapid e-learning intrigued 210 individuals. The evaluation group attracted only 151 participants. Instructional design attracted by far the largest number, with 337 on board. Now, as I review this chapter, the number of participants has skyrocketed.

What are they talking about? One gent asked about software for performance support and advised vendors to stay out of the conversation. Cost is also a concern to participants. Members of the communities want to know how long this or that typically takes and how to wring costs out of the effort.

With an interesting parallel to the 2008 election campaign in the United States, participants at LearningTown seek change. The instructional design subgroup at LearningTown participated in a quick poll that illustrated their yearning for a new way of doing things, given more participatory and Web 2.0 approaches. Turn to the resources section for this book and find the url for an article recently published in ASTD's *Learning Circuits*, June, 2008. There, Allison Rossett and Joe Williams review the implications of Web 2.0 technologies for our topic, performance analysis.

Mining Wikis

Once a curiosity looking for application, wikis have taken their place among collaborative technologies in a significant way. According to Wikipedia, one of the most popular wiki sites, "A wiki is a collection of web pages designed to enable anyone who accesses it to contribute or modify content, using a simplified markup language." Generally, wiki pages are organized around a particular topic and provide a low-cost way to manage content. What's interesting about wikis is that they are democratically birthed, as anybody can contribute. That's good.

And that might not be so good. The major drawback to using wikis is that the content is not systematically authenticated. Erroneous content or poor organization can diminish usefulness. However, studies of Wikipedia suggest a surprisingly high level of accuracy. In fact, *Nature* magazine published a comparative study of Wikipedia and the Encyclopedia Britannica in which they found that the two were similar in terms of accuracy. Not surprisingly, Britannica disagreed, noting that their own studies found many factual errors in Wikipedia. The debate continues.

Wikis can be a fertile resource for us. For example, a learning executive for a mutual fund company solved a problem using a wiki. The problem was her access to top-notch experts. They didn't want to take time to talk to the learning group. What she decided to do was to use a wiki for a small, select group of industry experts, and to have them work together to define opportunities and trends. They did it because they liked being in that very special group and in seeing their messages take new and easily updated forms. Their combined efforts then educated others throughout the firm.

Data-Sharing Sites

When collaboration requires more than discussion, you can share files, media, and calendars using sites such as MS SharePoint, sites.google.com, Stixy, and www.drop.io. These sites support many kinds of collaboration, from the most basic file sharing to full-fledged virtual meeting spaces. For instance, the IT department for a national supermarket put together an ad hoc team to conduct an analysis to determine training needs for a new point-of-sale system. Within minutes, they had created a SharePoint workspace to document their project. During the life of the analysis, they easily pulled together discussion groups, created surveys, updated team contact information, and posted project announcements. At the end, all relevant project information resided in one place. They managed their knowledge in a way that would be useful not only on this project, but on future projects with similar characteristics.

Opportunities

This chapter is strikingly different from the technology chapter in the first edition of *First Things Fast*. New tools are suggested. New approaches are included. New software is introduced. New roles are possible, for everyone who is involved. Net. Net. This is a good time for the performance analyst, and technology contributes to that positive outlook.

Technology, as you can see, supports several "mantras" highlighted in this book:

- *Be systematic.* Technology supports you in an iterative process, that of collecting data from one phase and using it to focus subsequent questioning and data-collection efforts in the next phase.

- *More sources are better than just a few.* Technology helps you reach for many views and opinions.

- *Manage the project.* Technology helps you perform an essential duty as a responsible project manager: staying on time and within budget. For instance, email allows you to swiftly initiate activity, "nudge" key

Table 7.1. Technology Resources.

Products and Services	Implications for Analysis
Adobe Acrobat Connect Pro www.adobe.com/products/acrobatconnectpro/ GoToMeeting www.gotomeeting.com WebEx www.webex.com Microsoft Office LiveMeeting http://office.microsoft.com/en-us/livemeeting/ default.aspx Artafact www.artafact.com Dimdim www.dimdim.com WizIQ http://www.wiziq.com/downloads/moodle/ Yugma www.yugma.com Vyew www.vyew.com iLinc www.ilinc.com	Software that supports synchronous interviews, focus groups, conferencing, and collaboration. Some are costly; a few (Dimdim and WizIQ) are free. Yes, free.
Google Groups http://groups.google.com/ MS SharePoint http://www.microsoft.com/sharepoint/prodinfo/ what.mspx sites.google.com https://www.google.com/accounts/ServiceLogin Stixy www.stixy.com	Integrated online locations to store and access content and to enable ongoing collaboration and archiving.

(Continued)

Table 7.1. Technology Resources. *(Continued)*

Products and Services	Implications for Analysis
Drop.io www.drop.io Marratech www.marratech.com	Integrated online locations to store and access content and to enable ongoing collaboration and archiving.
SAS www.sas.com SPSS www.spss.com	Quantitative and qualitative data analysis. Data mining.
WordPress www.wordpress.org Blogger www.blogger.com TypePad www.typepad.com	Software to enable the analyst to create a blog.

sources, and monitor ongoing processes. Digital interactions also create instant records of ideas, decisions, and plans.

- *Avoid analysis-paralysis.* Shave time off the front end and avoid paralysis by continuously "checking in" with key players and getting quick turnaround when testing your hypotheses. You'll keep the project on track and ensure more buy-in.

- *Share results.* Technology makes it easy to grab opinions and present the findings, as the data is collected. One of my doctoral students used this as a lure to encourage people to participate in her survey using SurveyMonkey. Immediately after respondents had contributed, they could view their reactions in light of the others who had also served as respondents.

8

Finding Meaning, Communicating Results

Margie: I got into this. I tried to figure out the problem. I did a quick review of the literature. I interviewed forty-seven people. I put up an online survey, and hundreds responded. What am I going to do now? My good efforts are overwhelming me. I have to make sense of it all. Then I must report about what I found.

Ana: Well, it's a good idea to put some effort into the way you bring those recommendations forward. I've had some experiences with my customers not appreciating my results as much as I did. I thought I had ferreted out some mind-boggling things, real surprises, and then the executive committee wouldn't go along with my plan.

Margie: Sometimes the studies confirm their opinions and directions, and then it is no problem at all. But usually, when I get a chance to dig into it, the analysis reveals more than was expected or something altogether different. Then, reporting is trickier. What can we do to increase the likelihood that our evidence-based findings will be acted on?

There's much we can do.

In this chapter, we'll look at ways for examining data and then sharing results, highlighting those that can be done in small and informal ways as well as those that require a somewhat grander effort.

Making Meaning with Data

Technology allows us to collect data from near and far. An online survey with hundreds or thousands of responses yields boatloads of data. What do you do with the boatloads? What do the data mean? How do you find sense in it all? And how do you move from numbers to stories that compel attention?

Fortunately, the technology that creates the flood is also there to tame the profusion. This chapter tours options through the stories of several projects.

Consult with experts in the organization who specialize in crunching data. Be sure to do that *before* the responses are collected, as you are creating your plan and instruments. Experts can help anticipate how you are going to manage the responses you get. Many will also provide fresh, experienced views of the instruments that you are using to generate the data. They help screen for reliability and validity.

Are the questions that you are asking reliable? Will they be seen the same way by all respondents? We ran into problems with reliability when I queried learning professionals in a global organization about technology-based learning methods. Would they share understanding of words such as *blog, wiki, webinar*, or *work-based projects*? We decided that they would not. What we did was to attempt to increase reliability by providing definitions. Your other option is to stick to the familiar.

The second concern is validity. In a nutshell, valid questions are questions that ask about important, relevant matters. Valid inquiries go to the heart of the matter, and are predicated on what you have learned from experts, review of extant data, and individual interviews. Years ago, a former student forwarded an instrument that featured an item asking respondents to report their "highest college grade." Now why would you ask that question? How is it germane? How will you use responses to shape recommendations? And harkening back to shared meaning . . . is that question reliable? A respondent could answer, "I got an 'A' in my bowling class." Another might share her GPA for two years at community college. A third would be annoyed or flummoxed; he didn't go to college at all. That item is invalid *and* unreliable.

Once you have valid and reliable items and have sought data in some of the ways detailed in Chapter Seven, you are ready to do something with your responses. Does your organization include people who specialize in crunching large data sets? Many do. They might be found in the research group, in HR, in IT, or even in fledgling business intelligence units. What these people have in common are backgrounds in psychometrics and contemporary skills that take large data sets and discern patterns. What if you don't have such people in your organization? Take out your old statistics text, or better yet, visit a nearby university. Professors and their research classes will connect you to ideas and software to analyze and represent data. Look to the web, of course. There are numerous PowerPoint decks and web sites associated with statistics classics that present basic concepts and point to relevant tools. The dominant software packages, such as SPSS, also provide guides and coaches to enhance use.

Software helps see and understand responses to questions with speed and ease. In Table 8.1, you will find a quick overview of ways to use the familiar Excel and PowerPoint for performance analysis. Thanks to Rebecca Frazee for creating this table.

Let's use two examples to demonstrate how to move from data to meaning. One example demonstrates a performance analysis that was short, sweet, and typical. The second example is more complex, with data collected from thousands and statistical analysis of the responses. That effort resulted in a hundred-plus-page report for a global corporation. The situations depicted in these examples have been changed to mask the organizations.

1. Do Something About the Engineering Briefings!!!

Imagine yourself as the performance consultant for a large engineering group within an even larger company. The executive for that group, your customer, wants help in figuring out why the engineers get lousy reactions to their presentations, also known as briefings. The engineers offer briefings about technical products to internal and external business partners and customers a few times each year.

What is up with the engineers' briefings? Why do audiences avoid the briefs? The executive was hoping that a training class devoted to "presentation skills" would solve the problem, but is willing to hear what you think ought to be done, based on a speedy analysis of the situation.

Table 8.1. Using Familiar Software for Performance Analysis.

I want to:	Excel would be good to:	PowerPoint would be good to:
Show who responded to the survey.	Present quantitative demographic data broken down into subgroups. Easily turn rows and columns of numbers into nice visual displays such as tables, histograms, and pie charts.	Use photos or graphics to present relevant characteristics of individuals or the setting. For example, use pictures showing age, gender, or ethnicity; a map showing where your global sample is located.
Make the data come alive with attractive and interactive presentations.	Generate several types of graphs from the same data. See Microsoft Office Labs for free plug-ins to enhance the functionality of your Office programs, such as plug-ins for creating graphics in Excel [http://www.officelabs.com/Pages/Default.aspx].	Present real quotes and stories from your participants using text, audio, or video clips. Why not a podcast that combines quotes, encouraging discussion about what those opinions mean and how to respond? Tell a story. Dramatize with visuals. Provide interactivity with animations, reveals, and nonlinear navigation through the deck. Check out PPTPlex, a free plug-in for PowerPoint that allows you to zoom in and out of your slides to present overall findings in context, with more detail, and show how details fit into the larger report.

	See a video example at http://communityclips.officelabs.com/Video.aspx?videoId=f362631f-c86c-4547-a544-9b8eda9975e3 and a review of the functionality at http://lifehacker.com/400546/ppt-plex-puts-powerpoint-slides-on-an-interactive-canvas.
Make data analysis easy and consistent.	Ask participants to complete surveys electronically so data can be automatically imported into Excel without re-entry. Import data directly from tables, databases, or online survey tools, such as SurveyMonkey. The newer Office suites make it easy to export and import across applications.

Create online forms from scratch or from a template for data entry. Forms can contain controls such as check boxes, radio buttons, and pull-down menus to make data entry and data coding consistent. While Excel is fine for this, consider opting for a database such as Microsoft Access to enable sophisticated or custom forms and reports.

Examine different facets of your data using filters, queries, and sorting. |

(Continued)

Table 8.1. Using Familiar Software for Performance Analysis. (Continued)

I want to:	Excel would be good to:	PowerPoint would be good to:
Involve customers along the way by sharing snippets of data.	Present "live data results" by creating bar charts that are linked to data cells in the spreadsheet so graphs are automatically updated as the numbers change. When using an online survey tool such as SurveyMonkey, you can provide a link to a "live data results" page so respondents can immediately see how their answers compare with the group to date.	Host a virtual meeting and use PowerPoint to focus attention and drive discussions.

You begin your analysis by finding out where engineers go wrong, in the view of their audiences. That involves reviewing email and phone complaints, and interviewing members of these audiences. That enables you to define the gap. You now know what their audiences see as the flaws in their briefings.

Our focus in this chapter is on the section of the analysis that reaches out to engineers to ask, via an anonymous online survey, what they think about impediments to successful briefings. Why do engineers stumble when they brief? Obviously, their view of the matter is important to tailoring the right solution.

You start by describing the executive's concern to the population of engineers ($N = 200$) in a preliminary email message. In this first short note, you describe the issue and solicit their participation, informing them that you will be asking for their ideas soon. A few days later, you send the email message presented as Exhibit 8.1. Note that Exhibit 8.1 asks for answers to two important

---

Exhibit 8.1. Email Letter.

Dear Colleague:

When I emailed you late last week, I told you that Ray Trahn and the Executive Engineering Council are eager for your opinions about ways to strengthen the engineering briefings. There are many complaints, as you know. And the briefings are important to help us communicate our programs to the field and to customers as well.

I'm sending you this email message because we want YOUR opinion. We've reviewed the views of the people the engineers have briefed in the past, and have a good idea about the strengths and limitations of past efforts. Now we want to hear from you. Your opinion is critical to help us construct our approach.

What you say will be held in the strictest confidence. When I report these data, they will be aggregated, reflecting what groups of people recommend, not the beliefs or statements of any one engineer.

Here is a web site for you to visit: https://xyzxyzxyz123. This short survey will enable you to easily provide your answers and also to maintain anonymity. Please take a few moments to respond to the survey now. It should take no more than five minutes. I'll expect to see your responses within 48 hours of the time and date on this message. And I'll be back to you to share results.

Thank you in advance for helping us improve our briefings.

Exhibit 8.2. Two Questions Seeking Engineers' Opinions About Drivers and Solutions.

1. Please tell us how much you think this contributes to the problems we have with our engineering briefings.

	Major Factor	A Factor	Not a Factor
A. Engineers aren't given sufficient time to plan briefings.	○	○	○
B. Engineers don't care about doing the briefings.	○	○	○
C. Engineers don't know how to do briefings.	○	○	○
D. Engineers are pulled away from their real work by the briefings.	○	○	○
E. Engineers aren't good at making briefings.	○	○	○
F. Engineering supervisors don't encourage engineers to do briefings.	○	○	○
G. Giving a good briefing doesn't count on performance appraisals.	○	○	○
H. The people who give the good briefings aren't usually the best engineers.	○	○	○
I. Engineers don't know how to plan and develop effective briefings.	○	○	○
J. The audiences are the ones with the problem. They don't understand technical content.	○	○	○

2. If you were in a position to fix the engineering briefings, what would you do? Help us. What approach or approaches would you use?

questions, one quantitative (how they rate the factors that could be causing the problem) and the other qualitative (their views on solutions). The email also points engineers to the URL where they will respond to an online survey. The example presented as Exhibit 8.2 was made available via SurveyMonkey.

One hundred and sixty engineers, of two hundred possible respondents, went to the web site and responded to the two queries. The data summarized just below adds value to the conversation. What you discovered reveals engineers' perceptions of the causes of the problem, across all engineers and departments. Listed in order of decreasing contribution to the problem, they are as follows:

1. Giving a good briefing doesn't count on performance appraisals.

2. Engineers are the wrong people to do the briefings.

3. Engineers are pulled away from their *real* work by the briefings.

4. Engineering supervisors don't encourage engineers to do briefings.

5. Engineers don't know how to do briefings and presentations.

Table 8.2. Engineers' Perceptions of the Causes of Problems with Briefings (*N* = 160).

Question	Major factor %	A factor %	Total %
Giving a good briefing doesn't count on performance appraisals.	81	12	93
Engineers are the wrong people to do the briefings.	21	69	90
Engineers are pulled away from their *real* work by the briefings.	71	19	90
Engineering supervisors don't encourage engineers to do briefings.	58	30	88
Engineers don't know how to do briefings and presentations.	30	37	67

The five contributors cited in Exhibit 8.2 are interesting. They raise questions about the value of a rush to develop and deliver a presentation skills workshop. The list points to other, substantive drivers.

But look at how the numbers clarify the situation. Table 8.2 shows the strength of the engineers' opinions. What do they see as a major factor contributing to the problems with the briefings? What do they see as only a factor, or as no factor at all?

Exhibit 8.3 features slides from a PowerPoint deck. The deck shows how the analyst talked about the results of this study. Discussion about the engineers' ratings is presented in slides 4, 5, and 6. The numbers, pie chart, and discussion add texture to the finding, taking us beyond the list of five in Exhibit 8.2 and far beyond the list of five at the top of page 175.

Slide 5 summarizes the results from online question 2, the question about how engineers would fix the problem with the briefs. The analyst counted mentions, not an unreasonable approach, since only 37 of the 160 respondents chose to answer the open-ended inquiry. Their views are depicted in a pie chart on slide 5.

Not surprisingly, engineers told us that, in order of preference, the organization must give incentives to engineers for doing the briefs, expect them to do the briefs, or skip them altogether. No doubt, the strategic value for the briefings is either not there or not articulated to the people who deliver them. Engineers do not understand the rationale for their briefing efforts. Supervisors, also, are in the dark.

Sending these engineers to a workshop to buff up their presentation skills is not going to solve this problem, not in isolation from other approaches, and it might even increase their cynicism. More than half the responses point to cultural solutions, not to an engineering skills gap.

Don't forget the promise made to respondents. They deserve an email about what was gleaned from online survey responses. Exhibit 8.4 is an example.

2. Are We Ready for Blended Learning?

This performance analysis looked at the readiness of a large international pharmaceutical company to move to blended learning. It explored employee, supervisory, and organizational factors likely to hinder or advance execution

Exhibit 8.3. What Engineers Say About Their Briefings.

What We Learned About Our Engineering Briefings

Three weeks ago, you said...

- "Never-ending stream of complaints from units across the company and even from our external customers."
- "We ask them to go out and brief about their projects twice, sometimes three times, each year."
- "I don't know why. They are good at engineering. But the briefs . . . people do not like them."
- "Maybe we should bring in presentations skills workshops?"

(Continued)

Exhibit 8.3. What Engineers Say About Their Briefings. *(Continued)*

What I Did

1. Reviewed complaints found in the phone logs and in email messages.
2. Interviewed nearly fifteen people, randomly pulled, from across the company. All had attended at least two briefings by our staff.
3. Conducted an online survey that reached out to engineers about their views of the situation. I want to focus on those results here.
4. Two more focus groups to go, with engineering supervisors.

What Our Engineers Told Us About Why Their Briefs Fail

- The organization is not telling them that it values efforts associated with briefings.
  - It's not considered when they receive their appraisals.
  - It's not their "real"work, in their views.
  - Their supervisors often do not encourage them to do the briefings, with 58% of the supervisors admitting this was a major factor.

- While they strongly state that briefings do not "count"and are not their real work, engineers are far less clear about whether or not they should be the ones doing briefings.

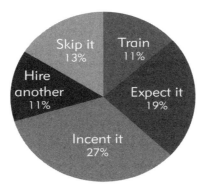

**What Engineers Told Us About
How to Solve the Problem with Briefs**

A Presentation Skills Workshop?!?

- Most engineers think that incentives and clear expectations are the best way to improve the briefs, with 27% urging incentives for briefing and 19% pointing to clarity of expectations.

- More than two-thirds (67%) think that engineers possess skills gaps about how to do the briefings.
  - A workshop should be part of the solution mix, but is not sufficient in itself. We need to look to the culture that wraps around these briefs. Eighty-eight percent do not get encouragement from their supervisors, and most see that as a major factor also.

(Continued)

Exhibit 8.3. What Engineers Say About Their Briefings. *(Continued)*

Where to Go from Here?

- We must talk about WHY we do these briefings—and if they remain a strategic priority, we must look to the performance management that wraps around the effort.
  – A workshop in and of itself will not solve our problem.

- I have two focus groups yet to run with engineering supervisors. I want to see where they weigh in here, especially now that I have data that reflect rank-and-file engineering views on this matter.

---

of the blended strategy. The company prioritized research, sales, and compliance and was eager to update skills and information access without scheduling more classes.

Because the leadership of this company favored data, triangulation, and certainty, analysis was more comprehensive than speedy. A handful of interviews or focus groups would not have sufficed here. Time (three months) and people (two, not full time, but significantly) were invested in looking at their questions about readiness. Several people within the organization also helped out on tasks that only they could perform, such as accessing internal employee databases to enable randomization.

The effort commenced with a review of the literature about blended and independent learning. Next up, forty-three learning and line leaders were interviewed. Finally, data were collected from several thousand employees and supervisors, all randomly and anonymously selected to participate in the effort.

Exhibit 8.4. Follow-Up Email for the Engineering Briefing Project.

Dear Colleagues,

Last week I reminded you that Ray Trahn and the Executive Engineering Council are looking to improve the engineering briefings. I sent you to a short online survey that sought your opinion on why the quality of engineering briefings is declining and what you think should be done to improve them. Thanks for your responses. We got a good mix of participation from engineers in all departments with a wide range of experiences with the company. Your insights and suggestions will help us improve the briefs.

As I promised, here is a quick overview of the results:

When asked why you think the engineering briefs are not appreciated by customers, you rated these as the main reasons:

1. Giving a good briefing doesn't count on performance appraisals.

2. Engineers are the wrong people to do the briefings.

3. Engineers are pulled away from their *real* work by the briefings.

4. Engineering supervisors don't encourage engineers to do briefings.

5. Engineers don't know how to do briefings and presentations.

When asked what you would suggest to improve the briefings, we received thirty-seven comments. Here is one: "No one seems to appreciate that we do these briefings. It just seems like more work with no reward. In fact, we get just the opposite—more pressure because we get behind in our work when we have to do these briefings." Several engineers' opinions are summed up in this comment: "My supervisor tries to get me out of doing the briefs. She has more important things for me to do." While two-thirds admit that not knowing how to do the briefings is a contributing factor, more influential is how the briefs are treated within the organization at large. If it's really important, how does the culture make that clear to engineers?

Thanks again for your help. If you have more to say about this, feel free to contact me by email or phone.

What We Did with the Blended Readiness Data. *Interviews:* Data from the interviews were entered, coded, and analyzed using a Microsoft Access database. Each comment or response to a question was entered as a record, coded as to the theme of the comment, and then linked to the associated question. Each interviewee was given a unique identifier that ensured anonymity while also allowing analysis of responses by role and unit.

Surveys: Both Excel and SPSS were used. First, the team computed descriptive statistics for the employee and the supervisor online survey items, including frequency distributions and means, when appropriate. To explore differences by groups (for example, generation group, gender, and work location), we used inferential statistics such as analysis of variance (ANOVA) and Chi-square, and post-hoc analyses to seek significant differences.

Even though our approach was comprehensive, we acknowledged its limitations in conversations, reports, and briefings. First, we reminded our client that these findings were based on respondents' opinions and self-reports. Second, although survey samples were generated according to accepted selection guidelines, participation was voluntary. Those who *chose* to respond might represent an inherently more tech-savvy group, a factor with relevance to the matters under study.

What We Learned. The final report weighed in at over eighty pages. While our customer expected that, and appreciated it, most customers would not. Typically, less is more, with supportive materials placed in relevant appendices. Even though this customer admired detail, not everyone in their company would. We provided an overview, in seven pages at the beginning of the lengthy document, for people who were interested but not willing to commit hours to perusing the full package. Our goal was to use the front seven pages to lure busy readers into the body of the text. We also included a detailed table of contents and hefty appendices.

We reported results in three sections, including an initial review of the literature about the benefits and risks associated with blended and independent learning.

Then we moved to the sections that spoke to their context and our findings: (1) Are employees ready and willing? (2) Are supervisors ready and willing? (3) Is the organization ready?

Let's look at how we reported, but only in part. The point here, of course, is not their answers, as interesting as they were, but rather how the data added value to the client company. Our purpose was to use the findings to inspire subsequent decisions about how to develop the people and the organization for success with blended learning and support, a goal of interest in many organizations today.

Were Employees Ready and Willing? Survey respondents were asked to rate their interest in fifteen learning activities. Rating options were

- Very much look forward to the learning activity.

- Willing to give it a try.

- Not interested. Would rather not take part in this.

- Can't rate this. I do not know about it.

For purposes of analysis, the team recoded the data—with the first two choices representing a *positive* position and the third choice a *negative* position. "Can't rate" was calculated and presented, and then excluded from further analysis. All learning activities received positive reviews. In fact, even the item with the most negative ratings (participating in an online community) *attracted four of five positive responses*. The item receiving the highest percentage of *Very much look forward to the learning activity* ratings was not particularly technological; it was *learning from an expert or supervisor on the job*.

Table 8.3 is a small example of how we set up the table that reported on employee interest in various ways of learning.

There were significant differences when responses were compared by group using a Chi-square test. Generation X and generation Y employees reported more enthusiasm than their boomer co-workers.

Were Supervisors Ready and Willing? Indeed they were. They were ready, willing, and enthusiastic, significantly so, and more so than was predicted by the pharma leaders we interviewed.

The results of Chi-square tests for comparisons between supervisors and employees revealed a statistically significant difference in their reactions to *all* learning activities. Note, however, that even though supervisors responded with *more* enthusiasm than employees about all learning activities, *both* supervisors and employees were favorably inclined toward the shift to independent and blended approaches. Lest you think that this is always the case, a recent study for another client found resistance from supervisors to these same ideas. Such negative supervisory views are a death knell for blended and workplace-based approaches.

Table 8.3. Employee Responses to Learning Activities.

Learning activity	Employee rating			
	Very much look forward to the learning activity	Willing to give it a try	Not interested. Would rather not take part in this	Can't rate this. I do not know about it
Learning from an expert or supervisor on the job n = 1,886	1,393 75%	424 23%	34 2%	35
Attending classroom training led by an instructor n = 1,914	1,397 73%	447 23%	63 3%	7
Accessing online resources, databases, or tools to find information I need as I do my job n = 1,887	1,151 62%	629 34%	62 3%	45

Table 8.4. Supervisors Rate Blended Learning and Responsibilities.

		Supervisors	
Survey item	*Response*	*Count*	*Percent*
I am enthusiastic about blended and other technology-based initiatives.		$n = 366$ $M = 3.22$	
	Strongly agree (4)	88	29%
	Agree (3)	199	65%
	Disagree (2)	13	4%
	Strongly disagree (1)	4	1%
	Don't know/No opinion	62	
I am interested in becoming more involved in my employees' learning and development.		$n = 366$ $M = 3.21$	
	Strongly agree (4)	91	26%
	Agree (3)	245	70%
	Disagree (2)	14	4%
	Strongly disagree (1)	1	0%
	Don't know/No opinion	15	

That was not the case for supervisors in this global pharmaceutical company. Table 8.4 shows a snippet of supervisory response to this move to blending and to their new responsibilities.

Was the Organization Seen as Ready? Yes and no in the view of sources, with anonymous employees and supervisors more optimistic than the leaders. More than 85 percent reported that they had a computer for use at work, a factor considered important if they hoped to deliver programs and information as needed.

We also briefed the client in a PowerPoint presentation. Exhibit 8.5 presents a few of the slides included in that briefing. We used signal lights,

Exhibit 8.5. Readiness for Blended Learning.

Are You Ready for Blended Learning?

A performance analysis
for XYZ global company

Blending Earns a Green Light

- Provides consistent messages and standards of practice
- Provides access no matter where or when
- Fosters collegial connections and taps into existing expertise
- Brings support, information, and education into the workplace

Green Light for Blending

How respondents saw the shift to BL

	Good or Great Idea
Employees	88%
Supervisors	93%
Interviewees	95%

"Not an opportunity, it is a **requirement**... Must deliver learning to where it is needed." —*Senior Manager*

- Provides more timely, nimble, and situated learning, support, and information.
- Enables us to be responsive to expectations and needs of younger workers.

Are Our People Ready?

- Generally they say they are.
- BUT... 1 in 8 employees (12%) reports they are not keen on blended learning.
- Supervisory readiness...
  - Supervisors themselves acknowledge they need additional training and support in order to guide employees in learning, reference, and development at work.

(Continued)

Exhibit 8.5. Readiness for Blended Learning. *(Continued)*

Company Cautions

- Blending is new for everybody, recognized by many respondents, in interviews and surveys.

- Classroom learning is part of the current sales-dominated culture, a fact that cannot be ignored.

- Although the learning department is eager to move toward blending, they are humble. Neither they nor the line organizations are confident they are yet ready to *deliver* on the promise of blended learning.

Start with supervisors, then...

1) Alter job descriptions, performance reviews, and reward systems to reflect new supervisory role, *to support all the new roles* inherent in BL.

2) Modify the orientation process to both reflect and model the new roles and expectations for supervisors and others.

3) Give supervisors their own top-notch blended program. Let them experience it first.

4) Further examine risks in the learning organization to install solutions to boost capacity and confidence.

included throughout the report, as well as in the briefing, to draw attention to areas for caution (yellow), concern (red), or delight (green).

What to Do with Wordy Data? As you can see from the preceding examples, and from instances throughout the book, performance analysis sometimes includes quantitative data and just about always generates qualitative responses. If you interviewed nineteen people and ran a focus group with five, it is possible to eyeball the data. Here is one example of the words used to explain systematic, human handling of qualitative data.

> The qualitative data derived from this study were organized in a FileMaker Pro database. A coding scheme was developed to categorize each comment. The coding scheme included general categories such as skills and knowledge, tools and infrastructure, methods and processes, roles and responsibilities, and other cultural factors. For more specificity, themes were tagged with terms or key words such as *learning approach, centralized/decentralized, supervisory support,* and *hype.* Some of these key words were predetermined, aligned with themes we were also exploring in the surveys, and others emerged through focus groups and interviews.

> Two independent raters coded a handful of interviews and compared their codes to ensure inter-rater reliability. When the original coding scheme did not prove sufficiently useful, it was altered. Again, the two raters independently coded data for comparison. This time the effort yielded more consistency and reliability. One rater then coded all data, and both raters interpreted the coded comments.

When larger numbers of interviews are involved, software can be helpful. Software for qualitative analysis peers inside text-based analysis, to help the researcher parse the data and explore relationships between responses. There are many software options, neatly detailed for you at the web site of the American Evaluation Association: http://www.eval.org/Resources/QDA.htm.

Which one is familiar? Which one is favored by your consultant or the internal person working with you on the project? How detailed or precise does your exploration need to be? How much time do you have for slicing, dicing, coding, and living with the data?

Price, of course, matters. The table at the close of Chapter Seven presents options that range from freeware to thousands of dollars. Some tools even devote themselves to handling data from audio and video files. They allow the researcher to link transcripts, key words, and notes to video and audio clips. These clips can be organized, searched, and presented in a variety of ways to yield a picture of the subject under study.

Guidelines for Effective Reporting

Report throughout the process. People in our business are sometimes guilty of trying to be saviors. Customers and clients—many of whom will eagerly wash their hands of the situation, given the opportunity to do so—might even encourage this sort of behavior. The customer is, in essence, asking us to wave a magic wand to meet his or her needs, whether that need is customer service or contemporary skills and perspectives for hospital administrators. Don't fall for it.

Although we might be eager to delight our customers with sorcery, sorcery is pretty much what it would be, if we attempted to go it alone without their involvement. Successful performance initiatives involve partnerships characterized by concerted efforts that are installed and nurtured close to where the work gets done. The executive who wishes to toss people over to training to get them ready for the new global initiative or who expects human resources to change the forms so that appraisals will improve is headed for disappointment.

We report throughout the process so that the customers are learning as we are learning. They hear about managers' concerns. They see that the errors, in the view of the engineers, are being caused by this and not that. They review unattributed quotes from job incumbents that show the complexity and texture of the situation. From beginning to end, they should be hearing what you are finding and conversing with you about meaning and implications.

Avoid surprises. This is no time to pull a rabbit out of a hat for customers. They won't like the rabbit or the hat. Then they will discredit the magician.

Use technology to provide updates. Create a shared online space where data is available. Create a blog where data is presented and conversation about implications is fostered. Customers are more likely to enact recommendations that they participated in hatching.

One other factor is relevant here. In a world of new media and workplace-based learning, data gathering must be pervasive and continuous. There is much we don't know about these new forms. The picture will emerge over time and use. The solution is often a pervasive system or blend, with no set beginning or end. We must establish ways to collect, examine, and report on data continuously.

Inform sources about what their contributions mean to the effort. It is important to cultivate your sources. A good way to do that is by reversing the flow of information. Share what you are learning during each stage in the analysis effort.

When you visit organizations, it is typical to hear strong sentiments regarding participation in studies: "What for? It doesn't make any difference what we say." "What for? They ask us so they can say they asked us. They already knew what they were going to do."

The only way to counter this accumulated cynicism is to make sources' contributions mean something. Report back to them. See Exhibit 8.2 as an example. Share selected results about key questions. Provide them with quotes and solicit further reactions. Share examples of the ways that their perspectives are going to influence the initiative. I'm not suggesting that you distribute your final report to all or that you visit many groups and offer oral briefings. You will achieve more credibility if you communicate frequently and in short, pointed bursts.

Share what you are learning with the others we've talked about throughout this book. It might be the folks in information technology, or your colleagues in compensation, or the management development team, or the specialists who manage selection, or the process reengineers who are reworking the sales-quality effort, or . . .

You are confronting the realities presented by "otherness," or organizational white space, as Geary Rummler and Alan Brache would talk about it in their fine book *Improving Performance: How to Manage the White Space on the Organization Chart* (1990). While you're working on the sales project, your associates around the organization aren't giving it much thought. It's your project. Or it is a project owned by your group. You cannot assume that these colleagues are going to jump on board just because your study suggests that the effort requires their contributions. Sharing the effort and data with colleagues and their leadership is critical if a cross-functional solution system is to be installed as a result of the performance analysis.

Show your customer that you have a handle on the situation, have taken a lean and appropriate look at it, and now possess a plan about how to proceed. This is the opportunity to present what you've discovered with related recommendations. Describe what you did; what you found, in the words and opinions of your sources; and what you think it might mean. Present options for where to go next, as well as any potholes that concern you. Admit to the limitations of your study. If you only had a few days to talk to a dozen people, explain that. Tone is important here. This is your opportunity to make a case for the direction(s) you want the customer to select. Look at the slide shows presented earlier as samples. Look at the sample report that concludes this chapter. They are partial statements that report on the effort and point toward action.

Although clarity and command are good, some circumstances call for more finesse and less masterfulness. Yes, some clients prefer strong direction. They want this tone: "We did this. We found this. We recommend that you do this." They sought your expertise and expect you to demonstrate it. In those cases, tell them what you found and what you think they ought to do. Be sure to include your rationale, based on the data from your analysis.

You could, however, be more open ended and collaborative about presentation of the results. That works for some clients, but not at all for others. A client in the transportation business is a good example. Telling him what to do would not have worked. No matter how sound the recommendations, from the get-go he wanted to be involved in hatching solutions. That was a desirable situation. In fact, it makes sense that a client who comes along on the analysis journey, including considering the meaning of data, will be committed to executing on the plan.

Our clients and customers are the only ones who are in a position to turn these suggestions into action. We need them to believe in the outcomes of the performance analysis and to carry them from paper and PowerPoint to action.

This more discovery-oriented approach to reporting is not hard to do, especially not when you are meeting with your client. Look, please, at Exhibit 8.3. Rather than taking your findings all the way to recommendations, stop with the data. Ask the client, Now that you look at these quotes or these responses, are you surprised? What questions do the data raise for you? What do these findings mean? We were talking about putting together a workshop about presentation skills. Will the workshop do the trick, given what the supervisors and engineers are reporting? As you look at these results, do other approaches become a priority?

Share quotes and numbers. If the client is uncertain about how to handle an element of the data, then step forward to present possibilities. In this approach, it is important to come to the client prepared to share a formed view of what you think is required. But rather than laying it all out on the table at the get-go, create an evidence-based conversation.

Capture attention. Write and brief with your audience in mind. Use quotes. Refer to the literature. Tell a story. Dramatize with visuals, when appropriate.

Exhibit 8.6 is a short, complete report. The situation is a familiar one. The performance appraisals are not up to snuff. Three years ago, they trained managers. Two years ago, they changed the form. Now what? Here is the performance analysis report. Nobody wanted a long report. But they required something that would shake them from entrenched habits and views. Note that there are specific sections and that each is defined. Then an example of each is provided.

Exhibit 8.6. What Are We Going to Do About the Appraisals?

Background

Description	Explain the reasons for the study. Why did you do this? What got the organization or you involved in it? Why is this important? What circumstances and assumptions served as underpinnings for this effort? Who were the key players and what were their concerns?
Example	Mary Detmer, director of human resources and training for Quick-Pro Co, called in early February to talk about a long-term and vexing problem in the organization. In her words, "Our performance appraisals are an ongoing problem for us, undermining many of our efforts, I believe."
	They've tried everything, she thinks. They've trained managers in how to write the appraisals. They've revised the forms. Then they've retrained. Then they've put the forms online.
	When asked about the exact nature of the flawed appraisals, she isn't entirely certain. Generally, she thinks that managers and supervisors "do them in a perfunctory fashion, just to get them filed."
	She thinks that the whole situation needs a fresh look, although she has some preference for a computer-based training program that would directly hook into the online forms.

Outcomes

Description	This section could be consolidated with the prior section.
	This is where you describe what it is that the client or customer is seeking. What is the vision that you heard from the client and other sources? How did the client respond to your questions regarding aspirations for improvement? What did experts say? What are the lessons provided by the literature and documentation? What do they want their people and organization to become? What new skills, knowledge, perspectives, and organizational patterns are sought?
Example	Mary Detmer, human resources director, directed attention to the corporate personnel policy manual (1/15/06), pages 23–32, for the precise expectations regarding performance appraisals. In addition, she named Juanita Omega and Curtis Sanders as her two colleagues most capable of "filling in the details."

Meetings with Ms. Omega and Mr. Sanders were very useful. They talked about criteria for what constitutes successful performance appraisals. With a blank appraisal in front of us, we discussed each line and standards associated with it. Ms. Omega and Mr. Sanders had randomly pulled a dozen appraisals from the files that they believe are good models. We studied each of them, with Ms. Omega and Mr. Sanders identifying what they liked about each, pointing to particularly successful instances of the eight lines on the form. Appendix A is a blank copy of the QuickPro appraisal form. Appendix B is an expanded version of the form with two tables added beneath each line. Table 1 provides examples of successful entries. Table 2 is a listing of criteria to use in judging each line.

The form, criteria, and attached examples were shared with Ms. Detmer and several line managers (Al Gordon, Franco Moldano, and Mitchell Lee) that she selected. They made suggestions and comments enabling us to strengthen the criteria. A review of the literature associated with performance appraisals yielded additional details regarding what constitutes an excellent appraisal.

Current Situation

Description This is where you state in detail what sources report about the current performance of the people and the organization. What are they doing? What are they doing right? What are they doing wrong? From the perspectives of executives, supervisors, job incumbents, and records you've examined, what are current strengths and weaknesses? This is your opportunity to present a clear picture of the current activities of the incumbents, in light of the goals of the customer or client. Where are the opportunities for improvement? What is going right?

Example Ms. Omega and Mr. Sanders randomly selected thirty appraisals for study. Prior to examining them in light of the criteria for effective appraisals described earlier, the identities of employees and supervisors were masked.

These appraisals were compared to Appendix B. On the basis of that review of the real appraisals, we are now able to clarify the details of the problem with the appraisals.

(Continued)

Exhibit 8.6. What Are We Going to Do About the Appraisals? *(Continued)*

Appendix C presents a precise picture of how QuickPro supervisors and managers fill out the eight lines of the appraisals. Ms. Detmer and her colleagues examined these data with us and were somewhat surprised. Rather than a general problem with appraisals, they saw the details of specific flaws associated with lines 6 and 7. In addition, while some leaders were concerned that appraisals were tardy, a check of the dates on submissions showed that 82 percent were "on time." Ms. Detmer decided that she can live with that number at this time.

The problems are lines 6 and 7. Line 6 is described around the company as the place where the "rubber meets the road." Here the supervisor is asked to identify areas for improvement. Criteria include specificity, links to job performance, use of behavioral words, descriptions of authentic work problems and challenges, examples that are familiar to the employee, and measurability. As the review of the thirty appraisals showed, just under one-third of employee appraisals have line 6 responses that are judged appropriate. The overwhelming problem is that few appraisals even bother to include anything in this line, even though they have been told in training that "every employee, including the CEO, has ways to grow in the job."

Line 7 is the other problem. This line requests supervisors to identify ways that the employee can address or improve performance. Acceptable responses must be specific, must be linked to the area for improvement, must include details on how to access the resource(s), and must display some expression of optimism regarding positive changes. Since only about 40 percent of supervisors bothered to fill in line 7, we had many fewer line 7 responses to examine. Of the twelve that were perused, four were judged to be acceptable, suggesting that most supervisors who try with line 6 run out of gas when they get to line 7. The next question that must be answered in regard to lines 6 and 7 is why. Why do people have problems with those two lines and what can be done about it?

Drivers and Causes

Description   For each gap and barrier, answer the following questions: Do the employees know how to do this? Do they want to? Do managers encourage it? Does the organization recognize it? Are the necessary tools or processes or incentives in place? By answering these questions you are determining the causes or drivers of the desired performance.

All these questions, in sum, enable you to explain what is keeping the organization and people from achieving its vision—and what needs to be done about it.

Example | Before computer-based training, or training of any flavor, is developed, it is essential to examine the reasons for the problems with lines 6 and 7. We did that by meeting with managers, supervisors, personnel experts, and job incumbents.

Managers and supervisors are nearly unanimous in their dislike of line 6. They don't like telling their employees what's less than perfect about them. If the organization feels that this is important, they will have to support the effort far more tangibly than they currently do. Here are some of the trends and findings associated with line 6:

- In focus group meetings, when mock detailed descriptions of employees were offered, 90 percent of participating supervisors and managers were able to fill out line 6 for the make-believe employees. Their efforts were compared to Appendix B and judged to be successful by the personnel experts.
- In individual interviews with twelve randomly selected supervisors and managers, nearly everyone agreed or strongly agreed with these statements: "Supervisors make less and less difference in how individual employees perform since reorganization," "Job incumbents don't take appraisals seriously," "I have my doubts about whether or not the appraisals make any difference," "Telling employees how they can improve makes little difference in their work performance."
- Eight of twelve supervisors expressed some doubt about what they ought to put in the areas of improvement. Although they could obviously "do it" for mock employees, they appeared to be in some confusion regarding the level of detail and what constituted a good answer.

(Continued)

Exhibit 8.6. What Are We Going to Do About the Appraisals? *(Continued)*

- These same interviews yielded a mixed picture regarding the confidence of employees. It was a nearly even split on the following three options: I am confident that I can identify ways that my employees can improve; I am not confident that I can identify ways that my employees can improve; I am not certain about my ability to find ways that my employees can improve their performance.
- When asked why they think that supervisors and managers fail to do an adequate job on line 6, the responses from interviewees clustered as follows:
  - Most said that filling in that line leads inevitably to problems with the employee, such as "getting stuck in grievance procedures" or, as one veteran said, "making enemies."
  - Close to three-fourths of respondents said that their managers do not back them when they are critical of employee performance.

  Line 7 is another story. In the focus groups, when given a series of line 6 areas for improvement, just under half of participants were able to identify strategies to improve performance. Ms. Detmer says that this is a critical concern. Participants were queried as to why they said they didn't know what to suggest to the employee or how the company would provide support if it would.

Solution Systems

Description   What will help this organization and its people? What interventions must come together to improve performance? Why are you making these particular recommendations? What options do they have and what are your preferences? What benefits and business results will come from the solution system being proposed? Why these solutions? Provide a rationale linked to the data.

Example   The drivers described just above provide a reasonably clear road map to QuickPro. If the company wants its supervisors and managers to address areas for employee improvement, no amount of training will get it done. It is not a matter of an absence of skills or knowledge. The problem is caused by the fact that supervisors and managers (and employees) are given mixed messages about how important this is. While the training says do it, if they do it, they are pitched into what they perceive as an endless and numbing array of organizational procedures. One supervisor pointed to the personnel manual and said, "There are two pages on the importance of identifying areas for improvement and continuous employee growth and ten pages on what an employee can do if he or she disagrees. That's a pretty clear message." In addition, many supervisors said they won't get sufficient backing from their bosses if they really "bite the bullet." This problem of the clash between organizational commitment and the training for line 6 has successfully eroded supervisor belief in the value of the activity. Too many doubt that it even matters whether or not you cite areas for individual improvement.

The problem with line 7 appears to be driven by an absence of familiarity with what to do to help employees improve. They didn't know what to recommend to mock employees with mock problems and, fortunately, almost all agree it is important to prompt employees as to what to do when they wish to improve their performance.

The table below identifies a solution system for the performance appraisal problem. The recommendations are linked to analysis results.

Recommendation	Rationale
Create an online database that specifies the criteria for lines 6 and 7 and provides examples. Use Appendix B as the basis for this effort.	Eight of twelve supervisors expressed some doubt about what constitutes a good line 6 answer. Only one-third of respondents said they were confident about filling out this line. They need an easy reference, and an online system is it.
Create a web portal that takes the twenty most commonly identified areas for improvement and links them to local and QuickPro resources.	Just under half of participants were able to identify strategies to improve performance for typical areas for improvement, a critical problem, according to Ms. Detmer. A friendly database of resources is a quick way to address this concern.

(Continued)

Exhibit 8.6. What Are We Going to Do About the Appraisals? *(Continued)*

Recommendation	Rationale
Develop and conduct short training for mid- and upper-level managers regarding the philosophy and values surrounding identification of areas for improvement. If this is expected, share the expectations and the reasons for those expectations.	Supervisors and managers do not believe that they are supported by their bosses when they bite the bullet and suggest areas for growth. Until they feel this support, they won't do it in any but perfunctory ways.
Work with human resources to establish a recognition program that honors the attempt to help employees develop via the appraisal system. Consider adding this element to their appraisals. It is critical to simplify grievance procedures and to update the policy manual to reflect those changes.	Supervisors and managers are clearer about the hassles associated with line 6 than its importance. The organization must address this issue or line 6 will continue as a problem.
Create a mentor program that pairs successful (on filling out lines 6 and 7) supervisors with others. Ask them to work together to plan appraisals, to fill them out, and then to support the supervisors after the performance appraisal meetings with employees.	Confidence is a problem for many supervisors. In addition, this kind of institutionalized program will show that these lines on the appraisal matter to the organization.

Conclusions

Description	In this section summarize recommendations and next steps. It is also appropriate to note any lingering ambiguities and questions that must be resolved prior to moving forward. What should the client do? What should the client do next? What qualifications or gray areas remain regarding this situation? How should the organization proceed?

Example	QuickPro doesn't have a big problem with their performance appraisals. It is a small and narrowly defined problem. But it will take a sincere and significant cross-functional effort to solve it.
	Before doing anything, executives need to commit themselves anew to the importance of identifying areas for growth to employees during the appraisal process. If they can't generate and communicate strong business reasons, perhaps the best solution is to drop lines 6 and 7. If they can find those reasons, they must show that they intend to stand behind them.
	Lines 6 and 7 will not improve until the organization shows that it really wants its supervisors and managers to tackle this difficult issue. We've proposed a solution system that will accomplish it. Changes are necessary in policies and the policy manual, in grievance processes and in the ways that upper-level people show that they will back up their supervisors and managers in these difficult issues.
	A web portal and a small training program for managers is also proposed. This will provide supervisors and managers with the details they need to do a good job with lines 6 and 7.
	Our organization has prepared a budget and budget justification that is presented as Appendix D. We are eager to chat with you about this report and the related proposal.

Provide Materials That Customers Can Use to Communicate with Their Audiences

There's never too much we can do to help clients make good use of the work we do for them. Our slide show briefings should be constructed with this in mind. In fact, for a California government client, we created two PowerPoint slide shows, one for the customer, an instructional design manager, and one that he could use with audiences in his organization. That work was done two years ago. In a recent phone conversation, he told me that he had pulled out those slides, edited a bit, and used them to move the initiative forward, because now the time is right. Always, you are endeavoring to increase the likelihood that your analysis will move off the shelf and into the mainstream of the organization.

Admit to Limitations

Every analysis has limitations. Here is a listing of limitations that were included in an analysis done recently. Consider it an example. Your limitations statement will be derived from your setting, circumstances, and resources.

The findings from our study can guide decision makers here in the Omicron-Delta organization. However, it's important to note the limitations associated with our effort, even though we've attempted to triangulate from several sources.

- Findings were based on individual self-reports and opinions.

- The quantitative data were not based on a random sample. Survey respondents self-selected, and those who chose to answer might be atypical.

- Shared language and concepts was a continuous problem, casting shadows on the reliability of the quantitative study. Did our respondents have shared meanings for "learning management systems" and "performance support tools"? We fear that they did not, even though we provided a glossary of definitions. If they lacked a shared definition, and we point to concerns here, how can we be certain about our reported results?

- The sample size for the survey was small, consisting of fifty-seven respondents, as was the number of interviewees—thirty-six individuals, thirty-one learning and education professionals and five line executives.

- These results reflect opinions about a particular moment in time (for example, in the summer of 20XX). Progress and initiatives are ongoing; these results do not reflect the most recent efforts and accomplishments.

9

Tales from the Trenches

In this chapter, eight professionals describe how they used analysis to respond to problems and opportunities in diverse settings and organizations. In several cases, names have been changed. In all cases, the stories will ring true.

1. Charlotte Donaldson opens this chapter with stories about projects done in banking. She "opens the kimono" and talks about how analysis improved the quality of decision making.

2. Let's revisit Kendra Sheldon's work in technology innovation in public education.

3. Next up, two tales from the U.S. Coast Guard. Terry Bickham, then with the Coast Guard and now with Deloitte, describes a program to help Coast Guard people enforce complicated government regulations for fish and fishing. Then follows a report from Captain Chris Hall about how he used analysis to improve on Search and Rescue.

4. Another new case comes next. Let's hear from Shirley Gresham about fault investigation and performance analysis.

5. Next up is an old favorite from Susan Madeira. She describes the study she and Leah Antignas did to develop an orientation program for a franchise sales company.

6. Laura Handrick describes her work for The Maids International. She tackles real challenges in vivid ways.

Training Is Not the Only Solution—Charlotte Donaldson's Banking Vignettes

Like many of you, I stumbled into a career as a learning professional. Years ago, I was a product manager for savings at a large southern bank. We were redoing all our savings products, to make them more attractive to consumers. Our research indicated that savings was where the real profit was—attracting solid deposits that stayed at the bank for some reasonable period was our goal. "The tellers just don't know how to sell our savings products—put together some classes fast!" was what our stakeholder asked for.

In starting our project, we incorrectly assumed we only had to have the Training Department create a new and more effective training program about existing savings products, take it on the road, and be finished, with kudos all around, when savings deposits increased. In wisely doing some research, however, we found there was one group of branches in the western part of the state that had savings growth stronger than any other group. It was only logical that we needed to inquire about why this was the case and then to learn from them.

When we visited that area to do some focus groups, we hoped to hear a magical sales formula for increasing savings deposits. You know, something that we could have the Training Department train everyone else to do or say. However, things took a different turn, as they often do. We learned that this group used something other than the traditional passbook (very popular at that time) that everyone else was using. They offered instead savings products with pre-encoded deposit slips in a checkbook cover package, which made it "OK" if the customers forgot their passbooks—it was just very, very easy for the customers to make their deposits. The tellers even jotted down the transaction and new balance in the savings register for them. This was a retirement area, and the customers loved that personal service!

So we took this idea back and convinced our stakeholder we needed an operational change, not just a snazzy training course on an old product. We then changed our operational approach systemwide to those pre-encoded savings deposit slips. We even chose a bright gold "checkbook" cover with our logo on the front. (Years later when I met my husband, he had one of these!) My next task was to ensure that the Training Department teach everyone "the why and the what." Wouldn't you know . . . the Training Department had no bandwidth! So, almost single-handedly, I designed and delivered the training—first time ever! It went swimmingly well, if I say so myself! I was then hooked *forever* to be involved in training and all the surrounding processes.

Circling back to our business problem, savings deposits *did* increase. The project was deemed a success. I feel we would not have achieved that goal if we did had not uncovered how the "star" banking group was approaching it.

Lessons learned: (1) Talk to "the stars" and find out how they make it work. Be prepared to be surprised. (2) Don't assume the Training Department has time to do the training. (3) Don't be afraid to ask questions, think, and recommend a change in processes and systems.

"You Trained Them Wrong"

At the same bank, another huge project I worked on was to lead the development of training for all the back-room data-entry staff on a brand-new mainframe system—we switched from Honeywell to IBM, and the conversion project took two years! Our training team worked with programmers, business analysts, subject matter experts, and end users to make sure we were on target with the training.

Finally, the conversion day arrived. That afternoon, as the data-entry people began keying transactions, the program came to a screeching halt. After some quick and frantic analysis, the programmers told the "big boss" that "training had really messed up by training people wrong." Of course, my heart almost stopped beating—we were talking about over a hundred end users being taught something wrong. I immediately asked the programmer to show me what was wrong. Remember, this was in the days before PCs, and these were dumb terminals we were using. A few of the end users were (accidentally) hitting a nearby function key, as they were using the numerical keypad to enter financial transactions. "You should have taught them not to touch that key! Your training was bad!"

Fortunately, the big boss had walked up and heard that comment. Being a very smart fellow, he replied, "Why that's the silliest thing I've ever heard. You can't train people to not accidentally hit a wrong key at the top of the numerical key pad! Why don't *you* program things to protect the system from this honest and unavoidable mistake?"

I could have hugged him! The programmer quickly found a way to protect from this situation, and within a few hours, all was well, on our conversion D-Day.

Lessons learned: I picked up another valuable lesson that day. People can know how to do something well, and do it well many, many times correctly. But an honest *mistake of the fingers (or the mind!)* for a power end user is not a training issue; rather, it is a problem with the system. Interestingly, this experience prepared me well for other subsequent system issues, when I had to go "head to head" with the programmers. The system must work perfectly, and it must protect the end users from reasonable mistakes.

One Branch Was Just Fine—All the Rest Were a "Hot Mess"

Several years later, I had left that bank and was working for a banking software company, in the training area once again. Our learners were our customers. We were preparing for a conversion to the operating system of a fairly large commercial bank in the northeast. My task was to lead the training efforts for what the tellers would be doing at the branches. My team came onsite and spent weeks training all the branch managers, who in turn trained their staff at their branches. Conversion day was just around the corner. Little did I know, our training efforts would once again be attacked in a mighty way.

The branches went live on the system on a hot Monday in August. We could see the lobby of the main branch from our position in the second-floor boardroom, where our team was armed and ready for answering questions as they rolled in by phone from the branches. As we watched the lobby traffic below, the lines got longer, and longer. No one was leaving the bank. The tellers were hunched over their terminals, and we could seldom see their faces. When we did see them, it was not a pretty sight. Uh-oh. My stomach started to tie up in knots.

Tellers started throwing their hands in the air. Supervisors began running back and forth, and customer body language was scary. About then, calls started rolling in from the branches . . . no one could make the system work, and the tellers could not post the customers' transactions. Again, my heart almost stopped. We were on the phone walking freaked-out tellers through individual transactions, one-by-one, and this gave new meaning to the term, "drinking from a fire hose."

It was nearly noon, and in marched the CEO. He was fuming. "Get your staff together in five minutes—we're going to have a conference call with all the branch managers, and find out why your training didn't work. You have a lot to answer for!" With the feeling my career was going down the tubes, I gathered the training staff around the boardroom table. The conference call began. The north branch said the lobby was full, and several of the tellers were crying. Only 10 percent of the normal amount of Monday morning transactions had been accomplished so far. "We need some help out here!" the branch manager screamed. Similar reports and additional reports of teller and customer "hissy fits" were added by the south and west branches. One teller even spat on the hardware.

Then, a clear, calm voice from the east branch changed my life and made me question my decision to jump out the second-story window. "Well, we're doing fine over here. The lobby traffic is normal, the tellers have posted all transactions, and in fact, half of them have already balanced and are ready for the afternoon rush. All is well—we love the new system and its speed and convenient features." A hush fell over the call. Strangely, I became calm and knew I would learn something of great significance that very day.

"What do you mean, Carol?" asked the CEO. "You had the same training everyone else did, and it is *hell* at all the rest of the branches. Why?" "Well, I can't speak for everyone, but we followed the action plan provided at the end of the training class to make sure we were ready for this day." "Tell me more," the CEO said, his voice full of interest.

"Well," Carol said softly, "the software trainers told us to go back and test that all our terminals would in fact connect to the mainframe. We did that last week, and found two problems, which were corrected immediately by the Data Center team. Then, the training staff advised me to sit down with each teller and ask what concerns each had about the conversion and the new system. I found out two tellers feared their jobs would be lost. We got that taken care of right away, and now they are my biggest supporters of the new system. Also, the trainers told us to create samples of the most common transactions, and let each teller practice on a daily basis until conversion weekend. We did that and actually, we found three transactions that were coded wrong and got the programmers to fix those. I celebrated the tellers who found those discrepancies with a king-sized Hershey bar, and we had a pizza party Thursday to celebrate everyone's training success. On Saturday afternoon, we all came in and did the mail transactions on the new system, just to get some live experience under our belts, so to speak.

"Also, I let everyone know I expected them to do their very best, maintain a positive attitude, and help each other out. As the trainers also suggested, I put a sign in the lobby that we were serving free orange juice on Monday, so even if we were a bit slower because of the new system, the customers had a little refreshment while they waited. Last, I bought t-shirts for everyone that said, 'Bankers do it with interest.' I asked for feedback on what I could do to support the conversion and their work, because they were the face of the bank, and I wanted them to know they were part of something very big. So things have been fine here—what a great new system!"

You could have heard a pin drop. I could have hugged Carol! The other branch managers began backpedaling—"I didn't know we could buy pizza—is there a budget for that?" "What do you mean sample transaction practice—which transactions did you use, Carol? Can I have a copy?" "You told them your expectations and showed your appreciation, huh? Nice idea." "Can some of your folks come help us?"

It was evident that the conversion had turned a corner. As the week wore on, each branch manager spent evenings and off hours following Carol's plan. The conversion was deemed a success. I sent Carol flowers.

Lessons learned: Follow up after training, and see if folks are really doing what you advised around action plans. When you find someone that is, find a way to "share the success in the workplace." And, sometimes, you are not going to get thanked. The CEO never did admit our training was fine. *But it was.* That glorious Carol proved it.

Summing It Up

We learning professionals have a huge responsibility and should be held accountable to find ways to develop and deliver successful training and to find ways to make sure that training works to solve the business problem. Part of that responsibility will always involve being aware that training is only part of the solution. Our jobs are also to speak up, when we are asked to develop training: "Great! . . . *What's the business problem we're trying to solve?*"

> —Charlotte Donaldson is a learning strategist for Leadership Development at Booz Allen Hamilton, a leading global consulting firm.

Who Wouldn't Want Computers in Their Classroom? Kendra Sheldon's Story

The cry "A computer in every classroom!" was heard across the land. Cookie sales, car washes, and bingo nights were epidemic as schools zealously raised money for technology. Parents, starry-eyed with dreams of computer-literate, Internet-savvy children, reached deep into their pockets to support their dreams. Educators, under pressure to prepare students for the twenty-first-century workplace, gave their support.

This massive technology rollout has created a need for professional development, as educators are expected not only to use the technology but also to crank out computer-literate students. If ever there was a need for analysis before action, this was it, and considering that school officials value education and training more than most professionals, making the case for performance analysis should have been a piece of cake, right?

Case One: Rancho Bizarro Elementary School

In Northern California, a decade ago, the strong economy fueled a growth spurt in once-sleepy suburbs. Competition for home buyers was fierce.

In one affluent suburb, Mr. McBuild, a large construction company, decided that the way to buyers' hearts was not with brass bathroom fixtures or bonus rooms but with a brand-new, high-tech elementary school. After all, what parent could resist the dream of computer-literate children taking their rightful places in Silicon Valley?

Mr. McBuild's new homes sold like hotcakes as the airwaves were flooded with ads: "Nothing is more important than your child's education. Rancho Bizarro Elementary, with computers in every classroom, email and Internet access for all, will prepare your child for the twenty-first century. Why settle for anything less? Buy a Mr. McBuild home today . . . for your child's future." Rancho Bizarro Elementary was a success story . . . or was it?

As time went on, parents began to complain that their children were not developing computer skills, only better game strategies. Students gradually lost interest in technology as they came to see computers as second-rate Nintendo sets. Teachers endured countless mind-numbing sermons on the power of technology but failed to develop the necessary computer skills. Most used the computer as a typewriter. Support for Rancho Bizarro school waned as the community wondered what went wrong.

For Rancho Bizarro and other schools, reality bites. Administrators, teachers, and librarians asked themselves, "Now that we have it, how will we use it?" They realized that computer use is anything but intuitive; many educators had never used one, let alone taught others how. It seems that as the PTA busily calculated how much technology they could purchase, nobody thought to train the teachers to use it well.

Rancho Bizarro's problems might have been avoided if school officials had invested in performance analysis. If they had, they would have discovered that teachers needed hands-on technology training, not lectures; they needed job aids, not technical manuals; and they needed long-term coaching and support, not a "one-day dip." A few interviews would have shed light on Rancho Bizarro's problems—and matched solutions to those problems.

Rancho Bizarro's situation was not unique. The problems came, in large part, from leaping without planning. The next case study shows that performance analysis can go a long way toward improving technology integration in the schools.

Case Two: Turtle Middle School

The Information Age has been a boon to small and midsize cities throughout the nation, as many high-tech companies have chosen clean air, hills of green, and ten-minute commutes over big-city woes. Affluent employees have happily relocated, taking their tax dollars with them.

Turtle Middle School, built during the prosperous Eisenhower years, enjoyed a solid academic reputation for decades, despite its location in a poor, big-city neighborhood. Many proud staff members had been at Turtle since the very first day. Though money was scarce, the school put together a technology program, one "hand-me-down" computer at a time. When the school reached the milestone "computer in every classroom," officials decided that it was time to launch an official technology program.

When a Plan Is Not a Plan Turtle Middle School was determined to make its technology program a success, and they hired media specialist Tiffany Banana to head up the effort. The first order of business was to write a technology plan. Tiffany's plan—a high-tech wish list of computer hardware, software, and speedy phone lines—was eagerly endorsed by city officials, school administrators, parents, and local businesses. They showed their support with donations. Turtle's teachers watched in stunned silence as their school was rapidly transformed into a "wired learning community."

Tiffany became well known to the faculty as she set up computing stations in every classroom and gave every teacher a pile of how-to manuals. Turtle's technology program appeared to be off to a running start—or was it?

An Ounce of Insight Is Worth a Pound of Technology As Tiffany traveled from classroom to classroom, installing "new-better-faster" software, she noticed two things: the teachers did not seem to be using their computers, and they seemed to resent her more than a little bit. Tiffany decided to call her friend Jack Bright, a performance specialist, and ask for his advice.

Tiffany: Jack, I don't know what to do. I've given these teachers the latest software, hardware, and documentation, but they are just not using them. Worse yet, they seem to resent me. What am I doing wrong?

Jack: Tiffany, did anyone ever think to ask the teachers how they felt about the new technology program? Technology is great, but the teachers are the ones who have to use it. Maybe you should talk to them to find out what's going on. Also, what are their skills? Are they novices or experts? Spend a day asking questions, and you'll know what's going on and what you might try next.

Tiffany: OK, I'll give it a try. But what do feelings have to do with computers? Everyone was so excited about my technology program; you'd think the teachers would plunge into those manuals so they could get online.

Analysis Turns Things Around Tiffany took Jack's advice and spoke to several teachers about the new technology program. She asked the following questions:

- How do you feel about the new technology program?
- Tell me a little about your computer skills.
- What would you like to use the computers to do?
- What questions do you want answered about computers in your classroom?
- Are you interested in hands-on training to develop computer skills?
- In what other ways might I support your efforts?

Tiffany also perused the manuals and spent some time using the new hardware and software.

A Data-Driven Solution System Tiffany found a widespread lack of enthusiasm, even resentment, toward the technology initiative. She also discovered that the how-to manuals were less than helpful and that using the new software was not intuitive. Tiffany also found herself struggling to understand the online help systems. Soon she came to understand the teachers' feelings about her and the great new opportunity.

Tiffany's findings are typical of new system rollouts that overlook the people side of things. Fortunately, the data she gleaned from analysis helped her design a customized solution system to make Turtle Middle School's technology program a success. It emphasizes the uses teachers most value and relies on a familiar instructor, available coaching, and simplified job aids. School officials and faculty, motivated to maintain Turtle's reputation for excellence, supported these recommendations, and the program is starting to become a high-tech success story.

—Kendra Sheldon is lead curriculum
developer at Cymer Inc.

Fish Things First: Terry Bickham's Story

Several years ago, a government study confirmed the commercial fishing industry's view that Coast Guard officers who enforced living marine resource laws weren't up to speed on fish, fishermen, or the process of catching fish. Admittedly, being a fish cop was not viewed by most as on par with the more glamorous missions of saving lives (see Chris Hall's case that follows) and catching drug smugglers. Proficiency on fish was not a priority.

To right the situation, Congress promptly legislated money to buy a training fix. Being largely responsible for performance improvement in the Pacific region, I got a call from headquarters in Washington, D.C., letting me know that additional staff and funding were on the way to help me put together a training program for the Coast Guard folks on the West Coast. I was expected to start formal classes on fisheries law enforcement in about two months.

I had a lot of questions that weren't getting answers. What really was the problem? What were we doing in that arena that was not so good or good enough? How could technology help? What exactly was headquarters attempting to achieve? This situation was ripe for performance analysis.

First Step

Soon, half a dozen new employees and a meager budget augmentation showed up on my office doorstep, all assigned to the fish challenge. What wasn't surprising was that these prospective "trainers" had neither fish nor instructional design expertise. The clock was ticking, so I promptly gave these folks a speedy indoctrination in performance analysis and divided them into three teams. One team would concentrate on the Pacific Northwest, one on California, and the last on the western Pacific islands. Each team would focus on gathering data from their respective geographic regions. Chunking it up helped make sense of the challenge. I left the teams to gather and review the literature on fisheries in their regions, records of inspections, court case packages, trade journals, and so on, while I pressed headquarters about expectations.

The fisheries enforcement office at headquarters didn't have the details I needed regarding optimals. Basically, they expected a formal regional fisheries training center to be established. Their vision focused on facilities and curriculum. The best I could determine, they wanted something like a week-long Fisheries Enforcement 101 course, and they wanted it fast. Reading the government study was slightly more enlightening. Although it lacked specific information about the Pacific region, it did point out that fisheries training to date was informal and inadequate. The reference section was a great source of professional writings on the subject.

After a couple of days of heavy-duty web surfing and good old library research, we found out that fisheries in the Pacific region were dissimilar. Salmon trolling off Washington state and tuna seining in the South Pacific were as different as baking and grilling. Sea urchin diving off of Southern California was one example of a myriad of small regional fisheries. Each fishery had its own set of complex and volatile laws and regulations.

Environmentalists and the fishing industry were at odds over species catch limits. All agreed that the fish were disappearing, and blamed each other. The outcome of this effort was that my teams had quickly amassed a good foundation on what types of fishing were going on in their regions and who the players were.

Next Steps

I sat down with the teams to sketch out the next several stages of our analysis. We set up a series of interviews for the following week with various sources in each geographic region. The teams would first go to the respective regional Coast Guard law enforcement manager (both a customer and a local sponsor) to get his or her view of the problem. Each team would then spend a couple of days out in the field interviewing

Coast Guard officers who were expected to do fish inspections (the job incumbents) and their immediate supervisors. Next, the teams would visit with state and federal game wardens (experts) and fishermen (experts, customers). We developed a structured interview job aid with questions for each source tailored to gathering facts and feelings about what was and should be happening.

What We Found

By the end of that week, we had an enormous amount of data. As expected, regional managers perceived training and enforcement efforts as inadequate. We learned that most Coast Guard officers shied away from enforcing fisheries laws because the regulations were too complex, all the fish looked the same, and the officers really felt uncomfortable trying to enforce something they admittedly knew little about. Besides, it was a smelly, thankless task that competed with their primary job of rescuing people. Though most felt professionalism required reasonable proficiency, the prospect of spending a week out of town in a class about fish law was not at all attractive.

Fishers, the preferred non–gender-specific term for fishermen, were riled up over officers who knew virtually nothing about what they were doing coming on their boats to inspect them. Short-staffed state and federal game wardens required experienced Coast Guard officers to help them out but lamented that there was little communication between them. For example, at one Coast Guard station, the Coasties complained they didn't know what the current fisheries laws were in their area and hadn't a clue how to find out. When I pointed out that a federal fisheries enforcement office was located in the building next door, it was news to them.

After about a week's investment in the performance analysis, it was obvious that a forty-hour resident course couldn't cure these ills. The situation differed as you moved fifty miles up or down the coast. Sure, training would be a key part of the solution, and I planned a full-blown training needs assessment to yield the meat for subsequent lesson plans and job aids. Right up front, though, the performance analysis showed the need for a solution system that established partnerships among the players to share information and eliminate barriers.

What Happened

Here's what we did. Knowledgeable state and federal officers mentored Coast Guard folks in fisheries enforcement and conducted joint enforcement patrols with them. A greater sense of professionalism emerged. Changes in regulations were shared via newly set up email and fax networks to demystify the law. State and federal fisheries biologists frequently visited Coast Guard stations with fresh-caught fish and provided clues on how to identify them. These scientists also shared data to show the status of depleted fish stocks and discussed the positive impact enforcement efforts were having on the health of species. The Coast Guard officers learned firsthand that they played an important part in living marine resource protection and contributed to the economic viability of their communities.

Coast Guard officers established relationships and a dialogue with local fishers and fishing organizations. Regular discussion groups were organized as a forum to clear up misunderstandings and balance enforcement with a sense of fairness. Fishers shared how being stopped for an inspection had an impact on their bottom line. Some of them invited local Coasties onto their boats and explained to them how the gear worked. A few even volunteered their boats as platforms for practice inspections. Coasties visited local wholesale fish auctions and net storage barns to further their knowledge about the industry.

Once the performance analysis was complete, my trainers continued to expand their expertise and develop specific one- or two-day training for each region and, in many cases, specialized modules appropriate to stretches of coastline in each region. Instead of a resident course, the trainers delivered their classes onsite at the local stations and spent time there to ensure relevance. These classes were hands-on and tailored to the locale, and involved community fishers. Demand for the classes was high, and the trainers were welcomed as part of the crew.

After a while, Coast Guard expertise and participation in fisheries enforcement increased, and complaints from fishers dwindled. Everyone seemed happier. Well, not everyone.

Some in Washington were still expecting us to produce that training center. They had pictured bricks and mortar, and I hadn't given it to them.

Of course, what we did on the West Coast went beyond just putting on a class. It was a successful systemic solution costing one-tenth what a comparable training center would have. Where did I go wrong? I had missed the boat by not adequately sharing the results of the performance analysis or selling our solution system to headquarters as we moved forward with it. I had concentrated on fixing the problem without bringing the sponsor along.

—Terry Bickham is learning and development
services leader for Deloitte Services LP.

Search and Rescue: Chris Hall's story

The United States Coast Guard has many responsibilities. While our missions range from fish regulation to ice-breaking to law enforcement, our foundation is built upon our most important mission—Search and Rescue (SAR). There are many types of SAR; a few examples include rescuing sinking vessels close to shore or a thousand miles from the coast; stranded hikers, hunters, rock climbers, and cross-country skiers; downed aircraft; overloaded migrant vessels; and injured fishermen. This case describes a particular type of SAR, when ships sink or aircraft go down far offshore in a place where help is not available. Under these conditions our focus is on the "search" portion of SAR. Our goal is to reduce or eliminate search time so we can get to the rescue.

To do this we have developed many tools and techniques over our history. One of the most important is the Self-Locating Data Marker Buoy (SLDMB). This is an extremely specialized piece of equipment that we primarily drop from aircraft in the area where we suspect the vessel sank. The SLDMB activates when it gets wet and sends a signal that is relayed by satellite to our search planners so they can calculate the drift (driven by currents and wind) of an object (usually a person or life raft). We can then design the search areas for our Coast Guard aircraft and vessels with the highest probability of success. The SLDMB is absolutely critical when the vessel sinks way offshore (cases thousands of miles offshore occur every year) or in unpredictable current areas such as near glaciers where the runoff from melting ice dramatically affects the drift.

The key to understanding the importance of the SLDMB is that it gives us real-time meteorological data. Without the SLDMB we have to rely on forecasted (based on historical) weather data. How much do you trust your weatherman? Would you stake your life on him?

Our story starts in October, three months after I took over as chief of the Office of Search and Rescue. Coast Guard Air Station Sitka, Alaska, had three major failures of SLDMBs during a one-week period on major SAR cases. All of the cases occurred near the mouth of glacial rivers where little tidal data existed. An additional failure occurred the same week from an SLDMB dropped on a SAR case in the Gulf of Mexico, by an aircraft from Clearwater, Florida.

First Steps

How big was the problem? To move quickly, we began by researching recent case files. We pulled out all SAR cases in 2007 in which SLDMBs were deployed. We found that 20 percent of deployed SLDMBs failed to send any data and only 63 percent met our standards for duration and accuracy. There was over a one-third failure rate, a staggering problem in our line of work. I immediately let the chain-of-command (my bosses) understand the magnitude of the problem and started analyzing it. I needed answers fast.

This was your classic "all-hands-on-deck" type of problem. I got the entire staff together to discuss what we knew about SLDMBs: their history; previous problems; how they are manufactured, distributed, powered, maintained, and serviced; what the "user" instructions were; whether there was training; and what documentation we had.

Our first discovery was that there were over a hundred expired SLDMBs still out in the field, on "ready racks" waiting to be grabbed and used in an emergency. I immediately issued a recall of the expired SLDMBs and had a staff member call every unit that had an expired SLDMB and explain how to send it to us for analysis. We quickly had a workable number and began the hands-on portion of the analysis. A team from both our Engineering Logistics Center (ELC) and headquarters met to dissect the returned equipment.

What We Found

Before examining a single SLDMB, it was evident from the variety of packaging (or lack thereof) that storage was a primary issue. For an SLDMB to activate when it gets wet, its packaging must keep it completely dry until it's needed. In the basic packaging design, the SLDMB is spring-loaded to activate, and held in place by water-soluble tape that melts when it gets wet.

The power source, ten D-cell batteries (like those in flashlights), is prevented from turning on by a small magnet, which holds a small switch open. The magnet is held in place by the same water-soluble tape. As can be easily seen, if water (or even moisture) gets to the tape the SLDMB would activate. The package is housed in a "Sonotube," which is used to protect the SLDMB as it is dropped out of an aircraft at speeds up to 180 miles per hour. The Sonotube is also held together by the same water-soluble tape that melts when it gets wet. The entire SLDMB is wrapped in a vapor barrier. The vapor barrier looks like an airtight tinfoil wrapper and should remain on the SLDMB until immediately before it is dropped during a case.

Many of our SLDMBs were returned with damaged and even missing vapor barriers. It was apparent that many units had opened the packaging of the SLDMB, including the vapor barrier wrap. As we analyzed this further we looked at the packaging. The instructions on the vapor wrap read, "Wrapper Must Be Removed Before Deploying." Problem number one was that our people were getting ahead of the game by removing the vapor wrap as soon as they opened the box—saving key time in the emergency but rendering the SLDMB useless after a few weeks. Rain or humidity melted the tape, causing the magnet to fall off and activate the power source, running down the batteries the same way you do if you leave your flashlight turned on. Unfortunately, the Sonotube protecting the SLDMB prevented users from seeing whether the tape had melted.

We also found that even on many of the SLDMBs that were returned with a still-intact vapor wrap, the magnet had been jarred loose, allowing the power source to activate. They too were long dead, and the batteries (also much like an old flashlight) had corroded into a mess. This problem was easy to deduce. Most of these had extremely small amounts of tape holding the magnets in place, which were easily loosened in shipping or when bounced around on a helicopter flight.

What We Did

There were many more problems we discovered in the design, labeling, and job aids, and in our logistics system (explaining why we had so many expired SLDMBs still on the shelf), but for the big smoking guns, we immediately replaced the label on the vapor barrier wrap. The new wording in large type reads: "STOP, do not open or remove sealed wrapper until deployment," and in smaller type: "Removal of the sealed wrapper exposes the water-soluble tape to moisture. Water-soluble tape holds the on/off magnet in place and the SLDMB deployment package together. Removal of the magnet turns the SLDMB on." We added wider water-soluble tape and additional layers of the tape around the SLDMB body to hold the switch magnet firmly in place. The added tape makes it less likely to stretch or be affected by low levels of moisture.

In addition, we conducted an assessment of all operational (nonexpired) SLDMBs. We provided criteria for inspection and specific requirements that must be met to keep an SLDMB in service. Further, we reached out to our inspection teams that evaluate our units' operational readiness. These teams have added SLDMB inspections to their checklists and have improved our accountability process. For one final measure of safety, we directed all of our units to drop two SLDMBs on every Search and Rescue case. All changes have been implemented.

Final Note

It's only been eight months, but we haven't had a SAR case with an SLDMB failure since we implemented the changes!

—Captain Chris Hall was the chief of the Office of Search and Rescue for the United States Coast Guard and now leads the Petaluma Training Center.

Shirley Gresham Tackles Failure Investigation Through Performance Analysis

"Good failure investigators have great intuition and judgment . . . but I have no idea how you're going to teach that."

—Manager in charge of the failure
investigation training rollout

For over twenty years, I've worked as an independent performance consultant for high-tech Fortune 500 companies. As a script writer for a video production company, I was assigned a project to "improve quality" at a chemical manufacturing plant. My intuition told me that the video the customer was requesting would not do the job, so I began researching how to approach the problem. The client ended up not pursuing the video, and I discovered performance analysis.

When a large medical device manufacturing company asked me to create training that would improve failure investigation at the company, I drew from my experience with NASA, the Navy, and Hewlett-Packard. Quality issues can cause a company to put production on hold, or to do a major recall. Millions of dollars are lost while failure investigators try to figure out why a problem is recurring. Like performance analysis, failure investigation must be done fast, without sacrificing quality.

During the performance analysis phase of the failure investigation training project, I was struck by how much these two disciplines have in common. Both

- Gather and analyze information in order to better understand a problem or need

- Look at a problem from multiple perspectives

- Remain nimble enough to change course as data are uncovered

- Look for deeper, systemic factors that may be contributing to a problem

What Is Failure Investigation?

Depending on the organization, a failure investigation might be triggered by a downed satellite, an injury to an operator, or the wrong medication being delivered to a patient. Failure investigators respond with actions similar to what you see on the television series *CSI: Crime Scene Investigation*. They gather and analyze evidence, try to reproduce the reported problem, form hypotheses, conduct experiments to test hypotheses, and decide how to proceed—often on the basis of incomplete information.

Failure investigation involves finding the root causes of problems or failures. Root causes are typically one of several factors that cause a malfunction. Once root causes are found, actions can be taken to prevent recurrence. Root causes are found in the following:

- Design of a product or system
- Processes or procedures
- Communication practices
- Maintenance practices
- Management decisions
- Resource management (budget, staff, training)

During the performance analysis for the failure investigation training, I found many challenges. I had access to five failure investigators at the company. It turns out that good investigators do the job differently. I found that they use different analysis techniques and tools, have different technical backgrounds and communication styles, and choose different paths on their journey to uncover root causes.

With about two-and-a-half months to do a performance analysis and produce a two-day, interactive workshop on failure investigation, time was tight and the goals were lofty. My client wanted comprehensive training for failure investigators that would improve their ability to swiftly find the root causes of problems. He also stressed the importance of experience, intuition, and good judgment when doing failure investigations, but had no idea how to teach those things.

These challenges were offset by the fact that the champion of the project was the president of the company. The sponsor (my direct manager) was a failure investigation expert who was committed to excellence and open-minded about how we might get there.

The Performance Analysis Plan

Here is my initial performance analysis plan:

- Look at causes of the performance problem
- Research how to improve judgment and intuition in failure investigators
- Meet with management to clarify goals and scope, and to get buy-in where necessary
- Gain access to the best failure investigators in the company
- Begin asking questions that would provide me with the following:
  - A failure investigation model
  - Failure investigation tools, techniques, and templates
  - Best practices and common errors
  - Case studies

Causes of the Performance Problem

The initial trigger for this effort was an audit by the Food and Drug Administration (FDA). A recurring quality issue was posing a risk to patient safety. The company had done a comprehensive failure investigation, but the problem continued to recur. The details of this and other "war stories" began to shed light on the problem. I learned that many of the people doing failure investigations did not have the skills or knowledge to do the job. They were making rookie mistakes, like not looking at the physical evidence and not digging deep enough to find systemic causes.

Besides talking to managers and experts, I reviewed the results of an internal study done by an FDA consultant. He was looking at the company's failure investigations from the point of view of the FDA, and proved to be an excellent resource. The study evaluated two years' worth of company reports on the causes of quality issues. I learned that a significant percentage did not accurately identify the root causes of problems. While they wanted to do it right, they didn't know how to nail the causes of the failures. They lacked necessary skills and knowledge.

Subject matter experts shed light on organizational causes of these problems. Investigators might wait weeks to get funding to do a particular experiment. Because failure investigations could spring from many units in the company, multiple teams could be investigating different parts of the same problem—without knowledge of each other's actions. In addition to a class, the organization must attend to establishing a coordinated way of examining failures.

Good Failure Investigators Have Good Intuition and Judgment

I required a strategy for improving intuition and judgment in failure investigators. Several years ago, I had worked with Allison Rossett to create training that would improve intuition and judgment in administrators of legal contracts. From a study done on Navy pilots, we learned that the ability to make sound judgments is affected by the difficulty of the judgment task, the number of relevant options one can draw from, and the level of stress present in the situation.

By thinking it through and talking to subject matter experts, we decided that we could improve judgment and intuition in failure investigators by addressing those three factors in our training. Here's how:

1. Everyone agreed that the less information available, the more difficult it is to exercise good judgment in failure investigations. Providing failure investigators with strategies and tools for gathering, organizing, and analyzing complex layers of information would help them understand the problem and make it easier to make sound judgments.

2. All of the subject matter experts looked at problems from several perspectives. This gave them more options to draw from during an investigation. They might ask, What did the user experience? What does field service know about the problem? What are the

assemblers on the production floor doing? Did the environment have an impact? What about shipping? Looking at a problem from different points of view expanded their options for how to proceed. Class activities related to looking at a problem from multiple perspectives would improve judgment.

3. Finally, we decided that the training and related supportive information could reduce stress by providing learners with the skills and knowledge to cope with the challenge.

Making the Most of Scant Moments

I had to get time with the experts. Having friends in high places helped me set up the initial meetings, but these experts were leading important failure investigations. There was pressure on them to get their investigations done fast. They politely made it clear that my time with them would be limited.

By being customer-oriented, I eventually got what I needed from these busy experts. Preparation, leadership, and demonstration of progress all helped earn their trust and create a sense of teamwork and partnership. By being prepared and anticipating their needs, I developed good relationships. I would send questions in advance, provide "friendly reminders" of action items, and set up meeting rooms before they arrived.

Leadership became another important factor in this performance analysis. Failure investigation is a complicated topic worthy of lengthy conversations. These experts had no idea what specifics I required. Some expressed skepticism that it was even possible to train someone to do failure investigation. Keeping performance analysis meetings focused on very specific goals helped me get the job done faster. One expert liked to talk about complex, technical details from his current project. To get back on track, I would ask him to help me connect his example to the bigger picture.

Years ago, I found a performance analysis technique in Rossett's book *Training Needs Assessment* that I often use to show progress and stay on track. During meetings, I capture information on large easel paper on the wall. It keeps everyone focused on the meeting's goals and helps organize the information into logical chunks. I used this strategy throughout the failure investigation performance analysis, and it worked well. Seeing a wall filled with information about failure investigations made everyone feel that something had been accomplished. This technique also helped me run the meetings. Once in a while, I would find myself not sure about where to go next. To get back on track, I would refer back to the wall of information and ask something about it: "Which items on this list do you think are most important?" or "Can you give me an example of this?" Ranking the importance of content, filling in holes, getting examples, and verifying that we were going in the right direction all helped refocus the effort. It is like active listening with visual aids!

Developing a Model

Developing a model for failure investigation that is flexible enough to work with any type of failure was one of my goals. Finding a model for a topic such as troubleshooting or failure investigation can be tricky because it is not a linear process. I usually begin finding a model by proposing an idea to the experts and getting their input.

This particular client uses the Six Sigma business management strategy, and it was suggested that I use a Six Sigma process called DMAIC (Define, Measure, Analyze, Improve, and Control) as a failure investigation model. I was thrilled to have my problem solved so easily, but the more I tried to organize what I learned about failure investigation into this DMAIC construct, the more I found it did not work. Failure investigation, like trouble-shooting, isn't linear. It does not fit into a five-step, linear process designed to improve manufacturing processes. In addition, the DMAIC process was missing key components that had to be present in failure investigations. However, it gave me a place to start, which was half the battle.

One expert remarked, "Failure investigation is like a puzzle. . . ." That was an "Aha" moment for me. I realized that if I could find the key pieces of that puzzle, then I would have a model that would work for failure investigation. I asked each of my five experts, "What pieces does every successful failure investigation include?" In separate meetings, they all identified the same key pieces. Eureka! I found it. I decided to represent our failure investigation model with a map of tropical islands. Each island was named after a key component present in every successful failure investigation. To solve the

Figure 9.1.

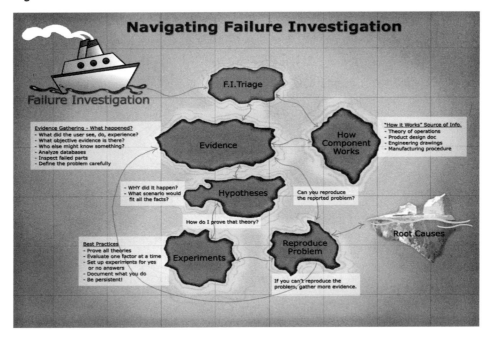

problem of failure investigation being nonlinear, the islands were connected by water currents that flowed in many directions. We named the map "Navigating Failure Investigation," and I used that conceptual map to structure the course (Figure 9.1).

Using Case Studies

Getting good case studies was critical to the success of this project. My plan was to have the case studies unfold as the course progressed, so that learners could experience discovery in failure investigations firsthand. This plan presented some design challenges, but in the end, it made for an engaging class.

Failure investigators always examine the physical evidence, so it made sense to bring evidence into the classroom. When I had trouble getting the failed part examples I needed, my manager stepped in and assigned someone to manufacture them. Perfect! One expert made sure that the failures accurately represented real failures from the field.

During the workshop pilot, I learned the value of simple case studies. I had to rework part of the course because two of the case study activities were too difficult for participants. Switching to a very simple case study about a burned birthday cake solved the problem. Everyone understood potential causes of burned cakes, and people had fun applying analysis tools and techniques to this familiar, mundane issue.

A Few Lessons Learned

Performance analysis depends on asking the right people the right questions at the right time. Following are some early questions I asked during this performance analysis:

- How do you know root causes when you see them?
- Which tools and techniques do you use to find root causes?
- What key components does every failure investigation have?
- If you were training a new investigator, what best practices would you share?
- What are the common errors that new investigators make?

Prepare thoroughly. With goals as the driver, think about what you need to get the job done and then do it. Anticipating obstacles and taking steps to overcome them, planning ahead, and keeping the momentum moving forward are all part of the job.

Get creative. Tough problems require creative solutions. Like a failure investigator, try thinking about the challenge from different points of view. Do research and draw from experience (both yours and others). Let information percolate in your head, and solutions will emerge. If they do not, then go get more information.

Do it with data. During this project, there was no time to survey other failure investigators or to go beyond my few experts to verify we were on the right track. In some areas I had too much information. I needed a quick way to home in on what would be most useful for our learners. I informally collected data by asking the experts to draw from their experience and tell me how frequently they did a particular task. For example, I had uncovered more failure investigation tools and techniques than we could possibly train. To narrow the focus, I asked each investigator, "Which failure investigation tools and techniques do you use most often?" By finding the tools and techniques each expert used most frequently, I found my focus.

Results

We trained over three hundred engineers in the first round of classes, and the feedback was extremely positive. Senior management told us, "The buzz is that the Failure Investigation Workshop is an excellent class." Attendee comments were also enthusiastic. The company recently opened the class to three hundred more engineers, and plans are in the works to roll it out to other locations.

—Shirley Gresham is president of training for Events Online in San Diego,
a full-service training and web site development company.

Susan Madeira Looks at Orientation

Here we see external consultants grapple with strategies to shift their customer from one view of what ought to be done to another. An additional wrinkle: the analysis unearthed a front-and-center role for line managers. What are you going to do when the managers are reluctant?

A franchising company's headquarters had for several years experienced increases in the number of employees. What was once a small business environment—where each person knew the other—had become a large, impersonal corporate headquarters. This increased number of employees along with a rising turnover rate ensured a pool of "new employees" at the headquarters. The new employees were expected to understand the corporate organization and learn new cultural, computer, phone, and other systems. Employees were also expected to know how corporate headquarters served the franchise offices throughout the world.

Prior to these years of growth, headquarters had grown slowly; there was not a strong need or desire for a formalized employee orientation program. As each new employee was hired, he or she was treated to a personalized orientation and introductions. However, as the number of new employees climbed, Ted Bryant, the director of human resources, realized that it was time to implement a formal orientation program. He had a pretty good idea about how the program ought to work.

Initial Plan

To implement his program, Ted turned to Cora Clay, the training director, for assistance in developing his orientation program. Ted felt the program should consist of four half-day sessions that included informational workshops and departmental tours, along with a hiring manager's checklist that would assist managers in orienting their new employees.

Due to resource constraints, Cora decided to hire two instructional design consultants, Leah Antignas and me, to develop Ted's orientation program. Leah and I had reservations about Ted's approach to orientation. Although orientation programs, now dubbed onboarding, are nothing new, and most companies have similar programs, we felt the need to perform further analysis before starting development.

Process

We approached senior and middle management and employees for insight into their needs and concerns associated with the orientation process. We used interviews, questionnaires, and a focus group to investigate and document the needs. We also scanned the published literature. The following paragraphs outline the data-collection process we used during the analysis.

Interviews. We began the data-collection process by conducting twelve interviews. Six of the interviews were with employees who had been with the company for less than six months. The other six were with those who had been with the company for at least one year. We asked the new employees to voice their orientation needs and to share the frustrations and problems they were experiencing. We asked the long-term employees what they felt would have helped them become better oriented to the company. Both groups provided information and resources that would benefit new hires. We also interviewed the CEO of the franchise company. His personality and presence set the tone for the organization, a spirit that should be reflected in the orientation program.

Questionnaire. We distributed a questionnaire to all employees at the headquarters. The questionnaire asked employees to identify their most important orientation topics, the biggest problems for new employees, and what they felt managers should do to orient new employees.

Focus Group. We summarized the findings gathered from these strategies and presented them to a nine-member focus group consisting of directors, managers, and a vice president. The goals of this group were to

- Report findings to management
- Discuss management's role in the orientation process
- Generate ideas, concerns, and constraints in regard to the orientation process
- Determine necessary resources to assist management in their new orientation roles, if any

Obstacles

The process to define and rejuvenate this orientation was not remarkable. Worth noting, however, are the obstacles we faced during and after the analysis.

For example, when Ted met with us, he told us what the orientation program would be; Ted's expectations were that we would immediately begin development of the program as he defined it.

With Cora's help, we explained to Ted the importance of taking a fresh look at the situation, of involving not only members of the human resources organization but also employees from all levels and organizations at headquarters, prior to defining the program. Getting Ted's support was not difficult. Ted had complete confidence in Cora, and Cora knew we were employing sound instructional design principles. As the project progressed, we sent frequent meeting minutes and other necessary correspondence. Throughout the process, we kept Ted informed about our activities and about how these efforts fit into the development of the orientation.

Time was another obstacle. Upper management wanted the orientation program delivered in less than two months. There were two obvious reasons for this push. First, at the previous corporate meeting attended by all employees, the suggestion for an orientation had been made and had received great response. Several months had passed since this meeting, and the leadership did not wish to dawdle in its response.

Second, the corporate mission and vision statements had recently been revised. The new statements included words such as *team* and *quality,* and the executive management team felt an orientation program for new employees would be a good place to start to make these statements come to life.

The reasons for the rush were certainly valid, but the time was insufficient for designing and developing the orientation program given the available resources. To deal with the constraints, we analyzed the reasons for the push. We determined that taking visible steps toward an orientation program and building enthusiasm for the development of the program would handle the concerns of upper management, even if the orientation program wasn't completed in two months. This time constraint was one of the reasons that we sent all employees questionnaires. It was critical that everyone saw some progress and felt a sense of ownership. This philosophy was congruent with the new corporate mission and vision.

The final obstacle was the political nature of the project. There were several issues, but two were particularly interesting. First, although managers' involvement and the ensuring of consistency were common themes throughout the interview and questionnaire responses, several managers saw an orientation program as one change they didn't need. Some seemed to fight the responsibility of orienting their new employees. This situation could not be ignored if the final orientation program was to be successful.

The second issue was that study had uncovered numerous requests for written job descriptions. Written job descriptions were not a standard practice, and Ted and Cora warned us about raising the issue to the executive management team. We felt we had to address the issue of job descriptions, but we had to do it without offending the management team or the people who had hired us.

The management focus group, besides fulfilling the objectives outlined earlier, was a means for addressing these political issues. We directed the discussion and presented results in such a way that the focus-group members themselves raised the subjects of management involvement and job descriptions. Thus the members of the focus group did not become defensive about these issues and willingly discussed them.

Results

From this performance analysis, we developed a plan for a major orientation program. The program contained some of Ted's original requests but differed in many respects, particularly pointing toward a larger and defined role for managers, a self-orientation for new employees, a video to provide a consistent message, print materials to which new employees could refer, and structured department tours by managers.

Although the orientation program was an important intervention, we recommended several other interventions that could help all employees adjust to the changing corporate environment. These recommendations included the following:

- A library for manuals, a centralized location for all office system documentation, policy and procedure manuals, training manuals, guides, and the like. The library would contain one or two copies of the most up-to-date version of the documentation. Employees would always know where they could go to find a needed reference.

- A letter of acceptance (and welcoming) sent out to all new employees.

- A complete set of job descriptions.

- A human resources pool for those who want to develop career paths. When job openings occur, offices in other areas of the country would look to corporate's human resources pool prior to looking outside the company, and vice versa.

- A series of mini-seminars presented at corporate. Seminars would include the "ins and outs" of a particular department and overviews of the business, of new office systems, of the computer software, and so on. A schedule and guidelines for attending the seminars would be sent out to all employees.

Lessons Learned

Everyone involved with the analysis viewed it as a success, but all of us had thoughts about what we could have done differently, what we might not do again, and what we will use in future projects:

- Increase communication about the process ahead of time, clarifying roles and responsibilities.

- Propose the study by using key words or "hot buttons" that make the process hard to refuse. For example, a key word for management might be *productivity*. If the performance analysis is defined as "a means of determining what the new employee needs in order to be productive," or as "a means of determining the topics to be addressed so that orientation is both effective and efficient," it will sell the concept more readily.

- Keep good documentation; it is critical. Not only was documentation useful in keeping all team members (external and internal) informed, but it has a post-project purpose as well. Cora says that she still refers to information contained in the report. The documentation reminds her of changes that still need to take place as well as provides her with a database and grounding point for future projects.

- Use focus groups. The focus group for this project, in which key decision makers were gathered to discuss the findings, concerns, and possible interventions, was and is a useful tool. It ensured buy-in and provided great insights!

—Susan (Olsen) Madeira provided performance improvement consultation and development for a variety of sales and marketing organizations, including SynOptics, Apple, and Microsoft Corp. She now leads a full-time homeschooling effort.

Habla Espanol: Laura Handrick's Story

On the surface, cleaning a house seems like pretty basic stuff—you vacuum the floor, dust the furniture, and pour some of the bubbly chemical stuff in the toilet, comprendo?

The Challenge

Required updates to training materials for The Maids Home Services seemed clear from the start. I reviewed the 1960s-era industrial-looking "manuals" and 1980s videos shot in shag-carpeted homes with blond actresses sporting bright toothy smiles as they washed floors on hands and knees. The materials were out of date, out of context, overly complex, and completely unbelievable. And they had been translated into Spanish just as they were!

While corporate management agreed that the materials needed to be updated in order to uphold our assertion that "Nobody outcleans the Maids," the subject matter experts were convinced no changes should be made to the procedures. At the same time, franchise owners for The Maids Home Services were desperate for trained maids able to service their customers *now*. Franchisees were turning away business during the holiday season for lack of trained employees.

The Data

We're a home service franchisor with over 160 entrepreneurial franchise owners, who each believe they know what to do and how to handle the training. They attended twelve years or more of public education after all. That makes them experts on training.

Sometimes the best way to reconcile differences between franchisees and the franchisor, or between executives and employees, is to gather and provide contextual data about what's really happening. So a task force was formed to gather their input and buy-in, and to begin educating them on the training development process, while leveraging their point of view as a first step in determining where to start.

Because The Maids Home Services provides cleaning in teams of four, and the cleaning procedures had been refined over twenty-five years and were solidly documented, it seemed obvious to me, with twenty years of experience, that the first order of business should be training team leaders on how to train, coach, and provide feedback to their teams. I was wrong.

The franchise partners on the task force met and reviewed data we'd gathered via SurveyMonkey online surveys to confirm that most business owners and managers wanted updated videos because "the shirts are the wrong color" and "videos are easy because you can bring Maria in on Monday, sit her in front of a videotape at 8:00 and send her out with the team at 8:45!" The franchise owners preferred a training solution that looked pretty and required little to no involvement on their part. And they wanted it to work fast—so that their employees could get to work.

The Problem

Maybe you're ahead of me here, but video allows the learner to remain passive. Conversations with field managers confirmed that new hires often fell asleep during the orientation videos. Team leaders reported that the new maids slowed down existing teams and often did not show up to work the next day. Another round of SurveyMonkey data confirmed that in over 50 percent of the teams, the new team member was treated as a "burden" to the team, slowing the team down, increasing breakage and damage. The team leaders were annoyed whenever a new hire was assigned to their team!

By focusing survey questions on the business and customer impact, and using that data to enlighten decision makers, we were able to convince subject matter experts and franchise owners that good performance on the job requires a blend of training, job aids, coaching, and feedback. Our goal—that each new hire not only learns how to do the job but chooses to do it correctly in home after home because they feel that they are part of a team that cares about their success. Industrial-era manuals, while detailed and accurate, feel cold and do little to educate and motivate novices.

The Surprise

Our survey results showed that home cleaning is complex. A cleanser that can be used on tile can stain marble. Products containing bleach when dripped on carpets leave stains, stainless steel scratches easily, and wiping a wooden picture frame with a cloth that has wood polish on it can leave a greasy brown mark on the wall. We tackled the basic cleaning functions first, replacing the videos with high-definition interactive game- and video-based programs built in Lectora and hosted on an LMS. But we didn't stop there.

Because over 60 percent of our learners are non–English speaking, we added telenovelas to the mix to illustrate twenty-five of the most critical

Figure 9.2.

Figure 9.3.

Team Leader Role
Your Team Leader has a big job

The Team Leader is the first person in the home, greeting the customer (if home), inspecting for safety, picking up trash and making note of special requests.

Half-way through the clean the team leader stops to do a half-time check, ensuring the team is on-track to meet budget minutes while delivering a quality clean. Sometimes the team leader will ask one team member to assist another to keep the clean on schedule.

If mistakes are found, the Team Leader may ask you to go back and re-clean. Learn from these corrections to improve your speed and quality.

At the end of the clean, the Team Leader inspects the team's work. She'll then comb fringe, remove footprints, spray Air Fresh and complete paperwork for the clean.

Nobody Outcleans The Maids.

procedures and mistakes to avoid, and provided just-in-time job aids to allow new employees to wear their instructions on their wrist, similar to a football player's game play wrist coach (Figure 9.2). Manuals were updated, reformatted with illustrations, and provided in a searchable online format (Figure 9.3).

Then we launched a pilot. Early feedback showed that updated materials with illustrations were eagerly received by franchise partners. In one office the prototype wrist coach was so well liked that copies were made and willingly duct-taped to the new hires' arms. Learners wanted to have their procedures visible to them in whatever room they happened to be cleaning. They wanted to know which product to use to clean ceramic stovetops and which cloth to use to wipe the face of an expensive television screen. They wanted to keep up with the team and didn't want to bother their team leader with basic procedural questions. They loved the illustrated telenovelas. They appreciated video examples showing real homes, real (looking) employees, with real dirt and real problems. Cat hair on a sofa, anyone? Soap scum on a glass shower door? Dirty ceiling fan blades? Dusty wicker furniture? A common response after first viewing the online programs is, "I need to go home now and re-clean my own house!"

We made some mistakes too. The Maids Home Services has franchise offices in the United States and Canada. Latinas in Texas and Latinas in Florida come from significantly different backgrounds. Our first set of translations was outsourced to five different translators, including one from Argentina, another from Panama, and two from Mexico. We mistakenly selected for audio translations and recording a translator who was born in Mexico and raised and educated in the United States, and had served as a bilingual broadcaster on a local TV station in California. She came with high recommendations. However, when our Ecuadorian maids watched the video they were puzzled, and some giggled and turned their eyes away. We immediately reached out to bilingual field managers for their feedback on the quality of the Spanish. Comments varied, but can be summed up as "it sounds as if someone's grandma from Mexico who never went to school translated this," and "Mexican street slang," and "Spanglish." While the Latinas from Mexico could understand the general intent, non-Mexican Spanish speakers were befuddled. We redid the Spanish translations using the one translator from Panama, Lydia Burgos, who received high praise from our own Spanish-speaking team leaders. Lydia (Burgos Translations) is fluent in both English and Spanish, and educated us about language and culture variations. We got a good laugh as we realized one of our manuals had the following line translated from "shake the wood polish" to "shake the wood pollock."

A phrase in our video script was even more offensive. Instead of "straighten rug fringe" it was translated to "straighten (pubic) hairs on rug."

Even our commonly used term "regular maid service" was mistranslated to imply "ordinary (common, base) maid service" instead of "regularly scheduled maid service." If we had not gone through this piloting phase, gathered data, and improved on the basis of what we learned, we would not have known to make these significant changes.

—Laura Handrick is engaged with strategic planning and operational innovation and has direct responsibility for R&D, training, and back office operations for The Maids International.

What are the lessons we can take away from these analysts' experiences?

As adept as our storytellers were, none of these efforts was a slam dunk. Success involved planning the planning, bringing customers along slowly, and selling and marketing solutions that often differed from the customer's original scope and vision.

Share the fun. Don't let them wonder what you're doing and why, and don't be satisfied with slipping your solution in through the back door. Make it their effort. Involving your client in the analysis process can be the best way to sell your approach and solution system while fertilizing the environment for future efforts. Include all relevant stakeholders and a variety of sources. Communicate your results, provide options, and elicit input in the planning and prioritizing phases of the project to create a common vision.

10

Into the Future

In this final chapter, I look at what I see as important influences on the field of human resources and training today. My intention here is to provide brief definitions of emergent trends and then to describe how each influences planning. I focus on five trends here: the convergence of learning and work; the convergence of analysis and evaluation; relationship management; all things 2.0; and dueling views of cognitive science. Technology, that other significant force, has been discussed throughout the book.

Converging Learning and Work

No trend is more obvious today than the convergence of learning, information, and work. I wrote about it on the first page of Chapter One of this new edition.

On July 18, 2007, Elliott Masie and M. David Merrill discussed it at the Learning Strategies Conference sponsored by the U.S. Navy's Human Performance Center. Masie touted the value of what he dubbed "fingertip knowledge," in which critical content is delivered in the context of work, not in the classroom. Merrill agreed with Masie, but pointed to the differences between knowledge and information: "It is not fingertip *knowledge,*" he noted. "It is fingertip *information.*" The job of learning professionals, according to Merrill, is to create experiences that turn information into knowledge.

Dave Merrill was right. Information and knowledge are not the same. *Information,* according to many sources, is there to reduce uncertainty. We reach for it in many forms, such as documentation, posters, and performance support tools, in order to get things done, such as changing the message on an answering machine, getting money out of the ATM, and reflecting on what to do to increase the visual street appeal of a residence we are eager to sell. On the other hand, the *Oxford English Dictionary* defines *knowledge* as (1) facts, information, and skills acquired by a person through experience or education; (2) the theoretical or practical understanding of a subject; (3) what is known in a particular field or in total, facts and information; or (4) awareness or familiarity gained by experience of a fact or situation.

Both information and knowledge belong in the mix. A customer service representative couldn't serve customers without knowledge about his products and access to updated information on the corporate web site. A real estate salesperson couldn't qualify customers without knowing how to build trust with customers and easy access to mobile data, materials, and rationale, all provided on her personal digital assistant. And Uncle Harry, who has tried to stop smoking ten times in the past two decades, finally succeeds with help from the online site QuitNet. He says, "Couldn't have done it without that web site, and all their lessons, community, nagging, and online meetings."

What the employee or citizen needs is not necessarily resident inside the brain. In part, what we rely on might be located in the environment as a checklist, an online help system, a reminder, a database, an example, or even the supportive words of an online adviser or community. Support, learning, and work now occur simultaneously and seamlessly. They converge, they dwell, where they are needed, close to the task.

As you can see, information is delivered into the context that matters, while knowledge, by definition, has found its way inside the individual, into memory, in a feat typically achieved through practice, feedback, and repetition over time. That transition of information into knowledge happens through education and training.

Should all information become knowledge? Should our goal be to move information from the outside to the inside of the employee? Not all of it, not at all. We dare not ignore the importance of learning, and of serious study and commitment, where appropriate. Nicholas Carr, in a 2008 article in Atlantic.com, put it in a question: Is Google making us stupid? One task confronted by the analyst is to determine what the chef, salesperson, or service rep must know by heart and what he or she can refer to as needed.

This is an organizational imperative, greatly aided by technology. U.S. Navy Vice-Admiral (retired) Pat Tracey, in a presentation at a Navy Learning Strategies conference, made that point: "Sending our people to residence programs is not compatible with our urgent needs in the field and our human capital strategy. . . ." ASTD's *State of the Industry Report* (2007) revealed that practice is beginning to match executive urgency. More learning, information, and coaching are residing where they are required—in work and in life.

This is important to the analyst because it moves our interventions from unique and special, such as three days of study at a retreat center or a class held at the workplace or online, to an array of learning and reference options available at work. Now, in the workplace, we (and our resources) must compete. Will the engineer reach for the guidelines? Will the manager listen to the podcast? Will the new employee turn to an e-coach or an e-learning module? Will the driver take the safety self-assessment and then follow up, when a question arises? Will the sales associate add her idea to the new products blog because it might help her colleagues?

The answer to all will be yes when the assets and experiences make sense to employees, when individuals can see reasons for effort, curiosity, and generosity. Analysis provides these revelations.

Converging Analysis and Evaluation

An Accenture study in 2003 asked two hundred executives from companies in the United States, Europe, and Australia about their companies' strategic priorities. More than half said their companies never or rarely measure their training investments against employee retention, and slightly more than one-third said their companies never or rarely measure investments in human resources or training against customer satisfaction.

There is work to be done. For starters, it's critical to get a handle on what is needed, what is happening, what is not, and why. This entails using analysis to define and document meaning and need; to craft solutions systems; to make selections that intrigue people across the organization; and then to use those findings as the basis for matched, lean evaluation efforts and continuous improvement.

What we need is more and actionable metrics, not the expectations that we will sign up for dichotomous camps dubbed analysis or evaluation.

Look at the question of need. Consider the success of current efforts. Peruse a set of questions raised by reps or engineers. Examine and sort customer complaints. Is the professional conducting analysis or evaluation through these activities? In a world that has gone much beyond the classroom to a blend of learning and information assets and experiences, analysis and evaluation do not parse.

The contention here is that analysis and evaluation are more similar than different, that in many ways they are and should be identified. Let's use an example to advance the point.

> You are rolling out a program to elevate attention to decisions surrounding ethics in your global organization. The initiative was grounded in reactions to the existing ethics class, interviews with instructors, recorded ethics complaints, outcomes associated with complaints, a review of the literature, interviews with people across the organization, and an anonymous online survey that asked hard questions about drivers. The resulting program involved a self-assessment, three virtual classroom sessions, a series of podcasts, a phone reporting line, two structured lunch chats for supervisors and their employees, an in-house coach, FAQs online, and a performance support tool to assist in decision making.

As the program is deployed, data are gathered on satisfaction, use, and recommendations for improvement. The podcasts were judged as too lengthy; within ten days, they were sliced and diced into smaller, targeted bites. A virtual classroom session was added because several questions were raised and the phone line recorded a half dozen inquiries and related reports about the topic. Four new questions and answers were added to the FAQ. The onboarding process now includes an introduction to the ethics blend, because this kind of workplace-based and multimodal program turned out to be different for employees.

Look at the groundwork on that ethics program. While that effort looks like performance analysis as discussed in this book, the professional also examined feedback and results associated with existing classes. Analysis or evaluation?

Once the program went "live," data were collected in order to continuously improve it. Changes were made and new assets were added. Analysis or evaluation?

Table 10.1 compares analysis and evaluation. Sources, techniques, and approaches are the same, with analysis focused on what *ought* to be happening in means and ends—and with more emphasis during evaluation on what has *already transpired*.

But really—as we move learning and support into work, with technology as a key aspect for delivery *and* data collection, what *is* the difference? And how does that distinction deliver value?

Table 10.2 puts these ideas to work on a challenge to help convenience store salespeople improve customer service. The data gathering *and* the data gathered look similar to me. What differs is how the findings are deployed. The analyst used what is learned to create and tailor the program. The evaluator uses it to make judgments and continuously improve the effort. In both cases, these professionals use data to enlighten the sponsor and enhance decisions.

It is not a matter of first and last or front and rear. More important is continuous, pervasive, transparent, and active metrics.

Table 10.1. Close Kin: Analysis and Evaluation.

	Analysis	*Evaluation*
Purpose	*Planning* approaches. (But don't we judge in order to plan?)	*Judging* approaches (But don't we use our plans to set criteria for judging?)
Key questions	What *should* we do? What drives or blocks success or what might?	How *well* did we do it?
Why bother?	To get the right program in place for this organization at this time.	To judge *existing* efforts, to determine what *has happened*, to use data to continuously improve the effort.
From whom? From what?	Multiple sources, such as sponsors, best practices, customers, supervisors, experts, work products, results . . .	Multiple sources, such as sponsors, best practices, customers, supervisors, experts, work products, results . . .
How?	Review work products and the literature; conduct interviews, scrutinize blogs and other social resources, use surveys, test, observe, use focus groups . . .	Review work products and the literature; conduct interviews, scrutinize blogs and other social resources, use surveys, test, observe, use focus groups . . .
When?	Looking *forward*.	Looking *backward* in order to go forward.
Net	Defines and articulates promises about how things will change, get better.	Determines if promises have been fulfilled, on the basis of purposes identified during analysis, and seeks opportunities for subsequent programming.

Table 10.2. Analysis and Evaluation: Customer Service in Convenience Stores.

	Analysis	Evaluation
Purpose	I've been asked to figure out how we should boost customer service in the stores across North America.	They asked me to look at the effectiveness of the program, to judge where it is working and where not.
Key questions	Why tackle this now? What would it look like if we did this wonderfully well? What is our customer service message? Where are the opportunities to exercise great customer service? Where do we go wrong now? When it's great, why? When it isn't, why not?	How *well* did we execute the program, given the goals and objectives derived from the analysis? Does the program happen as planned? What are reps' opinions about the customer service program? Are reps doing what is expected of them? What are supervisors' opinions? What do they do? What did they fail to do? How does it affect our numbers? Customer satisfaction and purchases?
Why bother?	Yes, why? Where are we meeting goals? Where are we failing? Why? How can this program further strategic goals for the stores, such as in purchases per visit and the likelihood of repeat visits?	Look at every aspect of the program. How do we improve the existing program? Are the classes satisfying? Does the supervisory coaching happen? Does it make a difference? What about the checklists? The self-assessments?
From whom?	Multiple sources, such as sponsors, best practices, customers, supervisors, published literature, experts . . .	Multiple sources, such as sponsors, best practices, customers, supervisors, experts . . . Focus here on the incumbents. Are they using the resources? Liking them? Are they asking for more? Returning to them repeatedly?

(Continued)

Table 10.2. Analysis and Evaluation: Customer Service in Convenience Stores. (Continued)

	Analysis	*Evaluation*
How?	Review work products and the literature; conduct interviews, surveys, focus groups; use secret shoppers . . .	Review work products and the literature; conduct interviews, surveys, focus groups; use secret shoppers . . . Use technology to track opinions, visits, and forwards.
When?	Seven weeks before the program is launched, the analysis commenced.	As elements of the program are in place, data are gathered. A pilot is done in New England in six stores, and customer satisfaction, supervisory checklists, sales, and secret shoppers results are compared to matched stores in nonpilot regions.

Relationship Management

In the past, many in our business have been perceived as "order takers." That is a far cry from relationship management.

Interactions too often go like this:

Professional: Glad you called. How can I help?

Customer: Well, we're trying to cope with deregulation in the utilities industry here in California. Suddenly we're going to be tossed into an increasingly competitive environment. Our folks are tense, very tense. I was thinking that you might come on out and do some stress management workshops for us. Mindy—you know, the woman from the mentor group in ASTD—said that you did a good one-day session for her. That's what we'd like for our supervisors too, although we'd prefer the half-day class, if you have one. Our people get it pretty fast.

Professional: Sure, I do have a half-day version. Happy to help out and glad you called. When were you thinking about scheduling the sessions? Let's get out our calendars.

There is a tendency for human resources professionals to deliver just what was sought, especially when it involves something in inventory, as in the example above.

That's not good enough, a point made convincingly in Cal Wick and colleagues' 2006 book, *The Six Disciplines of Breakthrough Learning.*

A better way to approach our work is through relationship management— that is, through long-term, deep, and constant interactions with the customer and with the customer's people, context, and strategy. You are not waiting to be asked to offer a class or to help with a product rollout or to solve a problem with error rates or time management. You knew these issues were percolating because you were in the room, at the table, when opportunities and problems were discussed.

Sandy Quesada, when she served as the leader of global learning at Eli Lilly Corporation, provided an example of internal relationship management. A lean central organization, headed by Quesada, worked closely with training and development professionals residing in business units and in global regions. These professionals were inside the operating fabric of the pharmaceutical business, working side by side with researchers, sales and marketing professionals, manufacturers, information technologists, and others. Their first view was that of the line unit and the geographic areas, recognizing that what China needs now is different from what Australia and Germany require. Quesada's goal was to help them maintain that business focus, while encouraging them also to enjoy and develop the robust professional identity associated with learning, technology, and performance. Her team did this by establishing common professional development opportunities, sharing best practices, and engaging in consultation across operating units.

Relationship management should be expected of the external consultant as well. What characterizes it is the inclination to serve customer needs rather than to sell whatever it is the consultant holds in inventory. Customization is the dominant spirit. Because the external consultant has worked to gain prior knowledge of the situation and continuously "studies up" on the organization and related topics, he or she can exercise well-reasoned curiosity and skepticism. From time to time, anticipation becomes a real possibility, even for an external provider.

There is a growing body of literature nudging us toward this focus on customers, relationships, and tailored responses. The publication of *Performance Consulting* (Robinson & Robinson, 1995, and an updated second edition in 2008) encouraged movement into the mainstream under the umbrella of performance consulting. On the basis of the work of Thomas Gilbert, Robert Mager, Peter Pipe, Joe Harless, Geary Rummler, Ron Zemke, and others, and on the impetus provided by the International Society for Performance Improvement and their CPT certification, internal trainers and human resources professionals and external consultants began to rethink and expand their roles. This emphasis has been ably advanced by ASTD in its CPLP certification.

The performance consultant and the instructional designer with a performance consulting viewpoint ground decisions in performance analysis. Analysis serves as the foundation and the glue for a profession and a perspective that demands study before recommendations, data before decisions, and involvement before actions.

Alice Cutter strongly advocates using a governance model within a learning organization. This model, which utilizes one or more employee committees across the organization, ensures accountability. Governance committees are particularly useful in firms that want to structure learning in an organized and standardized way. This model "brings consistency and reduces redundancy," creating a brand for learning.

Alice has seen numerous variations of the governance model succeed within many organizations and industries. She emphasizes that the model is never a hard sell; rather, people get excited about their involvement and they genuinely enjoy knowing about learning and performance initiatives. In the last governance model that Alice worked with, the committees were structured as follows:

1. An executive-level steering committee to guide strategic direction, as well as high-level oversight of learning and performance projects. The steering committee included the chief operating officer and that person's direct reports. These individuals come from *outside* the learning function and represent the operational and functional areas of the organization.

2. Regional and divisional councils offered practical advice and guidance for learning and performance initiatives. These councils were composed of

training leaders from within each region and division. The *regional training leaders* were field representatives of the learning function, and they helped to ensure the best way to implement and execute any learning initiatives. Both the regional and divisional training councils became huge advocates for the corporate learning initiatives.

Alice explains that responsibilities of governance committees vary depending upon the organizations they serve. Often, learning and development employees conduct performance analyses and training needs assessments. The committees then validate findings, solidify competencies, or offer alternative perspectives. Alice points out that the committees also set priorities when analysis reveals multiple possible performance solutions or learning products. Limited resources require careful decision making and planning. Governance committees provide an extra layer of assurance when making those decisions.

Governance councils can have an impact on both content and implementation details for learning projects. The councils can identify subject matter experts (SMEs) to create real-life situations for simulations as well as context that rings true with learners. Learning becomes authentic when "committees introduce reality," Alice states. They also offer guidance regarding the best and most effective way to roll out a project. "Committees have been extremely helpful in determining implementation time frames. If we have a rollout scheduled at a bad time—if something big is going on in the field—the councils let us know and we can immediately adjust schedules accordingly." In turn, council representatives see that corporate learning and development wants to work with frontline employees and be good stewards of organizational resources. The council carries that back to the front line, creating buy-in.

Governance committees can do many things, but Alice asserts that the most important thing they do is "help you realize the business need for *everything* that you do."

Alice Cutter currently works as the senior director of learning and development at Time Warner Cable. She has been involved in instructional design for more than three decades, including a stint as a partner of a small instructional design and strategy consulting firm. Alice began her working life as a commercial photographer, but after designing her first photography curriculum she knew even then that she wanted to help people learn. You can reach Alice at alice.cutter@twcable.com.

All Things 2.0

While a few do not like the 2.0 designation (see George Siemens [www
.elearnspace.org]), there is agreement that something significant is up, and
that the concepts are important and growing more so. Howard Jarche, in the
April 2008 *Learning Circuits,* defined 2.0 this way: "Web 2.0 is the growing
set of tools and processes that allows anyone to easily create digital content
and collaborate with others without any special programming skills."

Look at 2.0 in relation to the 1.0 world from which the first edition of
this book came. In the 1.0 world, knowledge, information, attitudes, views,
and experiences are captured by professionals through surveys, interviews, and
focus groups. The world that is 2.0 changes things as employees, customers,
and the rest of us seize the means to talk amongst ourselves through blogs,
wikis, and other community forms. Motorola customers get together online
to talk about how they are using their new Q phone. JetBlue instructors share
ideas about how to increase the power of their messages. Owners of standard
poodles find each other to appreciate their breed. And Army captains sta-
tioned in Iraq provide each other with up-to-the-minute advice about enemy
movements in alleys and kids' candy preferences. If you want to know what's
going on, and analysts must be in the know, all things 2.0 have value for us.

Every analyst must seek answers to questions such as these: How do we
tease the subtle know-how and perspectives from, for example, a contracts
administrator about strategies for maintaining productive and peaceful relationships with both the salesforce and the legal staff? How do we help her
describe the many things she considers and does, of which she isn't even
aware? In addition, how do we ensure that a steady flow of explicit customer
information is finding its way into databases so that, say, any salesperson
visiting Costco is familiar with the terms of its most current contracts and
formal and informal conversations? How do we find what it is that savvy
salespeople or responsive customer service reps or effective security personnel know? How do we make certain that the information reflects not just
the obvious but also the more subtle and cultural aspects that are essential to
success? How do we make it available to more people, so they can add their
views? How do we ensure that the information is refreshed? And how do we
make certain that it is easily located at the moment of need?

The answers to these questions are important to the organization and its people. Thomas Stewart (1997, p. 111) quotes Charles Paulk of Andersen Consulting on knowledge management: "When one of our consultants shows up, the client should get the best of the firm, not just the best of the consultant." When a professional contributes to Paulk's goal, he or she is nurturing a learning organization. Such an entity treasures its intellectual capital, encourages sharing not hoarding, and values teams more than individual stars. Pursuing knowledge stimulates additional questions, adds new sources, and ensures that those who know are helping those who do not. The analyst who uses 2.0 looks beyond the classroom to diverse ways for collecting, maintaining, honoring, and stirring up expertise.

2.0 is more than smarts *and* more than community. It is both. It is a great source for information, both explicit and tacit, that resides in the organization and its people. While 1.0 generates much that is seen as authoritative, 2.0 yields content that is natural, democratic, and timely. Analysts use both.

Dueling Views of Cognition

Although all practitioners can name the behaviorist B. F. Skinner, it is much harder to get a handle on the cognitivists. As Rita Richey (1986) of Wayne State University points out, cognitivists talk about many things: the readiness of the learner; organization of knowledge, most particularly mental models, or schemata, that people construct to represent what they know; insight; the relationship between computers and intelligence; short-term memory and strategies for ensuring storage and retrieval in long-term memory; individual perspectives on the material or job; and creating meaning by attaching new material to what is already familiar and useful. To all this John Keller (1983) of Florida State added the issue of motivation, a topic of great importance because of the convergence of learning, information, and work via technology. When there is no compelling instructor or concerned supervisor, what's going on inside the employee influences whether or not he or she will double-click on the web site or look in on the blog.

What are the implications of cognitive science for the analyst? First, cognitive science turns our attention inside learners, toward their eagerness, readiness, and enthusiasm. You can ask directly, of course, or look to their web presence. What engages them? Into what do they inquire? About what do they comment? Now that employees are no longer considered to be impenetrable "black boxes," front-end inquiry expands to include how individuals perceive the change, opportunity, or problem.

Second, you must "find" the subject matter, usually during the more expansive training needs assessment. You will be concerned with constructing the skeleton or scaffolding for the content and then adding meat to those bones through interactions with expert sources. Beyond a focus on what effective people do is the need to unearth what the star performer knows, considers, and thinks about. Cognitive science propels us to ask questions about the perspectives of able people as they approach their work. Finally, you must attend to employees' cognitive and metacognitive strategies. This expands the analysis to inquiry about the learning history and proclivities of employees and about their ability to manage their own growth and development. Again, independent and workplace-based learning and reference relies on knowing that your people are eager and able to go it alone, and that their supervisors will nudge, when necessary. A cognitive perspective has been represented throughout this book in the nature of the questions sprinkled throughout the tables.

There are two flavors of cognitivism. The first is objectivist. Famous objectivist cognitivists are Dave Merrill and author of this book's Preface, Ruth Clark. In a nutshell, they believe that you can and should derive and define outcomes. Such outcomes would come from the answers to the questions about what savvy performers think about, how they decided. The constructivists, in contrast, doubt the wisdom of articulating outcomes. Whereas an objectivist would present ideas, examples, practices, and feedback, a constructivist would provide access to examples and encourage employees to derive meaning independently.

With roots in John Dewey and Jerome Bruner, constructivists favor experiences that help individuals construct their own answers. This position is articulated by the University of Missouri's Dave Jonassen. While performance analysts labor to tame assets and experiences, Jonassen, in a 2001 interview in elearningpost, doubts it is possible: "Every amateur epistemologist knows that knowledge cannot be managed. Education has always assumed that knowledge can be transferred and that we can carefully control the process through education. That is a grand illusion."

Let's look at an example of a typical requirement. It is easy to imagine an executive saying, "We want managers to become better at dealing with conflict. We think we'd like to offer a class, or something, and maybe some individual coaching sessions. Please get back to me about this."

To make the point, I'll exaggerate a bit. The objectivist's performance analysis might look this: he would attempt to broadly define optimal outcomes associated with handling conflict. What would it look like if managers were in fact better at dealing with conflict? How does the literature summarize the challenges and approaches to conflict management? Are there a few acceptable and effective ways we wish to tout? How does an effective manager think about conflict, about getting positive outcomes from it and reducing the negatives that can result? What kinds of situations come up in which managers need this bag of skills? Where do they tend to mess up?

The objectivist would also seek barriers to successful performance. Why don't managers handle it well now? What gets in their way? What would it take for them to do it more effectively? How do managers feel about this aspect of their work? Answers to these questions would yield a set of outcomes and the drivers associated with them. Then it would be possible to put a solution system in place, including attaching a training needs assessment to those goals that involve skill, knowledge, and motivational concerns.

A constructivist would use analysis differently. Her approach might concentrate on finding numerous examples in the organization and seeking commentary to wrap around those examples. Whereas the objectivist would home in on the common core of attributes associated with a robust and perhaps standard way of approaching conflict, the constructivist is looking for instances and options. They become the grist for each individual's experience with handling conflict. This analyst might also use that planning time to establish a rubric that would enable individuals to self-assess their conflict management skills or to observe others in action. The purpose isn't to learn the right way to do it—according to the organization or an expert—but rather to construct a personally useful and realistic approach based on examples and commentary.

Although few organizations have signed up for full-dress constructivist approaches, these perspectives are influential. They lead to more learner control, multiple perspectives, no one right answer, inductive learning and performance processes and experiences, and active involvement by employees in finding answers for themselves for authentic challenges in their world of work. When I examine the earlier conflict management example, I see strengths in the objectivist *and* constructivist approaches. Wouldn't you be inclined to incorporate both in your planning and delivery? I would.

The roadblock for constructivism in most organizations comes from constructivists' reluctance regarding standard organizational approaches, established outcomes or objectives, and evaluation devices based on them. It took years for our profession to sell the importance of being clear about intentions, in performance terms, so that meaningful, targeted practice and measurement can occur. Although the constructivists make many good points, to revisit these issues in a way that might undo years of effort is counterproductive.

Allison: Well, that's it. Finito. I sure hope the book is helpful. When you work on something for this long, you get to wondering—and worrying.

Allison: Maybe it isn't helpful enough. Maybe I should rewrite Chapter Three, and take another whack at Chapter Six. I've wanted to redo Chapter . . .

Allison: I'll read it one more time. Get one more friend in the business to tell me what they think.

Allison: Enough already. Like you've said about analysis, and reiterated regarding constructivist approaches, there is no one right answer, no single silver bullet, and of course, no perfect book either. Enough is enough. Wrap it up. Say good-bye. Make it perfect in the next edition.

Allison: OK, OK. 'Bye.

WE TAKE TOO LONG. We don't focus on solutions. We're engulfed in "analysis paralysis." Sound familiar? It should; we've been hearing this for decades. We want to study a problem to be sure we address it in the least costly, most effective manner. We want to get it completely right, the first time, yet this admirable goal may not be the right approach for us in an increasingly "I need it now" world. In an era of constant speed and continuous change, should our approach to analysis also change?

Our field was born of linear thinking, the so-called systematic process. We lived and breathed ADDIE (Analysis, Design, Development, Implementation, and Evaluation) as *the* way we did our work. We didn't move on to the next phase of the process until we got sign-off on the previous one. So we studied the situation to be sure we could justify what's next and, in today's uncertain job market, so that we also didn't make a mistake. And we relied almost exclusively on subject matter experts to verify our findings, even when those experts were divorced from real users. We asked executives to bless our analysis, and we jumped through all kinds of hoops when they asked us to prove that what we would do would yield fabulous benefits, even before we had an opportunity to test it out.

We're also sometimes guilty of using analysis to justify the solution du jour. We've often been seduced by the latest technology, although new technology is not, in and of itself, a bad thing. In fact, new technologies for delivering learning—*and analyzing learning needs*—have many benefits and much promise. But our desire, and often the desire of our clients, to dive into the next great technology, sometimes blindly, can have an impact on our assessment of the problem at hand. When e-learning is mandated, we too often define a problem in a way e-learning can address. When the push is for more performance support, amazingly, more of our analyses seem to indicate that performance support is the way to go. Surprise, surprise.

It's time to rethink analysis. It's time to move away from a linear approach and a lockstep way of creating learning solutions. Analysis is no longer "step one," or any step for that matter. It is integrated into a way of thinking about learning design that is more of a spiral than a straight line. We look at a problem, listen to a lot of voices, gather the best intelligence we can, and then propose a solution, first as an idea, and then increasingly as a prototype, knowing full well that we'll get some of it wrong. We'll get feedback and rework our assumptions, collect new data, and build closer and closer approximations of the optimal solution. We'll discuss, propose, test, and evaluate technologies and refine as we go. We'll take analysis and evaluation and superimpose them; they go hand-in-hand. Every analysis finding drives an evaluation strategy, and every evaluation effort tells us how to sharpen our analysis. So not only does analysis evolve throughout a project, evaluation does as well. And we'll have our clients and users (learners), as well as experts, involved every step of the way.

We need to push back when asked to prove, before the fact, that our solution will *guarantee* a specific result. There are no guarantees, but if we do our work right, we can reasonably suggest an outcome, test that outcome on a small scale, and refine as we go, catching mistakes early, when they are more easily fixed. We'll convince management to support smaller demonstration projects, based on facts and reasonableness, but also on curiosity and faith, so that we can model and test a solution that can be scaled after we learn more about it. If we take more of a "new product development" approach to analysis and design of learning solutions, perhaps starting with some "consumer" research, then brainstorming, then moving on to modeling and mock-ups, all the while collecting data and getting feedback from key stakeholders—and do it fast—we stand a far better chance of finding the organizational support and funding we need.

When we approach learning analysis, evaluation, design, development, and implementation in this way, we create a vision of a solution that people can touch, a "picture" that they can more easily form in their mind of what the endgame will be. We satisfy that enduring need to "see it" and "try it" before we "buy it." And we begin to truly meet the needs of our clients not just through the language of learning, but increasingly in the business language and context *they* live and work in every day. We demonstrate that we understand their pain, and, because of this, they become more willing to invest—and trust—in us.

This investment need not be limited to traditional solutions. If we want to employ new technologies and approaches, what better way to sell their benefits than to allow our clients to see models and prototypes in action? Our traditional assumption, that clients only want what they've always wanted ("I want a course because a course is all I know") crumbles when they start to see the efficiencies and effectiveness of new ways of doing things. Most clients are pragmatists; they just want their problems solved. Show them (don't just tell them) a better way, even if it's not perfect, and they'll likely follow. Done right, it can be all downhill from there.

> "Truly successful decision making relies on a balance between deliberate and instinctive thinking."
>
> Malcolm Gladwell, *Blink: The Power of Thinking Without Thinking*, 2005

In the end, the new view of analysis, indeed the new view of learning design and development, is a delicate give-and-take between research and action, individual conviction and group consensus, architecture and construction, speed and quality, and evidence and "gut." No flowchart, tool, procedure, or process gets us there by itself. Recognizing that no two situations are ever quite the same, collaboration, ideation, risk taking, flexibility, and a willingness to learn as you go are equally essential, if not more so. The challenge for us all is to use our ever-increasing experience and wisdom to consistently pick the right blend of approaches—the right route—each time we navigate the journey. With swiftness and responsiveness as the increasingly overarching criteria of our work, we have no choice.

Marc J. Rosenberg, Ph.D.
October 2008

Dr. Marc J. Rosenberg (www.marcrosenberg.com) is a management consultant, educator, and leading expert in the world of training, organizational learning, e-learning, knowledge management, and performance improvement. He is the author of two books, the best-selling *E-Learning: Strategies for Delivering Knowledge in the Digital Age* (McGraw-Hill, 2001) and *Beyond E-Learning: Approaches and Technologies to Enhance Organizational Knowledge, Learning, and Performance* (Pfeiffer, 2006).

Allen, M. (2008). *Michael Allen's e-learning annual 2008.* San Francisco: Pfeiffer.

Argyris, C. (1990). *Overcoming organizational defenses.* Needham Heights, MA: Allyn & Bacon.

Argyris, C. (1993). *Knowledge for action: A guide to overcoming barriers to organizational change.* San Francisco: Jossey-Bass.

ASTD. (2007). *State of the industry report.* Alexandria, VA: ASTD.

Bailey-Hughes, B. (1997, May 14). Implementing survey results [13 paragraphs]. [Online]. Available: ftp://ftp.cac.psu.edu/pub/people/cxl18/summary/Implementing.

Bandura, A. (1977). Self-efficacy: Toward a unifying theory of behavioral change. *Psychological Review, 84,* 191–215.

Barwise, P., & Meehan, S. (2008, April). So you think you're a good listener. *Harvard Business Review, 86*(4), 22.

Benjamin, S. (1989). A closer look at needs analysis and needs assessment: Whatever happened to the systems approach? *Performance and Instruction, 28*(9), 12–16.

Berk, J. (2004, June). The state of learning analytics. *Training and Development, 58*(6), 34–39.

Bolman, L. G., & Deal, T. E. (1991). *Reframing organizations: Artistry, choice, and leadership.* San Francisco: Jossey-Bass.

Bridges, W. (1991). *Managing transitions.* Reading, MA: Addison-Wesley.

Brynjolfsson, E., & Hitt, L. (1996, September 9). The customer counts. *Information Week, 596,* 48–54.

Carlisle, K. (1986). *Job and task analysis.* Englewood Cliffs, NJ: Educational Technology Publications.

Carr, N. (2008, July–August). Is Google making us stupid? *The Atlantic.* Retrieved online September 15, 2008. Available: http://www.theatlantic .com/doc/200807/google.

Collis, D. J., & Montgomery, C. A. (2008, July–August). Best of HBR. Competing on resources. *Harvard Business Review, 86*(7/8), 140–150.

Connor, D. R. (1993). *Managing at the speed of change.* New York: Villard Books.

Crovitz, L. G. (2008, May 5, A13). Internet says: Me wants cookie. *Wall Street Journal.* Retrieved online May 6, 2008. Available: http://online.wsj .com/article/SB120994540824466285.html.

Davenport, T. H., & Prusak, L. (1998). *Working knowledge: How organizations manage what they know.* Boston: Harvard Business School Press.

Dean, P. (1996). Editorial: From where come performances in performance technology? *Performance Improvement Quarterly, 9*(2), 1–2.

Dean, P. J., & Ripley, D. E. (Eds.). (1998). *Performance improvement pathfinders: Models for organizational learning systems.* Washington, DC: ISPI.

Dennen, V. P., & Branch, R. C. (1995). *Considerations for designing instructional virtual environments.* (ERIC Document Reproduction Service No. ED 391 489).

Dlugan, A. (2008). *Six Minutes*: A public speaking and presentation skills blog. [Online]. Available: http://sixminutes.dlugan.com/.

Duarte, Nancy (2008). *slide:ology: The Art and Science of Creating Great Presentations*. Available: http://blog.duarte.com/. The author's company helped create Al Gore's presentation in *An Inconvenient Truth*.

elearningpost. (2001, January 31). Exclusive interview with Dave Jonassen. Retrieved September 15, 2008. Available: http://www.elearningpost.com/articles/archives/exclusive_interview_with_professor_david_jonassen/

Evans, B. (2008). Agents of change: A review of C. K. Prahalad and M. S. Krishnan's new book, *The New Age of Innovation. Information Week Research & Reports*. Retrieved May 8, 2008. Available: http://www.informationweek.com/news/business_intelligence/bpm/showArticle.jhtml?articleID=207100773.

Evans, P. B., & Wurster, T. S. (1997, September–October). Strategy and the new economics of information. *Harvard Business Review, 75*(5), 71–82.

Fulop, M., Loop-Bartick, K., & Rossett, A. (1997, July). Using the World Wide Web to conduct a needs assessment. *Performance Improvement, 36*(6), 22–27.

Gilbert, T. (1978). *Human competence: Engineering worthy performance*. New York: McGraw-Hill.

Graves, A. (2008, July 11). The boomer exodus: Ready to pass the torch? *HR World*. Available: http://www.hrworld.com/features/trendwatcher-boomer-exodus-071108/.

Gustafson, K. L., & Branch, R. M. (1997). *Survey of instructional development models* (3rd ed.). Syracuse, NY: ERIC Clearinghouse of Information and Technology.

Hamel, G., & Prahalad, C. K. (1994). *Competing for the future*. Cambridge, MA: Harvard Business School Press.

Hamilton, E. (1993). *The Greek way*. New York: Norton.

Hammer, M., & Champy, C. (1993). *Reengineering the corporation*. New York: HarperCollins.

Harless, J. H. (1975). *An ounce of analysis is worth a pound of objectives*. Newnan, GA: Harless Performance Guild.

Harrison, M. I. (1987). *Diagnosing organizations.* Thousand Oaks, CA: Sage.

Hart, I. (1997, March). ITForum Paper. In *Instructional Technology Research.* [Online]. Available: http://www2.gsu.edu/~wwwitr/docs/qual/index. html#Paper.

Hatcher, T., & Ward, S. E. (1997). Framing: A method to improve performance analyses. *Performance Improvement Quarterly, 10*(3), 84–103.

Helm, B. (2008, June 16). Online polls: How good are they? *Businessweek,* 86–87.

Hertzberg, H. (1998, January 5). The Narcissus survey. *New Yorker,* 27–29.

Jarche, H. (2008, April). Skills 2.0. *Training + Development.*

Jonassen, D. H. (1991). Objectivism vs. constructivism: Do we need a new philosophical paradigm? *Educational Technology Research and Development, 39,* 5–14.

Jonassen, D. H. (Ed.). (1996). *Handbook of research for educational communications and technology.* Old Tappan, NJ: Macmillan.

Juran, J. M. (1986, May). The quality trilogy. *Quality Progress,* 19–24.

Kelle, U. (Ed.). (1995). *Computer-aided qualitative data analysis.* Thousand Oaks, CA: Sage.

Keller, J. M. (1983). Motivational design of instruction. In C. M. Reigeluth (Ed.), *Instructional design theories and models: An overview of their current status* (pp. 335–382). Hillsdale, NJ: Erlbaum.

Kittleson, M. J. (1995). An assessment of the response rate via the postal service and e-mail. *Journal of Health Values, 18,* 27–29.

Kosslyn, Stephen M. (2007). *Clear and to the Point: 8 Psychological Principles for Compelling PowerPoint Presentations.* Oxford, UK: Oxford University Press.

Kotler, P., & Andreasen, A. (1987). *Strategic marketing for non-profit organizations* (3rd ed.). Engelwood Cliffs, NJ: Prentice Hall.

Lewis, T., & Bjorkquist, D. C. (1992). Needs assessment—a critical reappraisal. *Performance Improvement Quarterly, 5*(4), 33–53.

Mager, R. M. (1970). *Goal analysis.* Belmont, CA: Pitman Learning.

Mager, R. M. (1984). *Measuring instructional intent.* Belmont, CA: Pitman Learning.

Mager, R. M., & Pipe, P. (1984). *Analyzing performance problems.* Belmont, CA: Pitman Learning.

Mehta, R., & Sivadas, E. (1995). Comparing response rates and response content in mail versus electronic mail surveys. *Journal of the Market Research Society, 37,* 429–439.

Meister, J. (2008, May 13). *Jet Blue University Uses Own Faculty to Test Social Media Tools.* [Online]. Available: http://newlearningplaybook.com/blog/2008/05/13/jet-blue-university-uses-own-faculty-to-test-social-media-tools.

Merriam, S. B. (1998). *Qualitative research and case study applications in education.* San Francisco: Jossey-Bass.

Miles, M., & Huberman, A. M. (1984). *Qualitative data analysis.* Thousand Oaks, CA: Sage.

Patton, M. Q. (1987). *How to use qualitative methods in evaluation.* Thousand Oaks, CA: Sage.

Prahalad, C. K. & Krishnan, M. S. (2008). *New age of innovation.* New York: McGraw-Hill.

Rapaport, R. (1996, April–May). The network is the company. *Fast Company, 2,* 116–121.

Richey, R. C. (1986). *The theoretical and conceptual bases of instructional design.* London: Kogan Page.

Robinson, D. G., & Robinson, J. C. (2008). *Performance consulting* (2nd ed.). San Francisco: Berrett-Koehler.

Rodgers, E. M. (1983). *Diffusion of innovations* (3rd ed.). New York: Free Press.

Rodriguez, S. R. (1988). Needs assessment and analysis: Tools for change. *Journal of Instructional Development, 11*(1), 23–28.

Rosenberg, M. J. (1990, February). Performance technology working the system. *Training, 27*(2), 42–48.

Rosenberg, M. J. (2006). *Beyond e-learning: Approaches and technologies to enhance organizational knowledge, learning, and performance.* San Francisco: Pfeiffer.

Rosling, H. (2006). *Six Simple Techniques for Presenting Data: Hans Rosling (TED, 2006).* [Online]. Available: http://sixminutes.dlugan .com/2008/01/09/six-simple-techniques-for-presenting-data-hans-rosling-ted-2006.

Rossett, A. (1987). *Training needs assessment.* Englewood Cliffs, NJ: Educational Technology Publications.

Rossett, A. (1990, March). Overcoming obstacles to needs assessment. *Training, 27*(3), 36–41.

Rossett, A. (1996, March). Training and organizational development: Siblings separated at birth. *Training, 33*(4), 53–59.

Rossett, A. (1997, July). That was a great class, but . . . *Training and Development, 51*(7), 18–24.

Rossett, A., & Barnett, J. (1996, December). Designing under the influence: Instructional design for multimedia training. *Training, 33*(12), 33–43.

Rossett, A., & Czech, C. (1996). They really wanna but . . . The aftermath of professional preparation in performance technology. *Performance Improvement Quarterly, 8*(4), 114–132.

Rossett, A., & Downes-Gautier, J. H. (1991). *Handbook of job aids.* San Francisco: Jossey-Bass.

Rossett, A., & Schafer, L. (2007). *A handbook of job aids and performance support: Moving from knowledge in the classroom to knowledge everywhere.* San Francisco: John Wiley & Sons.

Rossett, A., & Williams, J. (2008, June). Performance analysis and Web 2.0. *Learning Circuits.* [Online]. Available: http://www.learningcircuits. org/0608_rossett.html.

Rummler, G. A. (1986). Organization redesign. In *National Society for Performance and Instruction, Introduction to Performance Technology.* Washington, DC: National Society for Performance and Instruction.

Rummler, G. A., & Brache, A. P. (1990). *Improving performance: How to manage the white space on the organization chart.* San Francisco: Jossey-Bass.

Schein, E. H. (1992). *Organizational culture and leadership* (2nd ed.). San Francisco: Jossey-Bass.

Seels, B., & Glasgow, Z. (1998). *Making instructional design decisions.* Columbus, OH: Merrill.

Senge, P. M. (1990). *The fifth discipline: The art and practice of the learning organization.* New York: Doubleday.

Sitzmann, T. M., Brown, K. G., Casper, W. J., Zimmerman, R., & Polliard, C. (2008). A meta-analysis of the nomological network of trainee reactions. *Journal of Applied Psychology, 93,* 280–295.

Sherman, R., & Webb, R. (1988). *Qualitative research in education.* London: Falmer.

Sleezer, C. M. (1993). Training needs assessment at work: A dynamic process. *Human Resource Development Quarterly, 4*(3), 247–264.

Stelter, B. (2008, July 25). Griping online? Cable company hears you and talks right back. *The New York Times.* A1, 16.

Stewart, T. A. (1997). *Intellectual capital: The new wealth of organizations.* New York: Doubleday.

Stolovitch, H. D. (2008, April). *The impact of expertise on the practice of performance technology and professional development.* Presentation at ISPI in New York City.

Stolovitch, H. D., & Keeps, E. J. (Eds.). (1992). *Handbook of human performance technology: A comprehensive guide for analyzing and solving performance problems in organizations.* San Francisco: Jossey-Bass.

Stone, D., Blomberg, S., & Villachica, S. (2008, April). *Using CTA (cognitive task analysis) to capture expert decision making and problem solving.* Presentation at ISPI in New York City.

Strauss, A., & Corbin, J. (1990). *Basics of qualitative research.* Thousand Oaks, CA: Sage.

Strauss, A., Schatzman, L., Bucher, R., and Sabshin, M. (1981). *Psychiatric ideologies and institutions.* New Brunswick, NJ: Transaction.

Strayer, J., & Rossett, A. (1994). Coaching sales performance: A case study. *Performance Improvement Quarterly, 7*(4), 39–53.

Svenson, R. A., & Rinderer, M. J. (1992). *The training and development strategic plan workbook.* Englewood Cliffs, NJ: Prentice-Hall.

Swanson, R. A. (1994). *Analysis for improving performance: Tools for diagnosing organizations and documenting workplace expertise.* San Francisco: Berrett-Koehler.

Thach, L. (1995). Using electronic mail to conduct survey research. *Educational Technology, 35,* 27–31.

This year's top IT users. (1996, September 9). *Information Week, 596,* 60–69.

Tufte, E. R. (2001). *The visual display of quantitative information.* Cheshire, CT: Graphics Press.

VizThink, http://www.vizthink.com/, is gathering visual thinkers from all corners of the world to create the first global community dedicated to the use of visualization in all forms of learning and communication.

Wademan, M. R., Spuches, C. M., & Doughty, P. L. (2007). The People Capability Maturity Model: Its approach and potential to improve workforce performance. *Performance Improvement Quarterly, 20*(1), 97–124.

Wick, C., Pollock, R., Jefferson, A., & Flanagan, R. (2006). *The six disciplines of breakthrough learning.* San Francisco: Pfeiffer.

Wildstrom, S. (1997, June 2). Desktop video: No longer a toy. *Business Week, 22,* n3529.

Witkin, R., & Altschuld, J. W. (1995). *Planning and conducting needs assessments: A practical guide.* Thousand Oaks, CA: Sage.

Zemke, R. (1998, March). How to do a needs assessment when you think you don't have time. *Training, 35*(3), 38–44.

Zemke, R., & Kramlinger, T. (1982). *Figuring things out: A trainer's guide to needs and task analysis.* Reading, MA: Addison-Wesley.

INDEX

Blended learning readiness example:
   (continued)
   qualitative data on, 189–190; on
   organizational, 185, 189; reporting results
   on, 186*e*–188*e*; results on employees, 183,
   184*t*; results on supervisors, 183, 185*t*;
   what we learned about, 182
Blogs (weblogs): data mining, 160–161;
   description of, 160
Boeing, 43, 103
Brache, A., 191
Brinkerhoff, R., 16, 17
British Petroleum, 31
Bruner, J., 254
Bryant, T., 230, 231, 233
Bucher, R., 117
Burgos, L., 238
Bush, S., 63
Businessweek magazine, 154

C

Carnegie Mellon University, 43
Carr, N., 243
Case studies: Charlotte Donaldson's banking
   vignettes, 203, 204–209; Chris Hall's
   Coast Guard SLDMB adoption, 203,
   217–220; Kendra Sheldon's computers in
   classrooms stories, 203, 209–213; Laura
   Handrick's The Maids Home Services
   story, 203, 234–239; lessons learned from
   the, 239; Shirley Gresham's failure
   investigation using performance analysis,
   203, 221–229; summary of, 203–204;
   Susan Madeira's look at manager
   orientation, 203, 229–234; Terry
   Bickham's commercial fishing story, 203,

213–217. *See also* External consultants;
   Performance analysis examples
Century 21 International, 23, 44
Chan, A., 94–95
Cincinnati, University of, 151
Cisco, 157
Clark, R., 13, 254
Clay, C., 230, 231, 232
Clinton, B., 55
Coast Guard. *See* U.S. Coast Guard
Cognitive science: implications for the
   analyst, 253–254; objectivist and
   constructivist schools of, 254–256;
   relevant perspectives and issues of, 253
Comcast, 160–161
Commercial fishing industry case study, 203,
   213–217
Communication: with each decision maker,
   39; principles for effective, 127–133,
   136–145; South African case study on,
   134–135; threats to, 140*t*. *See also* Email
   communication
Communication principles: 1. know your
   sources, 127–128; 2. be authentic, 128,
   136–137, 138*t*; 3. remember that
   performance analysis may be perceived as
   threatening, 137, 139–141; 4. emphasize
   planning, 141–145
Confidentiality issues, 152–153
Consultants. *See* External consultants
"Cookies," 152–153
Costco, 252
CPLP certification, 250
CPT certification, 250
Crovitz, L. G., 152, 153
"Culture of suspicion," 152

Reporting results: *(continued)*
   guidelines for effective, 190, 199–201;
   providing materials for customers on, 201;
   template for report format, 192*e*–199*e*. *See
   also* Meaning construction
Richey, R., 253
Robinson, D., 13, 37, 49, 50, 62, 250
Robinson, J., 37, 49, 50, 62, 250
Rollout: description as opportunity, 70;
   Floyd's operating system, 97*t*; performance
   analysis focus on, 76*t*, 79; performance
   analysis stages for addressing, 79, 83, 84*t*;
   rationales as, 71*t*
Rosenberg, M. J., 13, 260
Rossett, A., 23, 29, 51, 56, 91, 163,
   224, 225
RSS (Real Simple Subscription), 160
Rummler, G., 13, 191, 250

S

Sabshin, M., 117
SAIC (Science Applications International
   Corporation), 29, 55
San Diego State University, 37
Schafer, L., 56
Schatzman, L., 117
Scott, A., 26
Search and Rescue (SAR): Coast Guard
   mission of, 217; SLDMB adoption for,
   203, 217–220
Second Life, 3
Senge, P., 60, 107
Sheldon, K., 203, 209–213
Siemens, G., 252
Silver bullet, 28–29
Sivadas, E., 151, 152

Six Degrees Company, 4
The Six Disciplines of Breakthrough Learning
   (Wick and colleagues), 21, 249
Six Sigma, 226
Skills, knowledge, information: as
   performance drivers, 55–56, 62*t*; solutions
   matched with, 64*t*–65*t*. *See also*
   Information
Skinner, B. F., 253
SLDMB (Self-Locating Data Marker Buoy),
   203, 217–220
Smith, K., 26
Social networking: data mining sites for,
   161–163; LearningTown, 162; NING, 91;
   Twittering, 104
Software Engineering Institute (Carnegie
   Mellon University), 43
Solution partner perspective, 132*t*
Solution systems: analysis report section on,
   196*e*–197*e*; drivers matched with,
   64*t*–65*t*; IBM approach to, 63, 66*t*;
   performance analysis yielding
   recommendations for, 46*t*; performance
   drivers as defining, 63–66*t*; silver bullet
   versus, 28–29; Solution System Self-
   Check, 30*e*
Speed performance analysis: concerns about,
   11*t*, 109–110; issues to consider in,
   15–17; strategies for shaving time off,
   96–108; summary of methods for, 111.
   See also Performance analysis (PA)
Speed performance analysis strategies:
   1. clarify the effort, 96–99; 2. repurpose
   existing data, 99–102; 3. use "straw"
   approach to gathering data, 102–104,
   106–107; 4. establish hypotheses and test

Pfeiffer Publications Guide

This guide is designed to familiarize you with the various types of Pfeiffer publications. The formats section describes the various types of products that we publish; the methodologies section describes the many different ways that content might be provided within a product. We also provide a list of the topic areas in which we publish.

FORMATS

In addition to its extensive book-publishing program, Pfeiffer offers content in an array of formats, from fieldbooks for the practitioner to complete, ready-to-use training packages that support group learning.

FIELDBOOK Designed to provide information and guidance to practitioners in the midst of action. Most fieldbooks are companions to another, sometimes earlier, work, from which its ideas are derived; the fieldbook makes practical what was theoretical in the original text. Fieldbooks can certainly be read from cover to cover. More likely, though, you'll find yourself bouncing around following a particular theme, or dipping in as the mood, and the situation, dictate.

HANDBOOK A contributed volume of work on a single topic, comprising an eclectic mix of ideas, case studies, and best practices sourced by practitioners and experts in the field.

An editor or team of editors usually is appointed to seek out contributors and to evaluate content for relevance to the topic. Think of a handbook not as a ready-to-eat meal, but as a cookbook of ingredients that enables you to create the most fitting experience for the occasion.

RESOURCE Materials designed to support group learning. They come in many forms: a complete, ready-to-use exercise (such as a game); a comprehensive resource on one topic (such as conflict management) containing a variety of methods and approaches; or a collection of like-minded activities (such as icebreakers) on multiple subjects and situations.

TRAINING PACKAGE An entire, ready-to-use learning program that focuses on a particular topic or skill. All packages comprise a guide for the facilitator/trainer and a workbook for the participants. Some packages are supported with additional media—such as video—or learning aids, instruments, or other devices to help participants understand concepts or practice and develop skills.

- *Facilitator/trainer's guide* Contains an introduction to the program, advice on how to organize and facilitate the learning event, and step-by-step instructor notes. The guide also contains copies of presentation materials—handouts, presentations, and overhead designs, for example—used in the program.

- *Participant's workbook* Contains exercises and reading materials that support the learning goal and serves as a valuable reference and support guide for participants in the weeks and months that follow the learning event. Typically, each participant will require his or her own workbook.

ELECTRONIC CD-ROMs and web-based products transform static Pfeiffer content into dynamic, interactive experiences. Designed to take advantage of the searchability, automation, and ease-of-use that technology provides, our e-products bring convenience and immediate accessibility to your workspace.

METHODOLOGIES

CASE STUDY A presentation, in narrative form, of an actual event that has occurred inside an organization. Case studies are not prescriptive, nor are they used to prove a point; they are designed to develop critical analysis and decision-making skills. A case study has a specific time frame, specifies a sequence of events, is narrative in structure, and contains a plot structure—an issue (what should be/have been done?). Use case studies when the goal is to enable participants to apply previously learned theories to the circumstances in the case, decide what is pertinent, identify the real issues, decide what should have been done, and develop a plan of action.

ENERGIZER A short activity that develops readiness for the next session or learning event. Energizers are most commonly used after a break or lunch to stimulate or refocus the group. Many involve some form of physical activity, so they are a useful way to counter post-lunch lethargy. Other uses include transitioning from one topic to another, where "mental" distancing is important.

EXPERIENTIAL LEARNING ACTIVITY (ELA) A facilitator-led intervention that moves participants through the learning cycle from experience to application (also known as a Structured Experience). ELAs are carefully thought-out designs in which there is a definite learning purpose and intended outcome. Each step—everything that participants do during the activity—facilitates the accomplishment of the stated goal. Each ELA includes complete instructions for facilitating the intervention and a clear statement of goals, suggested group size and timing, materials required, an explanation of the process, and, where appropriate, possible variations to the activity. (For more detail on Experiential Learning Activities, see the Introduction to the *Reference Guide to Handbooks and Annuals*, 1999 edition, Pfeiffer, San Francisco.)

GAME A group activity that has the purpose of fostering team spirit and togetherness in addition to the achievement of a pre-stated goal. Usually contrived—undertaking a desert expedition, for example—this type of learning method offers an engaging means for participants to demonstrate and practice business and interpersonal skills. Games are effective for team building and personal development mainly because the goal is subordinate to the process—the means through which participants reach decisions, collaborate, communicate, and generate trust and understanding. Games often engage teams in "friendly" competition.

ICEBREAKER A (usually) short activity designed to help participants overcome initial anxiety in a training session and/or to acquaint the participants with one another. An icebreaker can be a fun activity or can be tied to specific topics or training goals. While a useful tool in itself, the icebreaker comes into its own in situations where tension or resistance exists within a group.

INSTRUMENT A device used to assess, appraise, evaluate, describe, classify, and summarize various aspects of human behavior. The term used to describe an instrument depends primarily on its format and purpose. These terms include survey, questionnaire, inventory, diagnostic, survey, and poll. Some uses of instruments include providing instrumental feedback to group members, studying here-and-now processes or functioning within a group, manipulating group composition, and evaluating outcomes of training and other interventions.

Instruments are popular in the training and HR field because, in general, more growth can occur if an individual is provided with a method for focusing specifically on his or her own behavior. Instruments also are used to obtain information that will serve as a basis for change and to assist in workforce planning efforts.

Paper-and-pencil tests still dominate the instrument landscape with a typical package comprising a facilitator's guide, which offers advice on administering the instrument and interpreting the collected data, and an initial set of instruments. Additional instruments are available separately. Pfeiffer, though, is investing heavily in e-instruments. Electronic instrumentation provides effortless distribution and, for larger groups particularly, offers advantages over paper-and-pencil tests in the time it takes to analyze data and provide feedback.

LECTURETTE A short talk that provides an explanation of a principle, model, or process that is pertinent to the participants' current learning needs. A lecturette is intended to establish a common language bond between the trainer and the participants by providing a mutual frame of reference. Use a lecturette as an introduction to a group activity or event, as an interjection during an event, or as a handout.

MODEL A graphic depiction of a system or process and the relationship among its elements. Models provide a frame of reference and something more tangible, and more easily remembered, than a verbal explanation. They also give participants something to "go on," enabling them to track their own progress as they experience the dynamics, processes, and relationships being depicted in the model.

ROLE PLAY A technique in which people assume a role in a situation/scenario: a customer service rep in an angry-customer exchange, for example. The way in which the role is approached is then discussed and feedback is offered. The role play is often repeated using a different approach and/or incorporating changes made based on feedback received. In other words, role playing is a spontaneous interaction involving realistic behavior under artificial (and safe) conditions.

SIMULATION A methodology for understanding the interrelationships among components of a system or process. Simulations differ from games in that they test or use a model that depicts or mirrors some aspect of reality in form, if not necessarily in content. Learning occurs by studying the effects of change on one or more factors of the model. Simulations are commonly used to test hypotheses about what happens in a system—often referred to as "what if?" analysis—or to examine best-case/worst-case scenarios.

THEORY A presentation of an idea from a conjectural perspective. Theories are useful because they encourage us to examine behavior and phenomena through a different lens.

TOPICS

The twin goals of providing effective and practical solutions for workforce training and organization development and meeting the educational needs of training and human resource professionals shape Pfeiffer's publishing program. Core topics include the following:

Leadership & Management

Communication & Presentation

Coaching & Mentoring

Training & Development

E-Learning

Teams & Collaboration

OD & Strategic Planning

Human Resources

Consulting

What will you find on pfeiffer.com?

- The best in workplace performance solutions for training and HR professionals
- Downloadable training tools, exercises, and content
- Web-exclusive offers
- Training tips, articles, and news
- Seamless on-line ordering
- Author guidelines, information on becoming a Pfeiffer Partner, and much more

Discover more at www.pfeiffer.com